Tasks of Passion:
Dennis Lee at Mid-Career

Tasks of Passion

Dennis Lee at Mid-Career

Edited by Karen Mulhallen, Donna Bennett, and Russell Brown

Descant Editions, Toronto

The following abbreviations of Dennis Lee's works have been uti-
lized in the essays. (References are to the last revision unless other-
wise indicated. For details of publication consult the Bibliography.)

KA	—	*Kingdom of Absence*
LADOO	—	*The Death of Harold Ladoo* (in *The Gods*)
CE	—	*Civil Elegies and Other Poems*
G	—	*The Gods*
SF	—	*Savage Fields*
CCS	—	'Cadence, Country, Silence'
GD	—	*Garbage Delight*
NK	—	*Nicholas Knock*

Published by DESCANT, P.O. Box 314, Station P, Toronto M5S 2S8
Ontario. DESCANT is published through the generosity of the *Canada
Council* and the *Ontario Arts Council*.

Typeset in Baskerville by Howarth & Smith (Toronto). Printed by
The Porcupine's Quill (Erin) in November of 1982. The stock is
Zephyr Antique Laid.

Photographs of Dennis Lee by Deborah Shackleton.

ISBN 0-9691167-0-5

Contents

The Epistolary Mode

Riffs

Epilogue

Chronology and Bibliography

Preface

This is the first in a series of books on important contemporary Canadian writers who have had insufficient recognition or whose work cannot be completely described by the use of traditional critical methodologies alone. An appropriate figure to begin with, Dennis Lee has had an unusually varied career — poet, editor, essayist, reviewer and journalist, children's writer, educator, lyricist (and this list is far from complete) — a career in which these roles so blend into one another that any account of his work tends to be, at best, partial. Thus, though we have created broad divisions in the book for the reader's convenience, many of the essays inevitably cut across the boundaries these categories suggest in order to locate Lee's work in contexts not available to the reader of any one poem or book. The importance of meditation and of music, the influence of German philosophy and poetry, the relationship between Lee's theory, his life, and his work, the place of his nonsense verse, the meaning of his continued struggle with Modernism, and the evolution of civil and personal *self* within his writing — these are some of the areas explored here. In their attempts to do justice to the body of the work, the essays may be seen approaching and moving around such topics reinforcing and modifying one another, until together they begin to provide a composite picture of a man who is so much in motion that the edges of the picture will always remain a blur.

We are particularly pleased to bring attention here to Lee's work as an editor — because that work has been extremely important and influential on the one hand, and almost invisible to the reading public on the other. Furthermore the editorial role has had profound effect on Lee's own writing as well, for he is a compulsive reviser of his own work, publishing new versions of poems and essays years after their first appearance. Because he is therefore a writer in process, his poetry and essays do not form a stable corpus of discrete units but become a single work in progress, one always subject to further revision, always in development, always aspiring to a philosophy of life that lies beyond the written page. Deep within this work is a religious impulse that brings together voices even more disparate than those of his civil and personal personae, and that manifests itself as an urge to create cosmologically, to edit out of the messy stuff of life a vision that is whole but not exclusive, one that contains comprehensively the nature of *being*.

We are also reminded of the ongoing nature of Lee's career by the first publication in this book of 'Riffs', his newest long poem, a poem which will undoubtedly continue to develop, as well as the first publication of 'Polyphony', Lee's newest statement on the nature of cadence. The poem and the essay grow organically out of Lee's earlier work and yet each signals new advances in that work, new challenges to future critics. Together the titles themselves affirm once more the continued importance of music in Lee's works, of the lyricist moving to the page his internal songs.

We would like to thank all those who took part in his volume, and ECW Press for permission to use excerpts from Mary MacPherson's forthcoming bibliography of Dennis Lee. We also wish to thank Ellen Pekilis for her editorial assistance in the making of this book.

Detachment from Self

George Bowering

Detachment from self is authentic love
even in autobiographical times;
need (but is it his or your uncaring
nerves him to scribe his acts from above?)
inches him toward confession and crimes,
sometimes called order, sometimes overbearing.

Losing that self is not simply to shove
ego aside while composing honest lines;
even loss of ego is a mantle for the wearing.

Dennis the Ed

Dennis Revisited

Margaret Atwood

WHEN I WAS ASKED to write a small piece on Dennis Lee, I began by counting up the number of years I've known him. It came as a slight shock to discover that it was over twenty. I first met him, ludicrously enough, at a Freshman Mixer at Victoria College, University of Toronto, in the fall of 1957. I was somewhat in awe of him, since, like everyone else, I knew he'd won the Prince of Wales Scholarship for the highest Grade 13 marks in the Province of Ontario; but nevertheless there I was, shuffling around the floor with him, while he explained that he was going to be a United Church Minister. I, on the other hand, was already doggedly set on being a writer, though I had scant ideas about how this was to be accomplished. At that time I thought, in my intolerant undergraduate way, that poetry and religion — especially the religion of the United Church — did not mix, which brought us to the end of the dance.

Then there was a gap, as Dennis was in mainstream English and I had digressed into Philosophy and English, foolishly thinking that my mind would thereby be broadened. But logic and poetry did not mix either, and in second year I switched back, having missed Bibliography forever. Some time later, Dennis and I became friends and collaborators. I suppose it was inevitable. Art of any kind, in the late 'fifties', in Toronto, at Victoria College, was not exactly a hot topic, and those of us who dared to risk incurring the pejorative label 'arty' practised herding and defensive dressing. We worked on ACTA, the literary magazine; we wrote on, and acted in, the yearly satirical revue. At one point, Dennis and I invented a pseudonym for literary parodies which combined both our names and which lingered on after our respective departures: Shakesbeat Latweed. 'Shakesbeat', because the first thing we wrote was a poem called 'Sprattire', variations on the first four lines of 'Jack Spratt', as if by various luminaries, from Shakespeare to a Beat poet. According to my mother, we laughed a lot while writing it. Dennis, then as now, had a faintly outrageous sense of humour concealed beneath his habitually worried look.

Dennis took fourth year off and went to Germany, thus enabling me to get a Woodrow Wilson (if he'd been there, *he'd* have got it). After that I was away from Toronto for the next ten years. So it must have been by letter, or during one of my infrequent visits back

(I seem to remember Hart House theatre, at intermission; but inter-mission of what?) that he contacted me about House of Anansi Press. Some people were starting a publishing house, he said, and they wanted to reprint my book of poems, *The Circle Game*, which had won the Governor General's Award that year but was out of print. He said they wanted to do 2,000 copies. I thought they were crazy. I also thought the idea of a publishing house was a little crazy too; it was still only 1967. But by this time both Dennis and I were cultural nationalists of a sort, though we'd come to it separately. We were both aware that the established publishing houses had been ti-morous about new writing, particularly in prose fiction, though also to a certain extent in poetry. The dreaded 'colonial mentality' was not yet a catchword but it was on its way. The first four Anansi au-thors got small grants from the Canada Council, most of which we bumped back into the company. It amazes me now to realize how lit-tle money it took to start Anansi. But it took a lot more blood and guts, much of both Dennis's.

During the late sixties, the period of Anansi's rapid growth and the establishment of Dennis's reputation as an editor, I was in Bos-ton, then Montreal, then Edmonton, so was in touch only by letter. At that period I worked in various ways on three Anansi books with Dennis: George Bowering's *The Gangs of Kosmos*, Bill Bissett's *Nobody Owns The Earth*, and, less intensively, Michael Ondaatje's *Billy the Kid*. When my own book, *Power Politics*, was ready to be seen, I felt it was an Anansi book and took it to Dennis. When I returned from England in 1971 I joined Anansi's Board and worked with various writers (sometimes with Dennis, sometimes alone), including Paulette Jiles, Eli Mandel, Terrence Heath, P.K. Page, John Thompson and Patrick Lane; and Dennis himself, with whom I edi-ted the second edition of *Civil Elegies*. Our most engrossing collabo-ration at that time, however, was his editing of my critical work *Survival*. Dennis was indispensable for the book, and in top editorial form: fast, incisive, full of helpful suggestions, and, by the end, just as exhausted as I was.

Small publishing is an energy-drainer, as anyone who has done it will testify. By 1973 Dennis was withdrawing more and more from Anansi, and shortly thereafter so was I.

I think it was in the summer of 1974 that Dennis read the first draft of *Lady Oracle* for me, with the usual helpful results. The edi-torial conference took place on the top of a rail fence, as I recall, which was typical of Dennis as an editor. The process was never what you would call formal. Given the choice of a dining room table

14

or a kitchen full of dirty dishes and chicken carcasses and cat boxes, Dennis would go for the kitchen every time.

This is as good a place as any to throw in my two cents' worth about Dennis-as-editor. The reputation is entirely deserved. When he's 'on', he can give another writer not only generous moral support but also an insightful, clear view of where a given book is trying to go. This is usually conveyed not in conversation alone but in pages and pages of single-spaced, detailed and amended notes. I have never worked with an editor who delivers so much in such a condensed mode. His willingness to enter so fully into a book's sources of energy make him more than usually vulnerable to invasion by the author's psyche and to the demands of the author's clamorous ego. At one stage of his life he was acting not only as surrogate midwife but as surrogate shrink and confessor to far too many people. It's no wonder that he's withdrawn from the editing process from time to time. It's no wonder too that he's sometimes become bored or impatient with the Super-editor uniform. He is also a writer, and both his own time and the attention and acclaim of others has often gone to the editing when it could or should have gone to the writing. It's his writing that's of primary importance for Dennis. It's also, I think, the hardest thing to talk to him about and the hardest thing for him to do.

When I try to picture Dennis to myself, it's the anxious wrinkles on his forehead that appear first, like the Cheshire Cat's grin. Next comes the pipe, eternally puffing, or sometimes a cigar. Then the rest of him appears, on the run, rumpled, harassed by invisible demons, replete with subterranean energy, slightly abstracted, sometimes perplexed, in spite of it all well-meaning, kindly in an embarrassed and hesitant way; and, when he's talking to you about something important, working very hard not only at but towards saying exactly what he wants to say, which is usually complex. Sometimes Dennis is less complex when he's had a few drinks and is playing the piano, for instance, or when he's making a terrible pun. This maniacal side of Dennis is most visible in *Alligator Pie* and its sequels, and probably keeps him sane; but friendly old Uncle Dennis is of course not the whole story.

I don't have the whole story, and it's clear to me after twenty-odd years that I'm not likely ever to have it. Dennis isn't what you'd call an easily accessible person. In any case, the whole story isn't finished yet. There's more to come.

Kind of Squash

Graeme Gibson

Wibbley Wobbley Woo
I don't know what to do
Wibbley wobbley wash
I'm feeling kind of squash   (*Traditional Lament*, D. Lee)

ONCE UPON A TIME there used to be publishers and editors who, after returning your manuscript, might bellow in parking lots, 'Now don't go committing suicide this week'. Or else they'd explain they didn't want to invest in 'just another publisher's author'.

While still considering *Five Legs*, chuckling hollowly in an elevator that was carrying us to the roof of the Park Plaza, one editor suggested I'd have to marry the daughter of a French Canadian pulp magnate before he could afford the paper for my book.

I told everyone all of this, of course. I blethered about it in the Pilot, which was still on Yonge Street, in the Embassy Tavern, and around countless kitchen tables. Such were those times, everyone agreed, 'That's the way it is'. There's no justice and precious little mercy. If they don't get you one way, they'll get you another.

'Graeme — I'd love to publish your book but New York won't let me. They only have so much money for experimental fiction and they spend it on Americans.' He, at least, bought me lunch and drinks. In fact he did such a good job, and was so decent, that I experienced a spasm of triumph. It was almost as if he'd accepted the book.

Trying to recall that period in my life is rather like trying to remember a long illness. Anyone who has had a book rejected by a bunch of publishers (even one can be enough) will recognize the way people say 'Oh' when they hear it. 'Oh', as if to say, 'I see . . .'. For many, the refusal is purely and simply a judgment on the book. It isn't published, presumably, because it isn't publishable. It doesn't work . . . .

If it happens often enough even the author begins to wonder.

So the first time I met Dennis, after 18 months of this sort of thing, I was pretty wild-eyed, spaced-out, I think we said back then. It seems to me he was up on a ladder. Perhaps he was changing his storm windows, or cleaning out eavestroughs, although in retrospect, that seems unlikely. Could he have been washing windows? I was standing on the sidewalk with the MS of *Five Legs*, which he'd agreed to consider for The House of Anansi, a publisher I hadn't even heard of a month before.

We didn't say much. I must have blurted something about how pleased I was he'd read it, that I hoped he'd like it, that sort of desperate politesse we shore ourselves up with. Certainly I insisted he be careful with the damned thing, explaining that it was the only real copy I had and that I'd already lost it in a suitcase once and had had to spend several days searching for it in a warehouse at the airport in Mexico City before I found it. Leaving him, I wandered off, mustering the old, almost reliable daydreams the best I could.

It must have been late in the summer of 1968 and I remember thinking he didn't look like a publisher. But since for almost a year and a half my MS had been consistently rejected by men who did look like publishers, who indeed *were* publishers, I can't have been too disturbed by Lee's rumpled diffidence. Besides, he looked more like the people I knew . . . .

Apart from his impeccable taste in choosing to publish *Five Legs*, my dominant memories of Dennis from that time are all associated with his cajoling, sometimes bullying but always persistent and enthusiastic talk as we edited the MS.

We started in the middle of December, 1968, and finished before mid-February. Many details are vague now but I do remember a certain number of rooms — his living room, with at least one overstuffed chair, a room in my apartment and another in Rochdale — that bedevilled experiment in idealism and good faith on Bloor Street. Since Dennis can make more smoke with pipe and cigar than a clutch of other people, and because I'm no slouch at that myself, those rooms were thick with it, a kind of tactical miasma as he forced me to think more clearly about my intentions, about the implications of my work, than I had previously thought possible. Or even decent.

So what sort of thing did he do? To begin with, since I have a strong weakness for over-writing, he insisted I cut stuff out. In one letter he said, '. . . there's a certain overinflated feeling — like . . . an air mattress that's been blown up 10% more than it needs to be'. Now I ask you, who could resist such blandishments?

Equally beguilingly he isolated what was cluttered or unfinished in characterization. In the book's final section, for example, where Felix approaches breakdown (or whatever it is that happens to him), the style in the edited version became much more fragmented and nervous. It still seems to me a wholly appropriate change . . . .

To illustrate the experience of Lee's contribution I don't think I can do better than, once again, quote from one of his letters. This

17

one came to me very early on in our marathon and did much to prepare me for his cunning mixture of flattery and challenge:

This is a real tour-de-force . . .
I have one major problem . . . To wit: Lucan's interior monologue goes on in 2 or 3 voices. The bumbly, discombobulated one is lovely. The whiny one is very nice. But then there's the anaemic lit-prof's weedy pastiche of every literary pre-Raphaelite cliche in the book. And thereby hangs the problem.
I can't remember the name of the fallacy, but somebody who claims he's triumphed because you find his book about boredom absolutely boring may be technically in the right; the only thing is, he's missed the boat completely. To overstate my case, I think that's what's happened here. You may have captured beautifully the moronic effect of a weak sub-literary mind coping with the flow of its experience by throwing up a constant stream of stereotypes, cliches, and grotesquely over-inflated romantic items of bilge. Good for you. But it doesn't work . . . my immediate nerve end reaction [tells me] it doesn't work . . . I've tried to mark, sneer at, jeer at, & in various other ways indicate my discomfort with most of the worser places . . . .

It is almost as impossible to describe this experience of detailed editing as it is to convey the process of writing because in both cases one forgets. Or at least I do. Looking at the MS, at the ticks in the margin, re-reading the notes and letters, I have a vague mnemonic stirring. The fact is we talked with marvellous intensity about those notes and the passages they referred to, but one thing remains clear. In his reading of the book Dennis was, more often than not, uncannily right, and he was almost never wrong.

Anyway, it seemed to me at the time, and it still does, that Dennis read *Five Legs* the way I'd written it. That is to say, with an extraordinary, even obsessive attention to detail. As a result, because he forced me to consider the words on the page in a way I'd forgotten, or sometimes never knew, he made it a better book and I came to see I was lucky to have been turned down by those mainstream Canadian, English and American publishers — none of them, at that time, could have helped me make the most of the book in the way Dennis did.

Perhaps it isn't odd, but it does seem notable, that during the months we worked on the MS I didn't get to know Dennis very well, not, at least, the man who existed apart from that flattering preoccupation with, and vision of, my work. I must have suspected much,

18

but it was only later, gradually, and of course it isn't finished, that I began to discover what a complex and driven man he is.

Thankless anonymity is a well-known editor's curse and springs from the rare, and often painful talent for complete attention to the work of others. It's an astonishing gift and never less so than when, like Dennis, an editor has the same lust for statement as any of his authors. Indeed more than many. I've never figured out how he's done it . . . .

Anyway, my first experience of him attacking the piano very late at night, or the shock of *Civil Elegies*, or the wonderful far-ranging and elaborate talk, the unfolding of Dennis and me (if you like), that is to say, my discovery of his humour and passion, his sense of destiny, all this led to my first recognition of what it means to be compatriotic.

This isn't the place to try and explain who the Dennis is that I know, even if I wanted to. Instead, I find myself thinking about the bunch of us back then, the writers (and those who supported us) who found in Anansi their first professional home.

Much has now been said about the renaissance, the enthusiasm and optimism that Anansi, and several other small publishers, encouraged and represented. Most of it is true, or true enough, but there's another, darker side to it. The fact is, it was often a hard, even tortuous and imperfect energy that we shared. Looking back at the injury of silence, the breakdown in egos and in marriages, the sad violence of suicide or murder, the often terrible but sometimes comic intensities, more often than not we find Dennis near the centre — as he was indeed with so many of the triumphs.

I guess that goes with the territory. But working close to the knife-edge with an amazing number of us, at a time when nothing was clear yet anything seemed possible, it sometimes appeared he was as much a sin-eater as editor. In works like 'Sibelius Park', and his poem for Sonny Ladoo, one can see him working this out, doing justice to the time far better than I could hope to do.

But that's a long time ago now and it almost does seem like another country. The fact I'm writing this to help celebrate Lee's presence among us, what better sign is there that time has passed?

Perhaps it is this fact that encourages me to feel that my relationship with Dennis Lee is neither just a professional one nor just a friendship — although fortunately it has been and is both. It somehow has more to do with the passage and time of my adult life so far.

Cut Down the Middle

Michael Ondaatje

THE IMPORTANT THING about Dennis Lee is that he is cut down the middle. Intensely private — suspicious of 'going public', and then the public cause — the desire to change the world. Both of these qualities also apply to his editorial work.

* * *

His grandest moment was when, as a critic, he took on Cohen's *Beautiful Losers*. An outrageous act because he approached the book as if it was still in manuscript, saying what *he* would do in editing the work. Even though the book had been out for 5 years. It doesn't matter if he was right or not, what matters is that he could assume the right to say those things. This is splendid. In my spare moments I think what Dennis would say to Dostoevsky about *The Brothers K.*, or Mickey Spillane about *I, the Jury*, or Stevenson about *Treasure Island*. Someday I want to see him do a book like this — essays on famous novels. This is partly to do with Eliot's *Tradition and the Individual Talent* and partly to do with Borges's take on *Don Quixote*.

* * *

I've worked with Dennis Lee often. He has pored over my work and I've pored over his. What still surprises me is how we continue to be friends, even though we often disagree very basically about certain things in the other's judgment. The problems I think stem from Dennis being a platonist, as I see it. Every thing returns to the purest image in the cave. He also takes what is *being said* more seriously than I do. I'm easily seduced by a strange tone or manner. I think we *do* both believe in 'neck-verses' — that song or poem or prayer where everything has to be said from the deepest layer in us, that last call.

* * *

He has infuriated me with some of his interpretations and judgments. And I am sure I have greatly disappointed him. What I am trying to stress here is that while Dennis has been very important for me, I would hate people to get the idea that he is the immaculate saintly doctor; he is human and his reactions are human, and so sometimes wrong. He is not the Broadway stage doc who knows what will make a flawed play a success with a built-in guarantee. He won't necessarily make the book a success but he will push the writer towards a truth — even if it means making the writer do something just to defend himself against Dennis' view. He does not do this as a devil's advocate either. Dennis is painfully honest. If something is bothering him about a section he will write you a four page (single spaced) letter questioning you, questioning himself, questioning the universe, questioning the liberal party, God, early jazz violinists, plant life in Argentina, the immorality of Basho, the failure of the villanelle in the 20th century. This can be exhausting.

Two things about this. 1. You think on what he says, you defend yourself, and in some way the book is improved. 2. This is also exhausting for him. He gives himself completely to the work, never in a casual way. You see why I'd love to see the Lee-Dostoevsky letters or the Lee-Spillane letters. What would he have done with that exhausting first chapter of *Under the Volcano*? What would he have done with 'The Intended' in *Heart of Darkness*?

There is a commitment on his part to the work and this commitment eats up his own creative time, and this commitment can make the author furious at him. I have wanted to emphasize the dark side of Dennis' work as an editor. I would hate to suggest literary fun and games and lunch at the Courtyard Cafe. (That has never happened yet and I keep waiting for it). And I want to stress he doesn't always have the answer and I still think he is often wrong — as he thinks I am often wrong. Each of us likes certain writers the other wouldn't be at all interested in. But he does push you towards something you may have been trying to avoid. He does leap on your flippant exit.

* * *

I tend to give a finished manuscript to four or five people with very different tastes, but Dennis is always one of them. His perspective — from the top of the mount or from his cigar-filled lair is something I value greatly. So, dear friend, you may not think so, but these notes *are* meant as a celebration. Till we meet again, as bp Nichol says, 'in the great noise among the languages'.

Dennis The Ed

Al Purdy

I HAD AN EDITOR once, and once only, who inserted the word 'that' between all my prose phrases where it could possibly bear the burden. And since I have a tendency to strip down language in some degree, this habit annoyed me. I still have a phobia about that editor.

However, most of them have been far wiser than me, since I'm good at spelling and they're good at grammar. Where poetry is concerned, I've generally been able to impress them that line breaks are holy and not to be tampered with on pain of exile from Parnassus; and that poetry and its practitioners should be treated with due reverence.

I take a different view when I'm doing the editing myself. One manuscript I worked on had several poems repeated in two or three different versions. It was a jumble of pages in no order whatever. It had also been rejected by a large publisher. Therefore it pleased me when the book was brought out later by the same publisher.

Which brings me to Dennis Lee. Dennis is knowledgeable, mild-mannered and tactful: he has all the virtues. Therefore I distrust him. He's much too good to be true. I expect a low whimper of discontent or snarl of outright disagreement to emanate from the publisher's eunuch-serfs at all times, indicating that they know their place and feel a proper respect.

But Dennis is not a eunuch: he writes himself. When it was arranged that he should edit *Being Alive*, my *Selected Poems*, for McStew and charming sweet-tempered Jack McC., I was pleased but apprehensive. For I am too mild-mannered and tactful, even if not notably knowledgeable. Our editorial meetings would be like a coming together of two mild zephyrs that wouldn't stir the curtains of an outhouse. Dennis and I are simply too much alike, except perhaps in physiognomy: he can see under a toy train and I can see over it.

A big problem with my *Selected*, as I saw it, was just that, the selection of the best poems. However, I had written so many poems over the years that they couldn't all be included within the bounds of 200 pages. And during our several sessions together, Dennis would say about 'The Drunk Tank' (for instance): 'The point of the poem is too obvious'. (I didn't think it was obvious at all, even if you didn't see Paul Newman's problems of communication in *Cool Hand Luke*.)

And he would say, feigning a puzzled look: 'I don't quite understand this passage — '.

'Migawd', I would rebut, 'a child of ten would understand what I'm getting at. It means, ah, that is to say, it means — '.

'It means,' Dennis said smoothly, 'that I am only nine years old and need to have things a little clearer. Now you take this other passage a little later in the same poem — '.

I have to explain here that a few of my things have been written for such a long time that they've assumed the character of an Unholy Writ for me, a rigidity that seems exactly right. And it was on several of these very poems that Dennis unassumingly pounced. Anyone who didn't know Dennis would think he was merely commenting, but Dennis's is a disguised pounce, an offhand pounce. And I would conceal my reaction to this, which didn't fool him at all. And both of us concealed our annoyance. And I would think: 'What is he thinking that he hasn't said?' And he would think: 'What does this retarded moron want besides unstinting admiration?' At least I think he thought that, and our unsaid thoughts met unimpeded by a cloud of cigar smoke that obscured the issue still further.

However, we generally agreed as to selection. And it was because of Dennis's continual remarks that a poem could be better that he was most valuable to me. 'Could be better' was repeated in dozens of different ways: clearer, less verbiage, more to the point, etc. He brought a different and fresh viewpoint to things I had thought rigid and permanent.

I suppose there is in your head a conception of what you think is good: a conception that is only valid when the good thing is there in front of you on the page as an example. Most of the time you are ruling out, in the brain's continual re-write, what you think is not good. And there is no real criterion about what is good except personal taste and a modicum of intelligence. (Literary taste is not a black and white thing, like a four-minute mile in running or a knockout in boxing.) The trouble is a writer wants to think, dearly desires to think, that everything he writes is good. Just because he (or she) wrote it. Of course it ain't so, not necessarily.

What Dennis thinks good is similar, at least related, to my own opinions. But again, with the concrete example before you, not something abstract. Therefore we were sometimes faced with the problem of too much agreement, which can be just as bad as too little. Or it may be that my tactfulness met his tactfulness in confrontation, and one said, 'I'll defer to you': and the other said, 'No no, I'll defer to *you*'. Life is hell, ain't it?

I remember Dennis saying, 'The reader should be led into the book as easily and rapidly as possible' — or something like that. Which has to do with the sequence of poems in a book. I have always liked jagged variety, the positioning of opposites next to each other, whether in verse form, language or subject. This method as opposed to uniting groups of poems under similar themes. And very often, as in writing itself, you can't say why you adopted a particular sequence and order.

Most of the ordering in *Being Alive* was done by Dennis. I still don't know why it is the way it is, and perhaps he doesn't. But if asked, I'm sure he could come up with some reasons. And sometimes, because of what he didn't say, I had a pretty good idea of what he was thinking. Underemphasis of a subject sometimes provides its own exaggeration.

What saying all this amounts to is: *Being Alive* is a much better book than it would have been without Dennis. He doesn't need testimonials, and I don't intend to provide them. There are perhaps a dozen poems in the book that owe their present form to him. He didn't re-write them or say what the changes should have been. He was tactfully dissatisfied. He was simply Dennis, devious, insightful, gaining his ends by misdirection and mind-reading brilliance. I wonder if he knew I knew he was all those things, and neither of us would admit it till now?

Generalissimo Lee

Scott Symons

HOW POSSIBLY TO DESCRIBE writing, working on a novel, with Dennis Lee as editor? You are fighting a jungle-battle. Guerilla warfare. The hidden enemy is . . . the Devil-and-all-his-works. You yourself may be part of said Devil-and-all-his-works, you're not quite sure. But for the moment you are certainly engaged in life and death struggle with such a Devil. With whatever equipment you have, which isn't much. The jungle is immense — the enemy's ambushes endless. You're not sure you can go on, or, if you can, just how. But behind you, supporting you, there's a Field Marshall, a hidden Generalissimo. You don't see him often (some never see him at all). He sends cryptic messages . . . telegrammatic, breathless, in code. 'Turn left at big tree with snakey leaves, fire bazooka . . . a large gate will open in rock wall directly ahead. Enter on your knees, keep head down.' About once a year the Generalissimo sends you a massive directive. You ponder over such a directive, knowing it must be right. But what does it truly mean? Short of a brain transplant?

Yes, it's like that, working on a book with Dennis Lee as editor. Precisely like that. With yourself, the author, as the guerilla warrior. And your subject matter, the jungle, full of hidden devils. And Lee . . . Lee of course as the hidden Generalissimo, pelting you with strategic ukases, almost always proved right.

And if it isn't like that, then you know you're *not* working on your book at the right level, or you're *not* responding to the tenor of his editorial missives. You're not really a writer at all, just a dilettante.

I first met Lee-as-editor in the Spring of 1973. I had a splendid but botched manuscript. And I had a cracked head from living some of the contents of the manuscript. I wasn't at all sure I could pull either the manuscript, or myself, together. The manuscript, without my knowing it, had been passed to Lee.

When Lee takes on the editing of a book, he is directly involved in the book, the fruition of the book, almost (and in some cases precisely) as a life and death matter. I believe this relates to the case he presents in *Savage Fields*. The case of a literature caught somewhere between Armageddon and the 'airless corridors of the mind'. It is Lee's necessity, and mission, to break this impasse. He chooses, then edits, books to this important end.

Thus he is totally committed to the book — not to the author, but to the book! An important distinction. He can forgive the author some weaknesses. He doesn't forgive the book any weaknesses. I can vouch for both facts.

Given that Lee takes on the editing of a book as a major personal commitment, and brings a formidable arsenal of capacities to bear on this editing, the question remains just *how* does he extort the best possible book from the author? The answer has to be that he climbs inside of the book's best possibilities, and works from, and to, there. Often enough those best possibilities lie beyond, not only the pen, but the quality of life of the author at that moment. It is my experience that Lee simply cajoles, bludgeons and drags the protesting, awed, frightened, irritated author after him. Thank God!

It would seem that I am an undiluted admirer of Lee-as-editor. Not so. What I have presented is Lee at his best (which is frequent). At his worst, dealing with Lee is a bit like being lectured by a Moderator of the United Church. An intellectual and literate version of same, of course. But Lee comes by this failing honourably. Both of his grandfathers (if I recollect rightly) were Methodist ministers. And he himself is a distinguished graduate of Victoria College (in the University of Toronto), that erstwhile heartland of Canadian Methodism.

But this tart statement happily leads to a larger and finer point about Lee — one which is important in assessing him as author and as editor. That is, he is probably the finest extant exemplar of a grand old Canadian tradition. I mean the Grit tradition, in its best sense. The Grit tradition as at once a social, and intellectual, and finally political stance in life. Lee as editor, like Lee as Lee, certainly embodies this culture in the best possible way. Its verbal astringencies, its moral austerities, its angular probities, its ironclad certainties (for example, about what properly constitutes 'social justice'). Not to mention its almost Breughelian reversions to a festive folk-yeoman sense of life (and here I think of Lee explosive at the piano!).

Lee himself, curiously, remains substantially ignorant of this culture, and its sources. But to work with him as editor is to know what that great Grit Canadian tradition once was . . . before it became flatulently plausible fat-cat, and announced that it alone was guardian of the meanings of Canada.

Such comment would be incomplete if I did not mention that Lee, in working as editor with me, was working with a latter-day exemplar of a Canadian tradition hostile to his own. For better and often worse, I derive from the rooted Canadian Tory culture. A culture that (in contrast to Grittery, or even to mere conservatism) is sensual, passional, non-cerebral, metaphysical, even neo-feudal . . . not to mention potentially ludicrously perverse. At least it must certainly have seemed that way to Lee, as he worked with me on my novel. To his immense credit he took all this in his stride. Though now and then he did shake his head in disbelief, and mutter 'It is all very exotic!'

Pass to the process of grappling with Lee as editor. In my case there were two aspects to this. The long-distance one, and the close quarter, hand-to-hand one. Often, Lee and I found ourselves thousands of miles apart. Geographically, I mean. I would be living in Mexico, and he in Toronto. Or I would be in Toronto, and Lee in Scotland. The result has been a massive exchange of editorial letters! His are ten, or fifteen, or twenty pages, typed single-spaced. How describe Lee's missives? First, they are delayed warhead missiles! They present themselves as simple, ho-hum, innocent commentary. But they're not. Once understood, they're nuclear detonations. Secondly, they truly require 'decoding'! One which I received in Mexico took a writer-friend and me two weeks to 'decode'. We each read it with care. Then set to work with scissors and paste, cutting the letter up, and reassembling it so that footnotes, addendums, tangential comments (often typed vertical in the margin of his letters!) were all in sequential order within the main body of the text. We then had a professional typist re-do the entire letter, double-spaced. Only then could we cope with the overall meaning of the text. Thirdly, the specific contents of such Lee-letters. Lee will mention that a 'small point' he is raising will only take two or three weeks of work on the author's part. It is my experience that if you substitute 'months' whenever Lee mentions weeks, you have it right. Such letters from Lee are tight, opaque, often verbally congealed. They are certainly the work of a literary genius.

Conclude with a close-quarter editing session with Lee. Face to face. Lee arrives chugging in his obsolescent Volkswagen. Invariably late, puffing, cherubic with apologies. Invariably carrying a mass of papers, inchoate in his arms. He plops onto the sofa, clears his throat, reaches for a large stogey. When the room is suitably permeated with the first blasts of smoke, he clears his throat for the second time. You know the editing session is about to begin. It starts in low key. He has some 'small point' he wants to raise. This takes anywhere up to an hour . . say two stogeys' worth. By the end of said 'small point' your entire book has been put into question, not to mention portions of your sanity. At this juncture Lee pauses, and shifts from a stogey to Calvados (or to milk, depending on the hang of the moon). He clears his throat again (always dire signal), and asks 'are you ready for this one?' You know it's the major point he's been solicitously saving. You're never ready. But fortunately he has invariably and with kindly tact, forewarned you what this 'major point' will be, during the earlier conversation. Two hours later it's all done. You both sit immersed in an iron fog of stogey-smoke, with empty brandy glasses. Clots of brain droop from the walls. Lee sits silent on the sofa. He looks relieved, satisfied, a little startled. The author, of course, sits wordless. His entire manuscript has just been carried, holus bolus, an entire step forward, despite his own best intentions.

I have no doubts. In dealing with Lee-as-editor we are really dealing with a National Asset, an editor who is better and stronger, than most of our national literature.

Working With Dennis Lee

Marian Engel

I HAD WRITTEN A NOVEL called *The Honeyman Festival* in about 1969, a successor to my first, *No Clouds of Glory*. My original New York publisher, and Longmans' of Canada, turned it down. They said it was sordid. Minn was pregnant.

I wasn't satisfied with it either. It seemed all wrong to me, kept turning into a bulgy *Anne of Green Gables*. Then Dennis Lee, whom I knew socially, persuaded me to let him have a look at it. 'I think we could do something with it.'

My New York agent was not well pleased, and made shoestring House of Anansi come up with a contract and a small ($200, I think) advance. Then Dennis set me down with the manuscript. We decided to eliminate everything in it that wasn't electric and rewrite the book around it.

Rumour has it that Dennis rewrote it. I distinctly remember doing it myself; but the fact was that both of us kept losing bits of paper, the twins were 3 or 4 and underfoot, and anybody could have written the book but I wouldn't have known. What was liberating was finding myself free of conventional narrative, and able to insert things like the Milton-Vacuum cleaner section.

We fought through the text word by word. Once I remember Dennis had someone use the word 'Golly'. I had a fit. It's not one of my words.

That was a jolly, messy, hectic time. Once he found me gardening and gave me a stern message I have not forgotten: writers haven't time. I am a great gardener — well, sort of — now. Once we went on TV together, author and publisher. My aunt phoned, 'I saw you on TV with Vida's nephew.' I asked my father who Dennis Lee was. 'Little Walter's boy', he said. Somehow that put the kibosh on things: we didn't much want that kind of connection.

Next we did my fatal *Monodromos*, which I first wrote as a flat nouveau roman. Even Dennis insisted I warm it up. It's an account of a year in Cyprus. It almost works and some of it is beautiful, but it still falls between two stools. It came at a hard time for Anansi: Dennis and Margaret Atwood were leaving. It was only a technical success, but professors love it.

We worked on it in terms of words and phrases, shape. Didn't talk much about character. I was more European than he was. We got into little wrangles, not big ones. I admired him tremendously, knew, though, that if I continued with him I'd grow dependent. I have to have my own way with my work or I lose my sense of direction.

He was an editor who allowed a writer a sense of dignity. I admired him totally, and still do.

A Chess Master in Control

Irving Layton

IT WAS LIKE PLAYING against a chess master in full control of all his emotions and moves. As poetry editor for McClelland and Stewart, he had been asked by the firm to assist me in fingering out those gems that would go into the composition of *A Wild Peculiar Joy, The Selected Poems of Irving Layton* 1945-1982. There was wariness at the beginning, on his part, on mine. After all, we came from opposite ends of the literary and cultural spectrum: WASP and Jew. To be candid, I was apprehensive that he would be unable to savour some of my poems because what after all could pogroms and gefilte fish mean to a WASP? Or corrupt black olives and herrings?

Of course, all the time I was wondering what was going on in his mind. Would the stereotype of me as arrogant bully and opinionated megalomaniac terrify him into easy acquiescence with my choices, or would he fight me line by line, verse by verse? Would he have the boldness to say nix to certain poems that I thought should be in the collection?

I'm not going to give a detailed account of our meetings which were numerous and always exciting. We both desired the same goal: the best possible selection that could be achieved from the hundreds of poems that I had written in a space of time that covered almost four decades. Lee's devotion to literature, it quickly became clear to me, was perfect. Also he had an excellent ear and superb taste. Several times he was persuaded to accept a poem after I had read it aloud and he caught the passion of it with the rhythm. Not always. Sometimes he'd shake his head, puff thoughtfully at his pipe, and tell me quietly he didn't think the poem quite made it. Three or four times, we were in adamant opposition. Sometimes I yielded, sometimes Lee did. Always with good grace because the disagreements were clearly stated and understood and ranged widely over theme, craft and everything else that delights literary chess masters.

All in all, working with Dennis Lee, someone who so marvellously fuses thought and passion, was an unforgettable experience. I shall always be grateful for those hours when he came to my tiny apartment on Bathurst. To give the reader some idea of the hard trading that went on between us during those exciting hours I should say that my count for the *Selected Poems* was one hundred and seventy. Lee thought the *Selected* should contain only one hundred and twenty-eight poems. The final count: one hundred and fifty.

Dennis Lee and Andy Warhol

Matt Cohen

Andy Warhol is famous for having said that in the modern world, every person is famous for at least fifteen minutes. Of course Andy Warhol has gone the way of the soupcan, and the modern world is now post-modern. Nonetheless, it is still true that the whole world has become showbusiness; we are all subject to the myths and pratfalls of fame. Thus it is that even the most archaic of beasts, the writer, has had to realize that no matter what the value or idiosyncracy of his work, it will ultimately be seen through the lens of his personality, judged by the stature of his image.

As this truth seeped through me, I felt myself lifted into a mood of uncontrollable elation. Unable to read further I threw the pamphlet to the floor, jumped on it, then dialled the number of my friend and *confidante* in such matters, Ann Gunnarson.

'Have you — ' I began excitedly.

'The spider is on its last legs,' she replied, in that deep and *confidante* voice I had first heard so many years ago.

'You know,' I confessed, 'I'm trying to write an article on Dennis Lee for Descant magazine. Can I come to interview you?'

'Me?' Anne Gunnarson is such a solitary person that she has removed the numbers from the front door of her modest Rosedale cottage.

'A sort of Paris Review type interview. You could give me a few free drinks and tell me about Dennis when he was younger — didn't you say you used to know him?'

'I was his babysitter,' Ann Gunnarson said.

'You babysat Dennis Lee?'

'He was a remarkable child. I remember once that he brought me some cookies and offered to rub my feet.'

'With the cookies?'

'No, with ski wax. You see, his parents had told him I was recently arrived from Norway, and he had thought I would be interested in skiing.'

IN THE EARLY DAYS of Anansi Press, a time which coincided with the initial and often unsure outbursts of writing by those who published there, Anansi was not so much a publishing company as a group of people convinced by Dennis Lee that they were entangled strands of a weird literary knot which would mark the division between past and future.

32

'This conversation will probably go down in literary history,' Dennis Lee said to me one day, while we were discussing something I've long since forgotten. And yet, ridiculous though his assertion then seemed, it was Dennis's belief in the mythic dimensions of apparently trivial arguments, the power of his total conviction about the potential and importance of a book — and its centrality to the history of the world — that made him such an effective editor.

Of course the 60s, though they can be but dimly remembered from this great distance, were a time of extravagant convictions. But Dennis Lee, it seemed to me then, was very much out of spirit with the times, because while the 60s extravagantly proclaimed that History Was Dead, Dennis Lee seemed to believe that it was the present that failed to exist — or that it existed only inasmuch as it was verified (even if in advance) by the future.

Of course it can be difficult to known what History's verdict will be. In its lieu, those of us who clustered about Anansi Press would often move along to the adjacent Red Lion on Jarvis Street, where we would drink beer and observe the traffic.

Among the hopeful drinkers was an intense West Indian writer called Harold Ladoo. Possessed by his own demons, he had been writing furiously for about a year when an Anansi writer came across his work and passed him onto Dennis. Eventually Anansi Press published two of the many novels he wrote. The first — *No Pain Like This Body* — was extremely well received. The second, *Yesterdays*, was published posthumously. In the midst of what seemed an unstoppable burst of writing, Ladoo had gone home to Trinidad to settle a family feud. To the immense regret of his Canadian admirers — but not to their surprise, for they had urged him not to go — the journey resulted in his murder.

The Death of Harold Ladoo is Dennis Lee's finest poem — perhaps a terrible way to describe a poem about a real person who died a real death — because it is his most personal poem. The subject is almost unforgivable, yet the purpose is not: to understand the death of a friend and colleague.

When I first read *The Death of Harold Ladoo*, I was totally transfixed — not a little because the poem was about a life that had existed in the same milieu as my own, and nor was Ladoo's death the first among Anansi writers — and yet as the manuscript went from draft to draft, for Dennis had the habit of showing drafts of his poems to various friends as he tightened them — it seemed to me that the poem crystallized into something beyond a letter to friends who had witnessed the same tragedy. Nonetheless, there was still the

33

question of what the poem might mean to people outside the tiny circle of Anansi's friends and acquaintances.

A couple of years later, when the poem had been published, I was visiting a friend in Winnipeg — a poetry editor and critic who has since become a published poet himself — who said to me that he considered *The Death of Harold Ladoo* not only Dennis's worst and most obscure effort, but an example of what was wrong with all Ontario (especially Toronto) poetry — i.e., its total self-absorption. It was *then* that I realized that I felt *The Death of Harold Ladoo* was not only a personally affecting poem, but a truly significant one. After all, where but in Canada does a poet get praised for being regional if he or she lives outside of Toronto, but damned for it if he lives *in* Toronto? Why is it so laudably human to write about the gulls of Vancouver, or the snakes and gophers of a Prairie childhood, but parochial and power-mongering to write about Jarvis Street or Yonge Street?

The Death of Harold Ladoo is, it seems to me, the ultimate Toronto poem — and Toronto, for all of its hatefulness (a myth it had the wit to invent for itself), is still the cultural centre of Canada. Technically sophisticated, steeped in a combination of guilt and the grasping for power, written to the rhythm of the machines of a city populated by those who distort and destroy their lives trying to succeed in its terms, *The Death of Harold Ladoo* is an act of biography that mines the particular instead of trying to deny and transcend it.

'Why,' asked my Winnipeg friend, 'should I care about what happened to someone in downtown Toronto?'

Even in Canada, the muse strikes in strange places.

* * *

Finding these places was, of course, Dennis Lee's speciality as an editor. In fact, even from Anansi's earliest days, Dennis had about him the aura of a man who could not only spot a superior work, or save a mediocre one, but also could see into the heart of the most twisted and unarticulated intentions.

It was this latter quality that made Dennis into such a sought-after reader (as he still is): a man who can see greatness in one's hopeless scribblings is a man to whom a manuscript should be sent.

Dennis gained this reputation, which eventually became an albatross, not only by sheer mythification, but as the result of a series of editorial interventions.

The first was when he took on the manuscript of a novel by Graeme Gibson. When it came to Anansi in 1967, it was a book desperately in search of a publisher. Dennis Lee, reading it, decided that what it really needed was an editor. By the simple expedient of cutting it almost in half — the deletions taking place on a line-by-line basis — he transformed the novel into Anansi's first big success. Then followed *The Collected Works of Billy The Kid* by Michael Ondaatje, still Ondaatje's best-known work; *Bartleby* by Chris Scott, a novel so wide-ranging in its use of the dictionary as to be virtually unreadable — and which, in consequence, attracted a reputation as *the* Anansi novel; *Technology and Empire* by George Grant; *Survival* by Margaret Atwood.

In each of these books Dennis's participation was not only crucial, but far beyond the role normally assigned to an editor. That is, he not only acted as a copy editor, or made structural suggestions, but he lent his energy to the day-by-day struggle of the writing and often — even usually — made suggestions so crucial that the books were fundamentally affected.

At the same time Dennis edited numerous books with which his involvement was more peripheral, though it seemed to the writers equally valuable. Into that category fell my own fiction, as well as the fiction of the other writers of Anansi's 'Spiderline' series of first novels, and most of the poetry Anansi published. My own first encounter with Dennis came in 1967, when he decided an article I had written for *This Magazine Is About Schools* — my first published piece, 4 pages of nonsense which took an almost equal number of months to write — should be republished in an anthology intended to be an attack on the educational system. The system survived, but in the meantime Dennis had asked me if I would consider submitting a novel to Anansi Press. Of course, I said, and shortly thereafter I purchased enough paper to make any writer's dream come true. As I worked on this novel, Dennis was starting to perform his miracles on other books: miracles of which he showed me tiny flashes as he sat hiding in my unmarked room at Rochdale College (where I had gotten my first job as writer-in-residence) smoking forbidden cigars and contemplating unspeakable sins.

Writers love a great editor because he saves their books — writers resent a great editor because he fails to save them. Into this second category I swiftly fell as the reviews informed me that my first novel was a talentless exploitation of a public who deserved better. Because my first novel had been released simultaneously with four others in what Anansi thought would be a brilliant publicity coup, I even had the pleasure of seeing my own lamentable production being compared — negatively — with those of equally hopeful writers. The most scathing of these occasions took place very close to The

35

Red Lion — at the CBC. In a studio there, William French of the *Globe And Mail* was seated at the head of a table around which the four writers cowered, and he delivered himself of a written speech spading each of us into our, no doubt well-deserved, place.

Unfortunately, like a recalcitrant Dickens schoolchild, I failed to grow in character as a result of this beneficial experience.

My next novel was such that Dennis not only failed to recognize its greatness, he even failed to offer to publish it. Nonetheless, by a weird series of twists, it ended up being accepted by McClelland and Stewart — an institution which, at that time, stood to Anansi Press in approximately the same moral relation as Torquemada stood to Joan of Arc.

Just the same, I was very happy. A writer of less saintly character would have chortled and rubbed salt in the Anansi wound: and so I did. And when the book was published and actually forgiven its existence by reviewers, I even dropped round to visit my former Anansi friends.

Instead of treating me as he should have, Dennis offered to look at whatever I was currently writing. That book was a volume of short stories which I enthusiastically sent to Dennis one-by-one as I wrote or revised them. After three months I had a book entirely different from the one which I had started. At that time in Anansi's history, Margaret Atwood had become Dennis Lee's coeditor on a number of projects: between their dual ministrations my stories had been exposed to such a combination of enthusiastic catalysis and skeptical dismay that whatever idea I'd had of what I was supposed to be writing was permanently shattered.

Whether this was a triumph or a tragedy I have never determined, but it seemed a logical conclusion to my years as an Anansi writer.

The Sheer Extent of It

Don Coles

WHAT AMAZES ME now is the sheer endless extent of it, of the patience and the spendthrift offering and re-offering of all that taste and tact and banked-up expertise. How *dared* I send or bring to him *three or four drafts* of so many of those poems (I'm speaking here mostly of my first book; recently I'm being allowed out on my own rather more) — and each of those drafts coming back with their margins thickly darkened with the economically-pencilled, tinglingly accurate notations!

To give a comprehensive picture of what I owe Dennis would fill up your issue. Briefly, here are some of his comments on just one poem, the opening poem in *Sometimes All Over*. It's called 'How We All Swiftly', and its focus is the novel thought that life is brief and its shiniest moments evanescent. A metaphor of children urgently unpacking birthday gifts plays a role.

A letter dated July 1974 is the first mention: 'I like it very much, though I query you sharply on the ending . . .'. The Xerox with pencilled comment followed: 'The last line-and-a-bit is wonky. Up above, the children are the "we" — running around distractedly and opening all the presents, but missing the real gift. But at the end they are "right" — why? for knowing that the real gift is there? One can only guess — you've changed the value of the children's response to gifts on the way through, but without telling the reader. As it stands the poem contradicts itself, virtually cancels itself out.'

In August another letter: '. . . I have suggestions for weaving the thing around a stage further; I wonder if the ending is at its fullest resonance yet. It may be because the journey image seems halfway a new one, at least in connection with the children (though it isn't really); I don't know what it is, it just feels to me as though it wants to be even righter than it is . . .'.

In September (having read another, evidently maladroit, redraft in the meantime): '. . . I'd suggest, with regard to that line, staying with the previous revision . . .'.

And later, on a Xerox: 'This is fine now — but is there another ounce somewhere?'

I have quoted here only those comments applicable to two lines in one poem; there are ten more remarks about the poem as a whole. And a comparable number on more than half of the poems in what eventually became that book. Some of them, by the way, very funny: 'A disgusting suggestion: crib some things from this (some discardable poem) for . . .?'; and again, 'On second thought, I'm not convinced that those last four lines *are* felt. They feel more like *angst de rigueur*.'; and again, 'Terribly false note. May be deliberate — but Pyrrhic!'

There's a lot of praise, too. Very important to me at the time (still is, of course, but you know what I mean).

Altogether it was rather splendid behaviour.

Dennis the Kid

Dennis Lee's Poetry for Children

The Tradition of Nonsense and Light Verse

Sheila Egoff

'A hill *can't* be a valley, you know.
That would be nonsense—'
The Red Queen shook her head.
'You may call it "nonsense" if you
like,' she said, 'but *I've* heard
nonsense, compared with which
that would be as sensible as a
dictionary!'

JUST A FEW MONTHS AGO, I asked a class of university graduates to quote a few lines from their favourite poems. After a long silence during which I thought they were summoning up lines from John Donne, T. S. Elliot or e. e. cummings, someone said cheerfully: 'Alligator pie, alligator pie', and the whole group burst into:

If I don't get some I think I'm gonna die
Give away the green grass, give away the sky;
But don't give away my alligator pie.

From there it was a natural step to 'Hey diddle diddle' and 'Hickory dickory dock'. All of which proves that Mother Goose and Dennis Lee are alive and well and living in the groves of Academe as well as in the kindergartens and that there is a connection between modern and old nonsense poetry. In his 'Postlude' to *Alligator Pie*, Dennis Lee quite rightly acknowledges his debt to the nursery rhymes just as almost one hundred and fifty years before Edward Lear quoted 'There was an old man of Tobago' as the inspiration for his limericks.

Nonsense is generally defined as no-sense. Nonsense verses do not contain any sparkling jests or parodies or ironies or wit or wisdom. Still less do they contain any noble thoughts. They are sheer nonsense and must be read as such.

I went to play in the park.
I didn't get home until dark.

But when I got back I had ants in my pants
And my father was feeding the shark.

I went to play in the park.
I didn't come home until dark.
And when I got back I had ants in my pants
And dirt in my shirt, and glue in my shoe,
And my father was tickling the shark. (AP)

One's first impression, after reading a group of nonsense verses is that anyone can do it. But in several ways, nonsense is more difficult to write than sense. Good nonsense verse demands just as much technical skill as that of any other kind of verse. The incongruity inherent in nonsense is produced 'not by ignoring the general laws of good poetry, but by upsetting them purposefully, and by making them, so to speak, stand on their heads'.[1] So the writer of nonsense verse must not only be a genuine poet, but must be an inhabitant of Topsyturvydom. It is a land where both Edward Lear and Lewis Carroll dwelled, Lear in the 'Gromboolian plain' in which grow the 'Calico Tree' and the 'Bong Tree' and Carroll on a seashore where a whiting asks a snail to 'walk a little faster'. Lee inhabits, at times, a more specifically Canadian physical and emotional geography, but where such places as Winnipeg and Nipigon take on an aura of make-believe.

In Kamloops
I'll eat your boots.

In the Gatineaus
I'll eat your toes.

In Napanee
I'll eat your knee. (AP)

In serious poetry the content is more important than any rhyme; indeed rhyme should be the perfect servant of the thought. But in nonsense verse — after the topsyturvy first line — the rhyme itself becomes the source of inspiration. Because it breaks all the rules it leads the poet into the most unusual situations. In the old nursery rhyme, 'a pocket full of rye' seems to demand 'four and twenty blackbirds baked in a pie'. And in his *Garbage Delight* (Macmillan, 1977), the nonsense refrain of 'Bitter batter' leads Lee to:

Bitter batter boop!
I'm swimming in your soup.

Bitter batter bout:
Kindly get me out!

Bitter batter boon:
Not upon your spoon!

Bitter batter bum!
Now I'm in your tum!

Nonsense rhythm is much more docile than nonsense rhyme. It adapts itself to the queerest words with a particular relish. Lewis Carroll has recorded the fact that 'The Hunting of the Snark' was really based on *one* line that came of itself into his mind one day, a line that eventually became the last line of a long poem. 'For the Snark *was* a Boojum, you see.' Lee has his rhythmical and fantastical animals too, 'The tickle tiger', 'The Lesser Glunk', 'The Enigmatic Grundiboob'. Sometimes too, the nonsense poet can dispense with new sounds or fantastic images; he can merely distort certain words in order to give them a proper ring as in:

What shall I do with McGonigle's tail?
It came off again, cause he swang on the rail (AP)

or

The tiniest man
I've ever seen
Sleeps deep in a heap
In a washing machine.

At eight each night
He goes downstairs
And he yawns and puts on
The pyjamas he wears; (GD)

Lewis Carroll's Bruno came close to an understanding of nonsense in his spelling lesson.

Sylvie was arranging some letters on a
board—E-V-I-L. 'Now Bruno,' she said,

'what does *that* spell?'
Bruno looked at it, in solemn silence,
for a minute. 'I know what it *doesn't*
spell!' he said at last.

Not all nonsense poems are first rate, and it is easier to show why
one is *not* than to explain why one *is*. Shel Silverstein is a much-
praised and popular American writer of nonsense verse, but not all
of it succeeds:

If I had a brontosaurus,
I would name him Horace or Morris.
But if suddenly one day he had
A lot of little brontosauri —
I would change his name
To Laurie. (Shel Silverstein. 'Where the Sidewalk Ends')

While such lines are humorous the rhymes are often awkward,
producing an equally awkward rhythm, and they are equally banal
in their word-play. Dennis Lee's poetic craftmanship and his talent
as a wordsmith never falters as can be seen in his memorable
Garbage Delight:

Now, I'm not the one
To say No to a bun,
And I always can manage some jelly;
If somebody gurgles,
'Please eat my hamburgles',
I try to make room in my belly.
I seem, if they scream,
Not to gag on ice-cream,
And with fudge I can choke down my fright;
But none is enticing
Or even worth slicing,
Compared with Garbage Delight.

With a nip and a nibble
A drip and a dribble
A dollop, a walloping bite:
If you want to see grins
All the way to my shins,
Then give me some Garbage Delight! (GD)

Garbage Delight can also be used to illustrate one of the greatest attributes of nonsense poetry — its musicality. If one of the essential tasks of the poet is to make music with words then nonsense poetry at least must rank first in its appeal to the ear. It is not the highest form of poetry but it is certainly the most purely poetical.

Not all of Lee's poetry falls into the nonsense vein. Much of it can be described as light verse, a category of poetry that, according to A. A. Milne

> observes the most exact laws of rhythm and metre as if by a happy accident, and in a sort of nonchalant spirit of mockery at the real poets who do it on purpose. But to describe it so leaves something unsaid; one must also say what it is not. Light Verse, then, is not the relaxation of a major poet in the intervals of writing an epic; it is not the kindly contribution of a minor poet to a little girl's album . . . It is a precise art which has only been taken seriously, and thus qualified as an art, in the nineteenth and twentieth centuries. It needs neither genealogical backing nor distinguished patronage to make it respectable.[2]

Many of Lee's lyrics have their roots in the versification of moral precepts — which was the standard fare for children in the 17th and 18th century — a light verse, light in the sense of cheerful, light-hearted, wistful, nostalgic. Lee has absorbed some of the cadences of the two best poets of this genre: for instance, his 'The Special Person' has the rhythm of Robert Louis Stevenson's 'My Shadow' while the cuteness of A. A. Milne can be seen in 'Being Five' and 'The Friends'. Lee's 'The Hockey Game' is even sub-titled 'With thanks to A. A. Milne'. In his light poetry Lee is at his best in lyrics such as 'Windshield Wipers', 'The Fishes of Kempenfelt Bay', 'A Song for Ookpik' and 'Skyscraper':

> Skyscraper, skyscraper,
> Scrape me some sky:
> Tickle the sun
> While the stars go by.

> Tickle the stars
> While the sun's climbing high,
> Then skyscraper, skyscraper
> Scrape me some sky.

Much of Lee's success in his poetry for young children is due to the fact that he is a traditionalist both in his nonsense verses and his light poetry. And there is no one more traditional and conservative than the young child. So Lee has retained all the qualities that make Lear and Carroll and Milne and Stevenson still appealing to to-day's child — a structured and consistent rhyme scheme that is pleasing to the ear; a musical rhythm that gets one's foot tapping in time to the verse; a good deal of humour and fun often combined with recognizable, gentle child situations.

However, Lee is no mere imitator; he has cooked the ingredients of the past in different measures and has added a few of his own. He is more concerned with the inner world of childhood than were his predecessors. This philosophy is best summed up in his ending to 'A Song for Ookpik':

Ookpik;
　Ookpik,
By your
　Grace,
Help us
　Live in
Our own
　Space (NK)

Lear and Carroll were interested in nonsense per se and this concentration gives their work a wild and an intellectual aura quite missing in poems such as Lee's 'On Tuesdays I Polish My Uncle' where the images of parks and sharks and 'beans in his jeans' and 'a bee on his knee' are more directly related to a child's experience than a 'slithy tove'.

In his domestic poetry Lee goes beyond the chiefly idyllic aspects of childhood as portrayed by Stevenson and Milne. Children, to him, are no longer the well-mannered mannequins of the past. He invests them with the qualities that are rightly theirs — spontaneity, vulnerability, curiosity, naughtiness and an ability to see through some of the shenanigans of the adult world. He subscribes to the belief that children are capable of experiencing life more openly and honestly than adults. In his own words — 'the point is to experience things directly, not to experience only nice things'.[3] So mixed in with the sheer nonsense are humorous looks at a child's frustrations from a child's point of view — 'The Bratty Brother (Sister)', whose title speaks for itself; 'Bloody Bill', a contact with bullydom; 'I Have My Father's Eyes', an acknowledgement that all kids have to listen to the parcelling out of family traits. This may make Dennis Lee sound like a child psychologist, which he is not. What he is, in the best tradition of nonsense and light verse, is a children's poet of our own time and place.

And for this he has been rewarded by the spontaneous affection of thousands of children (young and old). They may not remember the name Dennis Lee, and they certainly won't care that he is a Canadian, but his craftsmanship has already put much of his work into our national consciousness:

Alligator soup, alligator soup,
If I don't get some I think I'm gonna droop,
Give away my hockey stick, give away my hoop,
But don't give away my alligator soup.

[1] Cammaerts, Emile, *The Poetry of Nonsense*. George Rutledge & Sons Ltd., London, 1925, p.40.

[2] Milne, A. A., *Year In, Year Out*. London, Methuen, 1952, pp.198-9.

[3] Dennis Lee, 'Roots and Plays: Writing as a 35-Year-Old Children', *Canadian Children's Literature* No. 4, 1976, p.35.

Dennis Lee's Children's Poetry

Alison Acker

BEING SILLY IS serious business. To be as silly as a three-year-old drowning his shoes in the toilet or a six-year-old making mashed potato mountains — or as Dennis Lee writing children's poems — needs style, application and a sense of delicious anarchy. And without some parental disapproval, drowning shoes or reciting 'Bloody Bill the Pirate' wouldn't be half so much fun.

Dennis Lee obviously understands kids. He has the rhymes and rhythms down pat, and he shares their fascination with dirt and smells and bugs and all the 'squishiness' of the physical environment. If the *children* of fifty years ago had been the book buyers, Lee would have been just as successful then as he is now, but I doubt if our Depression grandfathers would have bought us *Garbage Delight*. They would have been shocked.

Today's parents are patsies. It is hardly worthwhile trying to shock them anymore. Tuned in to Bruno Bettelheim and the merits of the goriest Grimm, stamped out by so many child psychology theorists, and full of guilt about their own parental shortcomings, they shell out happily for Lee's books and keep asking for more. After all, they are so funny, aren't they?

And of course they are funny, but with the serious kind of fun that children take seriously, and which adults can only accept by dismissing as merely comic. Watching Dennis Lee read to an audience makes this obvious. The children squirm around his knees, eyes widening and screams just starting as Bigfoot emerges from the closet. The parents giggle politely. Dennis Lee is as solemn as a balding Ookpik. It's obvious whose side he is on.

The Canadian public, already so proud of Dennis Lee, would be even happier if they could turn him into a stand-up funny man. So articles written about him lean heavily on the arch or the frankly cute, such as a *Reader's Digest* profile of him as 'The Moppets' Minstrel'. Nobody expected Lewis Carroll to chortle over the Cheshire Cat or Edward Lear to have hysterics over 'The Pobble Who Had No Toes' and do a song and dance routine. But Disney, TV or perhaps our own wacky ideas about the joys of childhood have encouraged us to think that all children's literature and especially poetry, has to be funny, and those who write it slightly loony, too.

Sad things have happened to the figures who once stalked or

lurked in our childhood dreams, terrible and sublime. For the movies, Rudyard Kipling's dignified kings of the jungle have learned vaudeville. Hercules has become TV's The Hulk. Dragons have stopped breathing fire and begun to run errands and now even whales have to be funny to get an audience. Just as we have trivialized the experiences of childhood, so we trivialize its interpreters. E. B. White, author of *Charlotte's Web*, Maurice Sendak and even Dr. Seuss have lamented the fact that being a children's writer is not taken seriously as an occupation. It looks so easy.

Study of Dennis Lee's work, however, shows not only honest craft, originality and an understanding of children, but a delicate balance between anarchy and compliance with the contemporary mores. It is fine to beat up pirates and wash the 'blood and scum and rum' off your hands so long as you remember to buy a 'quart of two per cent' and take it home to Mum. Significantly, one of the favourites with children is the poem about the Bratty Brother who gets hurled off the CN tower and dumped into the furnace, while parents are happier with 'Windshield Wipers', a modern lullabye that puts the kids to sleep on the way home.

The content of Lee's poetry is a skilful mix to please both kids and parents. The kids enjoy the mud puddles, flies, songs about sitters and garbage and hockey and sharks. Best of all for the parents are the poems about food, that major gratification of the senses which so many of us never outgrow! But, for kids, it's the messy and outlandish food that is the real fun. *Alligator Soup* is more enjoyable than chicken, and *Garbage Delight* beats haute cuisine. Successful children's literature has always been a series of eating or being eaten, from ravenous giants to *The Tale of Peter Rabbit*, and now Dennis Lee's monster sings:

> I eat kids yum yum!
> I stuff them down my tum.
> I only leave the teeth and clothes.
> (I specially like the toes.) (GD)

But this monster runs away when threatened by a hungry girl, and even *Garbage Delight* is no more messy than a mix of butterscotch and 'hamburgles', which is tame stuff compared to the delicious messes scoffed down by Wilbur the pig in *Charlotte's Web*.

Lee's poems dive deepest into the cauldron of childhood fears and desires with their succession of monsters, but the tigers and sharks are never out of hand. When they make too much noise, they get sent to bed.

49

After all, Lee's world is still a very nice WASP world somewhere between Honest Ed's and Casa Loma, filled with laundromats and swings and dads and mums and bicycles, where the toughest problem for a kid is how to get your neck through the hole in a particularly stubborn sweater. It is a far cry from the world of many Canadian children, especially the immigrant kids just now getting attention from Canadian children's writers — as in *Come With Us*, by the Women's Education Press, where children speak for themselves about working every evening in dad's store at age ten, or getting punched out every day at school. Some of these kids might find Dennis Lee's content tame — but even they would undoubtedly enjoy his rhythms and his skill with words.

That's because Lee began with nursery rhymes, discarding the subject matter — all those jolly millers and shepherdesses — as exotic, and using instead good Canadian mailmen, Eaton's and Simpson's, Medicine Hat and the Mississauga rattlesnake. Occasionally, like the bored creators of the TV Saturday morning series, he slips in stuff intended to tickle the adults primarily, such as the sly references to William Lyon Mackenzie King and his mother. But generally he follows the time-tested practice — that goes back to cows jumping over moons and cats talking to kings — of mixing the familiar and the absurd.

Lee is great on diction. He gets exactly the right word to describe the 'swish' and 'fizz' of swinging and the 'fuzziness' of bears. Best of all are the poems that are almost entirely word play, like 'The Sitter and the Butter and the Better Batter Fritter' and the skipping rhymes.

Since traditions live on for centuries in the schoolyard, Canadian children still skip to rhymes about 'Engine Number Nine'. Now Lee's 'bouncing songs' about home-brew and ice cream pie have joined their repertoire. Lee's rhyming is solid. None of this fancy, half-rhyme stuff; instead 'thumbs' and 'bums' and 'jeans' and 'beans'. The finest poems are the cumulative ones that children delight in because they can join in, like 'On Tuesdays I Polish My Uncle'. For older kids there are puzzle poems like 'The Big Molice Pan and the Bertie Dumb'. And for parents to read to the very young there are lullabies with a nice A.A. Milne Teddy Bear feel to them, all snuggles and fur.

All these poems encourage language learning, sharpen the ear, open up a child's imagination to the joys of words, but that never becomes apparent. And maybe that is the trouble with Lee, because he makes it difficult for parents or teachers to go back to verse books with pretentious titles about 'flying with wings of fancy', books full of lovely but lifeless descriptions of trees and sheep. Despite their beautiful illustrations, other Canadian books of children's poetry have been pretty tame and boring.

A child brought up on Lee, however, could move up to Lear or Lewis Carroll with delight and acquire a love of language that might survive even high-school English classes. Let us hope, then, that that child never learns that Dennis Lee's poems are also educational. And that Dennis Lee never forgets whose side he is on, and never ceases to take seriously the fine art of being silly.

The Poetic Voice

The Poem as Score

Denise Levertov

DENNIS LEE'S POEMS are important to me above all because, more consistently than those of anyone else whose work I know, they manifest a full awareness of the poem as a form of musical score, in which melody — the pitchpatterns of the voice — is indicated to the reader by means of the deployment of the words on the page. He utilizes linebreaks and indentations with intelligent intuition to produce effects accessible to the reader without any need for special training: as long as the poem's structure is respected, and the typographical units are not disregarded, the melody emerges, audible out loud or to the inner ear — though of course the variations of individual or regional speech will modify it to some extent, just as the melodies of music (as distinct from those of speech and chant) are somewhat modified by one or another singer or instrumentalist, without radical disruption of the composer's intention.

A good example of his grasp of this technique is the second part of *Not Abstract Harmonies But*:

> How did I
> miss it? that
> haltingly, silently,
> openly, home
> each mortal being, hale or crippled or done,
> announces the pitch of itself in
> a piecemeal world. And
> here! it was always here, the living coherence!
> Not abstract harmonies but, rather, that
> each thing gropes to be itself in time and what is lovely
> is how, once brought to a pitch it holds & presides
> in the hum of its own galvanic being. (G)

The reader's attention is focused on the content, as is proper — but a subliminal directive is provided by the score, and in fact is precisely what *brings* the content into the understanding. I don't mean to suggest that layout is more important than diction and syntax! — rather it is the channel through which diction and syntax can move at the pace, and with the intonation, that bring them to full expression. Of course, Dennis Lee's content is interesting in itself, whether 'personal' in the accepted sense (as in the love poems) or in the greater complexity, equally personal, of the poems on Canadian history and politics, or of meditations on our time and on the artist in modern society, (as in *The Death of Harold Ladoo*) or in that searching out of the ground and air of reality and the sacred which gives its title to *The Gods*. If what he had to say lacked interest, his gift for structural precision would be a mere virtuosity, ornamental at best.

His diction, too, is very characteristic in its bold incorporation of unexpected words, often ugly in themselves, but accurate:

> . . . it lobs us aside, pale snot poor rags . . .

> power in tangible
> dollops . . .

> . . . smack in the clobber & flux
> coherence is born (G)

One could write also of the way his syntax reflects the movement of *inner speech*, that is, neither the broken and casual habits of our common utterance nor the articulation of preformed ideas that characterize prose but the fluent processes of a mature mind talking its way along interior paths. That, however, is inseparable from the melodic factor, the sense of score, which is to me, as I've said, his most notable attribute — especially in those poems where he has utilized interior spaces (or *articulations*), and indentations along with his sensitive line-breaks.

Lee's work is scarcely known in the United States (like much Canadian literature — much to my disgust, having seen Canadian bookstores full of American books) but I have been making a practice of getting my students to study his poems as illustrations of what my own theories of technique are. The techniques he exemplifies are not a manner, to be imitated — or to avoid imitating — but a *use of tools* which demonstrates their function, so that (given an ear and something to say) another person taking up the same tools is enabled to sound forth his or her *own* voice more clearly.

At Home In The Difficult World

Robert Bringhurst

IT HAS BEEN my good fortune to know Dennis Lee for close to a decade, not only as my slightly older, less foolish contemporary, but also as a valued friend. He has been my senior colleague and elder brother not only in the craft of words but in the craftlessness of living — the friend who had been there first in such quandaries as fatherhood, marriage, unmarriage, and scenting the acrid whiff of home. All this has been cushioned by distance — the physical distance between the Coast Range and Toronto — and by differences of heritage. He was born here, I am an immigrant; he is an easterner, I a westerner; he is a well-mannered, well-schooled urbanite, I a peasant outdoorsman; he in some measure a Greek, and I in some measure a Persian.

Be that as it may, I find in his work, as in him, neither the transient glitter and frittery hunches of urban concern, nor the wistful inconsequence of most well-mannered contemporary writing. I find there deep, unself-righteous good sense and trustworthy hunger, the praise of what is and what isn't, the manifold voice, flinty reticence, glee, the patient craftsmanship, wide scope and deep meditation which make him, in my view, the prince among Canadian poets. He is one of the few living poets known to me whom I am always, without exception, eager to read, and whom I can in honesty prod and castigate others to read.

It is not merely that he is very talented. Many poets are formidably talented; that is not enough. Lee has driven his talent courageously and warily against the central vacuum of our botched and thoughtless culture and, at great personal cost, has found words for us — which we might use, as he has, to begin to understand our sometimes beautiful, often ruinous presence in the world. He has not been content to make fine-tuned, lovely, essentially useless, ornamental poems around the edge of the gaping wound, or to blaze gorgeously and meaninglessly down the track of his own personal, heart-rending madness. He is that rarest of things in our age: not merely a poet, but a poet who knows, almost, what poetry is for.

Out of the darkness of that knowledge he has written poems which I am convinced are deeper and sturdier than those of any, bar none, among his predecessors in this country. Out of that knowledge too, he has worked tirelessly as editor, publisher, friend, and even functioned at times as a soft touch for money, to inspire his elders, juniors and contemporaries to better work, and to the invention at last of something worthy to be called Canadian literature. While espousing the conservative Canadian nationalism of George Grant, he has welcomed without reserve immigrant writers as various as Harold Ladoo, Michael Ondaatje, Giorgio di Cicco, Roo Borson and myself — not to mention the dean of immigrant writers in this country, George Faludy. The topic is touched on in *The Death of Harold Ladoo*, as Lee reviews briefly his years with the House of Anansi:

> For eight straight years of crud in public places
> we worked to incite a country to belong to
>
> . . .
> and every honest word on a page meant news of another comrade —
> like you, Harold.

In the first published version of that poem, the text read '*I* worked to incite a country'. The belated change reminds me to mention, also belatedly, another of Lee's qualities, hardwon and real — and that is his modesty.

Like every poet of stature, and particularly every modern poet of stature, he has had to reinvent his art in order to practice it. Like a smaller but rapidly increasing number of others — Dante Alighieri, William Butler Yeats and many third-world poets such as Okot p'Bitek come to mind — he has had to invent out of disparate pieces his very nation merely to write his first unimpeachable line.

For immigrant writers like myself, if I may dwell on that point for a moment, the problem is in some respects different. It is the necessary heresy of the uprooted always to reverse the terms of St. John's familiar sentence so that it says, 'In my house are many fathers' mansions,' while the native-born try to live up to the text as it stands. This puts the immigrant, from the looks of it, in league with technological man — world-man rather than earth-man, to borrow terms from Lee's *Savage Fields*. The immigrant, if he is ever to leave his cocoon, must fight that through in his own flesh until he reaches ground. But so it seems, increasingly in these days, must the stay-at-home — even though he come upon the problem from another side.

In Canada the two versions of the problem, for all their admitted differences, seem uncannily the same. First because colonization, like migration, muddles men's consanguinity with the earth. Second, because all of us — or rather, 99% of us — are still, in a deep sense, immigrants here.

How, out of this rootlessness, and how, out of the running sore and institutionalized idiocy of western civilization, its arms race, its rape of the earth, its poisoning of the rivers, lakes and air, its continuous conversion of footpaths into freeways and of ecologies into jobs, can a man write poetry which is neither irrelevant nor hideous nor insane? That very question — 'How can this be happening?' — persists in all Lee's writing. It is one of the great strengths of his work: that perpetual, attentive wonder.

Though it means repeating one or two things I have already said, I list here specifically some of the reasons his work as a poet has been important to me personally, as a slightly younger practitioner of the trade.

1 He has unconfused the poem and the text.

2 He churns up out of himself a multitude of selves and voices, and has learned through hard practice how to orchestrate and conduct them with magnificent skill. (Would that we could do so in our lives as well as in our writing.)

3 He has known that the true poem, as an outlaw in our society, must clear its own space before it can make itself heard, and has invented means for it to do so.

4 He has refused to be caught in the amber of his own illuminations.

5 He has known how necessary it is to start from scratch, to reground the language in earth and our lives. He has not, to my knowledge, published a glib page in more than a decade.

6 He has heard all around him the unresonant, nameless void, and has not for long supposed that that in itself was an answer to anything; nor has he ever ignored it.

7 There under his feet, where it was all along, he has truly discovered the ground.

8 He writes out of deep, continuous process instead of lugging a baited and set sensibility through airports and streets looking for something to 'write a poem about'. He doesn't waste his and the reader's time confecting 'occasional poems'. (He remarked once in

an interview with Alan Twigg: 'I have lots of private experiences and opinions, of course, but why clutter up the airwaves with more of that stuff? If that's all there is, better the paper stays empty. So I start from square one, which is silence. Often enough I just stay there.')

9 He thinks with his forearms, as a good musician must.

10 He knows — though how one learns it in Toronto is beyond me — that the poem is a route through mountains, twisting and climbing, picking up vistas now and again if the weather is clear, but always surrounded by things which are older and bigger than it is or we are.

11 He has learned how to speak to profound moral questions without either cringing or preaching.

12 He has never stopped growing.

I will speak to a few of these points in greater detail.

* * *

Lee's usual method of working is known not only to his friends but, through gossip and published interviews, to a wide circle of readers. That method is assiduous literary labor: many dozens or hundreds of drafts. Indeed, he has kept right on writing most of his best poems even after their first publication. His reverence is for the poem itself, not for the sometimes inspired but, by definition, always inadequate text which the poet may coax and cajole to the page.

Though it sounds like the most literary or writerly of methods, it in fact produces results markedly like those which we know from the oral tradition, in which poetic *technique* has its deepest ground. Among oral poets and storytellers, each performance is textually different from every other. Some presentations are better, some worse, but at a certain level of craft and of meditation, every version of the same story or poem may be equally worth hearing, because those versions are no longer successive drafts, no longer stations along a linear progression, so much as they are temporal incarnations attending upon and dancing *around* an unrealizable, and perhaps itself indeterminate, perfect form. Lee's late drafts too — that is to say, his published ones, and those he allows out in the mail to his friends — often partake of this quality, this radiant imperfection. (As a matter of fact, he is the only *literate* poet other than William Langland of whose work I care to own all the published versions.)

Behind this condition of radiant imperfection, the linear stage is still there — for me at least, often circuitous and snarly, but with a beginning, a middle (sometimes correctly spelled *muddle*) and, roughly speaking, an end. Part of Lee's genius is his skill at driving mulish, cantankerous humans along that path — both himself and others whose unpublished work has come into his hands. The first miles of that path are the miles of waiting — mooching around, as Lee likes to call it. The second leg is that of the early drafts, and the third is that at which something is more or less written, which the writer himself can begin to read. The work leaks out at some point along this latter stage — often not far enough along, for most of us are lazy or weak or harassed. We can call this last leg the editing stage, though that is to oversimplify matters greatly. I cannot speak concerning the earlier parts of the process, for there every traveller who is going anywhere is on his own. But in the final stage, where a certain amount of fellowship is possible, Lee is more selfless and determined than any other artist I have ever known.

That he is a compulsive and talented editor is, of course, public knowledge. He can be seen at work, in *Savage Fields*, where he cheerfully sets out to edit Leonard Cohen's *Beautiful Losers*, not in the least deterred by the fact that the book is already in print, and indeed had been so for ten years. That he is not just a good but in fact a great editor — and not just a great editor either, but the kind of great editor only a great writer can be — is known to those who have undergone the process with him, albeit painfully, reluctantly, or with the frostbitten energy of Protestant brides.

In the fall of 1981, Lee was editing my own selected poems, ultimately published as *The Beauty of the Weapons*. John Newlove and George Payerle had both combed through the text before Lee took his turn, and he and I began on it by trading marathon letters. It was then that I learned something I thought I already knew. I learned what an assiduous critic Dennis can be: perfectly capable of praising a poem up and down, all the while attacking it word by word, stanza by stanza until at first sight nothing seems to remain. Perfectly capable of saying, in effect, 'This is a beautiful poem, but all the words are wrong' — which, indeed, is sometimes the case. Early in this process Lee had phoned to say he wanted to edit the book in the flesh and was therefore flying to Vancouver. (The money to do so came, I am certain, out of his, not the publisher's, pocket.) By normal standards the editing was already done when, in

61

late November, he finally arrived. I put him up in my garret, and there for four days, sixteen hours a day, we went over the text syllable by syllable, stanza by stanza, page by page.

I had done something similar in my small way to a few others — none of them what you might think of as professional writers — and I am embarrassed to confess it had never occurred to me that anyone would, or indeed that anyone still could, do the same thing, twice as thoroughly, to me.

The occasion is memorable now for other reasons too, of course. Lee had at that time forbidden himself liquor, and in recompense was drinking vast quantities of an appalling concoction of coconut pulp and fruit juice, as well as smoking furiously, hustling back and forth between his pipe and his cigars. He was also mildly troubled by his back, and for that reason among others I had given him the only bed, while I slept on a folding cot, at home in my favorite sleeping bag. It was the first time in five or six years — the first time since I had myself given up tobacco — that I'd suffered smoker's cough, but the cause of it was plain enough. What puzzled me was that it seemed to grow worse each night, when Lee was at last asleep, breathing air instead of smoke, and when even his smoke-filled clothes were out of range, with him, in the other room. Only after he left did I discover that the tar-laden rags from his twice-daily pipe cleaning, as well as the cigar butts, had been piling up in the trash can hard by the head of the cot where, each night, I lay down hoping to breathe.

Those four pencil-to-pencil, nose-to-nose days were the crux of the process, though it continued in fits by mail for several more months and came more or less to its end the following June, in a Malaysian cafe on St. Clair Avenue in Toronto, with Lee plucking an errant comma out of a laggard page. Then the book went to Ellen Seligman, McClelland & Stewart's house editor, who started again from page one.

Two days after that final haggle, over satay sauce and beer on St. Clair Avenue, I met at a poetry festival a young woman who proudly informed me she was editing her *own* book, soon to be released by a reputable Toronto publisher — and I confess, with no embarrassment at all this time, I could have cried.

* * *

I have spoken too much about myself already in this essay, when its proper subject is the work and talent of Dennis Lee. I want however still to reflect on some shreds of our conversation during those days in the autumn of 1981.

Lee's essays on the subject of cadence and polyphony — which, oddly enough, I had not read at that time — are among the masterpieces of reverential explication. I know no writing which better exemplifies Lew Welch's splendid motto: 'Guard the mysteries! Constantly reveal them!' Yet their terms are often terms which feel unnatural to me with regard to my own work. In the evenings of those days, after long hours over the poems, we sometimes listened to favorite tape recordings of mine — John Lewis's compositions for jazz quartet, dead Ben Webster smoking his saxophone like a brass cigar, and Daniel Barenboim playing the late sonatas of Beethoven. (Lee when I visit him plays Charlie Parker, John Coltrane, and sometimes the pianist Jimmy Yancy.) And to this accompaniment I tried clumsily to explain things I still cannot explain, about chromatic and achromatic image clusters and chords, and interwoven sequences of images — polyphonies, I called them, though polychory might have been a better term. Casting about for common ground from which to triangulate the discussion, I asked if he had read Claude Lévi-Strauss's *Mythologiques*. No, came the answer. He was deeply uncomfortable with the whole approach, with what he had called 'its conviction that the ultimate use of reason is to map transformations between value-free structural grammars'.

I found myself still trying to talk about patterns, melodies, sequences, clusters — audible, visual, noetic; I do not know; but structures, themes — made of what I called images. I hope someday to know, now that I have read Lee's essays on *cadence*, whether he and I are pointing at the same or different things with these different metaphors — his enviably consistent and carefully thought, mine clumsily synaesthetic.

The answer does not lie, I agree, with the critics — even the most brilliant ones, like Lévi-Strauss. Yet I do not begrudge Lévi-Strauss his pretense (for it is a pretense) to value-free mapping. I do not ask him to tell me which stories or motives or themes coincide with which values. I turn to him rather as I turn to Banfield's *Mammals of Canada* or Peterson's *Guide to Western Birds*, for details of habitat, range, dentition and anatomy. It is value-free taxonomy in pretense, but compiled, I believe, *ad maiorem deorum gloriam*, whether the compiler might wish that or no.

I am often unable to follow Lévi-Strauss's analyses, which may for all I know be riddled with error; but I hear two dogs sniffing the same wind when Dennis talks, at first hand, about cadence, and Lévi-Strauss, writing at second hand, as a critic, and using different metaphors, says 'Nous ne prétendons donc pas montrer comment les hommes pensent dans les mythes, mais comment les mythes se pensent dans les hommes, et à leur insu'. Dennis speaks about hearing a music; I am more inclined to say that I see it, yet music seems to me the proper word. I have learned more about how to build poems from reading the scores of and from listening to Ludwig van Beethoven's later piano sonatas than from any writer I can name — and as much about metric from Miles Davis as from that other great master of airborne time and timed images, William Butler Yeats. But Dennis will not disagree with me there. Indeed, I could *think* a very interesting essay on Dennis Lee and Charlie Parker, though I could not write it, for I do not know the words.

And I don't know yet how to tie that conversation down, though I think I do know *where* to tie it. Bumblingly, borrowing phrases and words here and there, I should try to say it something like this. Men do not think; thought thinks. Thought is the function of life in the mind. And it is not that the mind affords insight into the world; rather the world presents itself in the mind, because the mind is of, is made out of, the world. Or call it the earth. It is the earth in Lee's terms. I am somehow prone myself to keep calling it the world. The mind is a natural outgrowth of the world, like appleblossoms or racoon fur, like snow crystals, toadstools or the knee. Images, myths, clusters and sequences of images, bouquets of voices, breed in recognizable forms in the minds of men on different continents and in different years just as, in the marshes of different continents, mosquitoes and monkshood and buttercups do. Myth, man, mind, mosquito, monkshood leaf and flower are all born out of the earth, all children of the world. *Les mythes se pensent dans les hommes, et à leur insu.*

Students of Buddhism sometimes face this proposition through a sentence of Seng-chao, an early fifth-century sage who was the principal student of Kumarajiva. The sentence says: *wù wō t'úng ken, shíh fei i ch'î*; beyond me to translate, but I will try: 'Things and ourselves have the same root; is and isn't are one thing, which is what we are.' To some of the thinking which this sentence urges upon us we will presently return.

For now it is time to listen more closely to some of the words of Dennis Lee.

* * *

I have said that Lee is an urban poet. In fact I had been reading him for several years before it dawned on me how deep and central was the presence of the earth in all his writing. I am at a loss to know now how I missed it, unless in my western arrogance I presumed

64

that it couldn't be there, and took what I saw for Ontario pastoralism. It is, of course, not that at all.

We can begin at the beginning, with the fourth poem in *Kingdom of Absence*. The shad flies are beating themselves to death against the screen of what I take to be a cottage near Lake Muskoka, and Lee is watching his daughter watching, when something else obtrudes on his consciousness:

> High above the Severn
> the loons beat north, barbaric, cold, serene.

This by itself could indeed be pastoralism of a kind. You could find it, for instance, in the best Sung poets, like Liu Yung. You would find nothing there, though, like these lines from later in the sequence:

> How should a man endure
> mere energy, crammed naked into flowers?
> . . .
> We explicate the trees but they go on sorrowing
> mutely beyond us, botched in our dimension.

These are the early stirrings. But it is between the first and second published versions of the *Civil Elegies* (which is when Lee says he really began to listen to cadence) that the vision of the earth takes hold. In the lead poem from the volume *Civil Elegies and Other Poems*, the speaker finds his enlightenment, if that is the right term, in the trees:

> . . . the
> birches dance, and they
> dance. They have
> their reasons. You do not know
> anything.

It occurs again with a simple patch of grass in 'Sibelius Park':

> The grass is wet, it
> gleams
> . . . till the green goes luminous and it does it
> does, it comes clear.

65

But it is in the reworked *Elegies* themselves that we find the hard-won, magnificent passages, beginning *moderato* in the 1st Elegy:

>   . . . in dread to live
> the land, our own harsh country, beloved, the prairie,
>   the foothills —
> and for me it is lake by rapids by stream-fed lake, threading
> north through the terminal vistas of black spruce, in a
> bitter, cherished land it is farm after
> farm in the waste of the continental outcrop —
> for me it is Shield but wherever terrain
>   informs our lives and claims us . . .

and *ritenuto*, concluding the final Elegy:

> Earth, you nearest, allow me.
> Green of the earth and civil grey:
> within me, without me and moment by
> moment allow me for to
> be here is enough and earth you
> strangest, you nearest, be home.

Is it possible that we might, at last, learn to hear those lines?

In the first published version of a poem entitled 'The Gods' (Kanchenjunga Press, 1978), the gods strode powerfully out of the landscape, seething:

>   I do say
>   gods
>   old ripples of presence
>   archaic eddies of being, a space ago
>   their strokes and carnal voltage, as
> *pineforce   potence-of-bearswipe   voicing-the-thunder.*
> In the middle of one more day, in a clearing maybe   say, birches
>   calm on the lope of its pads
>   furred   hot-breathing   erect, at ease, catastrophic
>   . . .
>   — thus, the god against us in clear air;
>   or simply
>   light that rises from lake-face,
>   melding with light
>   that drifts like a liquid
>   windfall down to

> evoke it —
> such grace in the shining air.
> All gods, all gods and none of them
> domesticated angels . . . .

In the revision of that poem (McClelland & Stewart, 1979), Lee backed off considerably. The wilderness images are gone, and instead we have such lines as:

> who, now, can speak of gods? for random example,
> a bear to our forebears, and even to
> grope in a pristine hunch back to that way of being on earth
> is nearly beyond me.

I do not admire the new pun nor applaud the new reticence, but I believe absolutely that it is genuine. I believe this is a man in terror of blasphemy drawing back from what he cannot claim to know. It is something I mentioned before. It is modesty.

Lee, I think, would say too that it is a man drawing back from idolatry. The fruitless progress from love to idolatry of a woman's body is, after all, the theme of the sequence of poems into which this one has settled home. This sequence (*also* called 'The Gods') begins:

> Wal   I got a gal
>   on my   kazoo
> and she looks real good,
> like a good gal
>   should,

and ends:

> Forgive me.

Women and earth. In tension, of course, with the city, Toronto. It is a duality which Lee speaks of elsewhere using Martin Heidegger's terms, *Erde und Welt*, earth and world; and we will face it in those words presently. It echoes in Lee's work with another duality, the duality mentioned by Seng-chao — who was telling us, you will recall, that these dualities are no more dual than single. 'Is and isn't are what we are.'

The complex relationship between earth and world on the one hand, and void and being on the other, will, I believe, come as clear in the following quotations as it comes in any writing elsewhere.

Once again, we can begin with the early poems in *Kingdom of Absence* (indeed, we might begin with its title):

> . . .
> To live that lie from courage, knowing leaf
> and loam for absolute, but speaking the objects,
> making it conscious, improvising cosmos,
> is much. Is human. But is not the ground.
> . . .
> I eat the darkness, . . .
> hearing the word that rides beneath the silence:
> 'My ground is your abyss,' and then my breathing.
> . . .
> He cannot speak what is, unless his words
> be uttered by the darkness where it rides.
> . . .
> Yes. Only in this absence . . .
> only in this poverty
> and absence can the simple-witted spring
> achieve right flowers in the fetid concrete,
> or lovers do their bughouse in the mind.
> . . .
> . . . and not the climb
> and kindling of the spirit, where it lifts
> and flowers, standing gently into Being,
> but this: in the blank heartlands of absence . . . .

Many modern poets could have written these words, if many modern poets could write this well. But Lee gave up wooing the void when he learned to hear something more interesting. In a little poem called 'Words for the Given' we are given these words:

> If I take up space in the silence, master, friend —
> let it be, we all live here and do not matter.
> . . .
> No listen, I still don't know but what does that
> matter? Listen.   It is.   It is.   It is.

Now that we have both halves of the equation, the absence acquires new presence. We encounter it full force in the *Elegies*:

> the Archer declares

that space is primal, raw, beyond control and drives toward a
living stillness, its own.
                . . . if a man strays into that
vast barbaric space it happens that he enters into
void and will go
under, or he must himself become void.
. . .
Small things ignite us, and the quirky particulars
flare on all sides.
A cluster of birches, in moonlight;
a jack pine, gnarled and
focussing heaven and earth —
these might fend off void.
. . .
But massy and knotted and still the Archer continues its space,
which violates our lives, and reminds us, and has no mercy upon us.
For a people which lays its whiskey and violent machines
on a land that is primal, and native, which takes that land in greedy
innocence but will not live it, which is not claimed by its own
and sells that land off even before it has owned it,
traducing the immemorial pacts of men and earth . . .
that people will botch its cities . . .
                        and prising wide
a civil space to live in, by the grace of its own invention it will
fill that space with the artifacts of death.

On Queen Street, therefore, in Long Branch, wherever the
people have come upon it, say that the
news is as bad as we thought:
we have spent the bankroll; here, in this place,
it is time to honour the void. (CE 3)

Those lines — strong enough to set beside the choruses of Sopho-
cles — take us to the end of the 3rd Elegy, and the theme is picked
up again without pause at the beginning of the 4th Elegy:

    Among the things which
    hesitate to be, is void our
    vocation? . . .
    Dwelling among the
    bruised and infinitely binding world
    are we not meant to

relinquish it all, to begin at last
the one abundant psalm of letting be?

If only it
held.
    . . . nothing
belongs to us, and
only that nothing is home.

Lee has learned (like Sophocles, though in terms more vicious
than Sophocles dreamed) that the theme embraces politics:

For a man who
fries the skin of kids with burning jelly is a
criminal. Even though he loves children he is a criminal. Even though his
money pumps your oil he is criminal, and though his programs infest
        the air you breathe he is
criminal and though his honest quislings run your
government he is criminal and though you do not love his enemies he is
criminal . . . .

And this is void, to participate in an
abomination larger than yourself. It is to fashion
other men's napalm and know it, to be a
Canadian safe in the square. . . . (CE 5)

And it embraces, or swallows, what passes for love:

                    for there are
    few among us who are competent at being, and few who can
    let our lovers be. (CE 6)

It is tested and questioned through the person of Hector de Saint-
Denys-Garneau, 'master of emptiness', and with Garneau's example
before him, Lee is finally free to draw back. The voice that rises to
speak here speaks against pursuing the void, even as a religious vo-
cation, for that is

    the graveyard of many for want of the lore of emptiness,
    which once was a sane thing, but now of those who begin
    their lonely inward procession I
    do not know a chastened handful who survive.
    . . .

70

And I will not enter void till I come to myself
nor silence the world till I learn its lovely syllables . . . . (CE 8)

By this hopscotch of quotations we have come to the end of the
penultimate elegy. In the final poem a new set of questions is asked,
and new answers propounded which ratify the decision already an-
nounced, not to follow Garneau but to stay in the world. We do not,
in fact, says the poem,

> have recourse to void.
> For void is not a place, nor
> negation of place.
> Void is not the high cessation of the lone self's burden,
> crowned with the early nostalgias;
> nor is it rampant around the corner, endlessly possible.
> We enter void when void no longer exists.
> . . .
> And I must learn to live it all again, depart again —
> . . .
> finding a place among the ones who live
> on earth somehow sustained in fits and starts
> by the deep ache and presence and sometimes the joy of what is.
> Freely out of its dignity the void must
> supplant itself. . . . (CE 9)

Out of this realization, concession or truce, issue the final lines (al-
ready quoted): 'Earth, you nearest, allow me . . . .'. To them we have
come, from the voice which saw, at the end of the 7th Elegy,

> no hope that we might come to our own
> and live, with our claimed selves, at home in the difficult world.

And we have traced one thread in the weave of the poem. One
thread which is two; two threads which are one.

By and large in the following volume, *The Gods*, we hear more of
what is than what isn't:

> Not abstract harmonies but, rather, that
> each thing gropes to be itself in time and what is lovely
> is how, once brought to a pitch it holds and presides
> in the hum of its own galvanic being.

This is the fruit of the decision, announced in the *Elegies*, to con-

tinue to live in the world. Some of the fruit. There is more; or you
may say there is husk and seed.

> For a civilization cannot sustain
> lobotomy, meaning the loss of awe,
> the numbing of *tremendum* . . .
> it cannot dispel the numinous, as we have done for
> centuries without those exiled gods and demons rushing back
> in subterranean concourse,
> altered, mocking . . . .

> A world that denies
> the gods, the gods
> make mad . . . .
> > Even that glorious dream
> > of opening space to be in, of saying
> > > the real words of that space —
> > that too was false, for we cannot
> > idolize a thing without it going infernal . . . .

The poem I am quoting here is as fine as any poem I know made
in this century. I put it with Federico García Lorca's 'Llanto por Ig-
nacio Sánchez Mejías'. What else can I say in its praise? It is called
The Death of Harold Ladoo. It begins with a fallen elm; it ends in the
dark beneath a living linden. Native tree gone down; hybrid import
thriving.

> Night inches through. It's cold. I wish I were sleeping,
> or stronger, more rooted in something real . . . .

And it is written in our language. It sings in the simple, banal,
quirky, eternally broke and obscenely rich tongue of its place and
time.

> I hope this is enough.
> And, to let the beings be.
> And also to honour the gods in their former selves,
> albeit obscurely, at a distance, unable
> to speak the older tongue; and to wait
> till their fury is spent and they call on us again
> for passionate awe in our lives, and a high clean style.

It is the work of a man with no appetite for cheap and easy answers. Count the poets, living or dead, of whom it is possible to say the same.

The answers he *has* found for himself, and has found for us, are: earth *and* the human world; void *and* being; gods *and* godlessness. Not one cancelling or greying the other, but each shining into and out of the face of the other. These are the difficult rules of being here, at home in the difficult world.

Yet if I say Lee has 'found' these answers, if I call them 'rules', have I not unsaid everything the poems, in their intricate, tentative dance, have been saying? Another sentence, plucked from the store; this one from Martin Heidegger: *Jede Antwort bleibt nur als Antwort in Kraft, solange sie im Fragen verwurzelt ist.* 'Every answer remains in power as an answer only so long as it is rooted in questioning.'

Let us return in that spirit to the second half of Seng-chao's sentence. *Shih fei i ch'i.* 'Is, isn't: one weather.' Or: 'Yes, no: one breath'. Or: 'To be and not be are one energy'. Or: 'To be breathed is to be and to not be'. None of these is correct, nor do the translations move successively toward the target, like the shots of a hunter finding his windage. They dance around, like the shots of one who has not yet learned how to breathe.

* * *

The larger poems we have been listening to — the *Civil Elegies, The Gods, The Death of Harold Ladoo* — are poems Lee calls meditations, and it will be well for us to consider how apt the name, and what it means.

Yet how shall we speak of these things? There are books to be quoted, names to be mentioned, connections to be described; but to what end? The process of meditation, not the literature which surrounds it, is what we must learn to hear in listening to these poems. So we encounter a familiar problem; those who know, know; those who do not must come to the knowledge in their own good time. The world divides into those to whom one cannot speak and those to whom one does not have to. Yet it is necessary to try.

No hints, no literary clues are needed to point to the meditative content of the poems, but one has been provided, and we may, out of courtesy, take it as a thread with which to begin.

The *Civil Elegies* in their revised form carry two epigraphs. One is from an essay by George Grant on political philosophy. The other consists of two conflated sentences from the *Dohakosha* of Saraha, a Buddhist text written in one of the ninth-century Prakrit vernaculars of eastern India. Tradition would have it that Saraha was a master archer — and who can say but what his presence haunts the

statue in Nathan Phillips Square? Be that as it may, the verses col-
lected under his name speak eloquently of the central thesis of the
Mahayana: that *śunyata*, meaning voidness, emptiness, the unreality
of the real — *and* meaning the wisdom of knowing that what is is
empty — is inseparable from *karuna*, meaning compassion, the deep
love of what is, standing open to the pain and glory of the living
world. These two together, *śunyata* and *karuna*, say the Mahayana
masters, are the principles of *bodhicitta*, the enlightened mind.

This is one of the dwelling points of Mahayana meditation.

Behind the verses of Saraha lie the writings of Nagarjuna, the
great Mahayana dialectician. And there (*Mulamadhyamikakarikas*
25:19) we find a famous formulation which can be summarized in a
symbol and two words: *samsara* = *nirvana*. That is to say, the world
of perfect enlightenment is *identical with* the empirical, frightened,
mucked-up, quotidian world. What you see is what you get. How
then do you choose to see it?

This is another dwelling point for meditation.

With these ideas in mind, we may listen again to some lines from
the 9th Elegy:

> And what if there is no regenerative absence?
> What if the void that compels us is only
> a mood gone absolute?
> We would have to live in the world.
> What if the dreary high-rise is nothing but
> banks of dreary high-rise, it does not
> release the spirit by fraying its attachment,
> for the excellent reason that there is no place else to go?
> We would have to live in it, making our lives on earth.
> . . .
> We enter void when void no longer exists.
> . . .
> Earth, you nearest, allow me . . . .

And we may listen to a few sentences from Lee's essay, 'Cadence,
Country, Silence':

> What we know is never a giant emptiness — unless we are
> merely playing with the idea of emptiness, which is a pursuit
> for dilettantes. We do not encounter Void, we encounter this
> void and that. And in the particular ground of their own
> lapsed existence . . . it is *this* friendship, *this* orange-tree, *this*

street-corner which take on resonance and demand to be written.

But each is true only in the embrace of the other. Nonbeing and what is: we cannot know either authentically by itself. Each is home to the other. Hence to give homage to the world for itself is idolatry — but to give homage to the void for itself is also idolatry. To accept nonbeing at home in what is, to accept what-is at home in nonbeing, is perhaps the essential act of being human.

How much actual acquaintance with Buddhist tradition underlies that essay and the *Elegies* I do not know and, in fact, do not especially care. Certainly there is no trace of dilettante orientalism in either. Nor do I want to imply that the only meditative tradition is the Mahayana tradition. Lee, if I am not mistaken, feels much nearer to Christian contemplative practice, as we know it through Hugh of St. Victor and John of the Cross. I speak to the poems myself in Buddhist terms because those are the terms I know, and because they happen to fit the shape of what I hear in the *Civil Elegies*. That does not make Lee a Buddhist, though it may indeed demonstrate the ecumenical strength of his writing. Even the epigraph from Saraha — missing from the first edition — may well be, as epigraphs often are, a discovery after the fact. The resemblances, the recurrences, are real in either case, and to encounter them is a source of joy — just as it is a joy, having known the alpine larches of the Hozameen Range in British Columbia, to come over a ridge into a grove of larches different yet the same, taller, with pinker bark, a different species, in the hills of northern Italy. Nor are these recurrences value-free. The rediscovery of the earth, in any language, and the reinvention of the world, are the rediscovery of value where it lies — not in real estate, not in minerals; those metaphors have turned vicious — but in earth and world somehow, somehow right there in the ground's touch upon us and the way we touch the ground.

There is more, of course. We could read the sequence of poems which forms Part I of *The Gods* in the light of the *Hevajra Tantra* or the *Cittaviśuddhi Prakarana* of Aryadeva, for instance, which tell us that passion both ties and releases the world, that 'the skillful know how to cure passion with passion itself . . . as the wise man cleanses himself with impurities' — but these investigations should be conducted by someone better schooled than I in the Buddhist tradition, lest they lead us from the theme.

75

Meditation, we were saying, has something to do not with melting dualities down, but with kindling them into illumination: wringing out of them at least a faint light. It is also the process of casting off selves until none remain, and until the spring they bubble up from is momentarily quiet. It is the casting off of voices — a process which, pursued as Lee pursues it, can produce what he calls polyphonies: ghosts of the self, multiple voices speaking the poem. Meditation in this sense means: *instrumentation*. It is the agency of the orchestral colors of the poem. It will be a useful exercise sometime, when we have learned more clearly how to listen, to try to count and name the voices — the violins, horns and hurdy-gurdies — which Lee blows in performing these poems.

After the meditation, what? For those of us who are not saints, the pool of selves will soon enough again begin to boil. And if it is true that the world is true and beautiful, who can complain? In *The Gods* is a poem entitled 'Remember, Woman':

Remember, woman, how we lay
Beside ourselves the livelong day
And tuned out all that heady fuss
And felt new lives invading us?

We loved, as though our bodies meant
To fire their own enlightenment,
And raise, despite our moral dread,
A carnal om on a rumpled bed.

Remember how the light that shone
Spilled from within you? Off and on
The switch was easy, and we lit
Eternal brightness for a bit.

. . .

Brothers, lovers, mothers, wives —
Glad ambush by a dozen lives.
Fresh selves of you, new many me,
A sacrament of letting be.

. . .

Cocky beatitude! which sank
To getting by in brain and flank.

The fire went out; our lives grew sane.
Sweet Christ, I long for then again!

This sometimes meditative, sometimes tantric, sometimes frayed
multiplicity of selves is, of course, another theme which can be
traced through the poems from the very beginning. It is not some-
thing that an impressionable author, orphaned by the death of one
culture, picked up by reading blithe, modish treatises on the exoti-
cism of another. It is something he has worked to name because it
confronted him in the deep midst of his living. By means of a
process called meditation — a process I have been saying is
analogous to, is botanically related to, not propagated *from*, the
dhyana or *ch'án* of Mahayana Buddhist tradition — Lee has put this
multiplicity to work. In *Kingdom of Absence*, the multiplicity is merely
named:

One by one my body turns to clay.
When I review my troop of scruffy selves
and count personae . . . .

In the *Civil Elegies*, in *The Death of Harold Ladoo*, it is enacted; the
voices are marshalled and tuned. Nor is the assemblage haphazard.

A man should not make of his friends a
blur of aesthetic alternatives:
nor of himself, though it feels good.
. . .
And I unsay nothing, friend I must continue
locked with you for keeps in this tug of cherishing war,
but always now I return to the deep unscheduled ground of caring
in which we lived our lives . . . . (LADOO)

* * *

I mentioned a moment ago three genera of multiplicity, calling
them for convenience's sake the meditative, the tantric, and the
frayed. The names will do, if we do not make too much use of them.
Concerning the third genus there is a sobering passage in *Savage
Fields*, a book to which, now, before this meditation is through with
us, we should turn.

When there is no longer any pattern for being human which

77

has absolute sanction, man must invent himself. It is the inception of radical freedom.

Yet the result is very bitter. A man has limitless scope to be anything at all — and nothing at all to be. For the meaning of being human no longer has any valuative content; and as men process the raw material of potential selfhoods, they find every new model of self going inert again before they have properly constructed it. Radical freedom means a plethora of alienated selves, free-floating I-systems, mocking a self which has been unselved of all but the will to create itself.

This is a part of Lee's diagnosis of our condition under the reign of expansionist western liberalism. It describes the terminal stage of a disease which, in its earlier forms, looked like an excess of health: the eager charge of humankind against the frontiers of history and knowledge, unlocking the fetters of superstition, conquering earth and sky. It is the legacy of a duality that wasn't one: a duality in which one term (man against nature, or in the words we must now begin to use, world against earth) has been allowed to supersede.

But *Savage Fields*, as that excerpt will remind us, is a work of expository, monophonic prose: a different fish from the polyphonic poems to which we have been listening. Moreover it masquerades, rather unfortunately, as a work of literary criticism — and it has readily been accepted as such in the intellectual subcultures where 'criticism' has become yet one more form of entertainment: the debased and ingenious metaphysics of yet one more paper world.

That problem aside, *Savage Fields* is still a difficult work to read intelligently. It is a book about our presence in the world, yet it comes to its position through the study of two other books — Michael Ondaatje's *Collected Works of Billy the Kid* and Leonard Cohen's *Beautiful Losers*. Both of these are works which investigate the energies of self-destruction; and the study pursues its subjects so tenaciously that it, even more than they, seems continuously on the verge of fission.

It is the thesis of the work that *world* (which means all that is, understood as acculturated, manipulated, taken) and *earth* (all that is, understood as natural, unconscious, given) are coextensive and at war. The metaphor is that of interpenetrating, contradictory magnetic fields.

It is a concept *like*, but not the same as, the interfused duality of voidness and affection, and the coextensive dualities of botched world and beautiful world, godless world and numinous world, which we have heard invoked and kindled in the poems. Like them in that one of its rules is: everything that is, is both. Unlike them, of

78

course, in the definition of its terms. Whether that is the only differ-
ence is harder to say. We are dealing here no longer with poems,
which say what they mean, but with systems, orthodoxies, cosmolog-
ical models, which say what they are forced to say under pressure of
a given argument at a given time. Shall we compare Lee's insistence
on the strife of world and earth to the Buddhist insistence on the
noble truth of pain? The results could only be inconclusive.

We are left with the thesis as we are given it: world and earth,
coextensive and at war.

We could name some other dualities it is *not* like. It is, for in-
stance, not very much like the old dichotomies, man and nature,
mind and body, object and subject, father and mother, intellect and
feeling. These familiar pairs do not follow the rule: everything that
is, is both. Nor do other, similar dualities that come to mind: culture
and nature, animus and anima, and so on.

Again we are left with the thesis as given.

In the system Lee has proposed, the old frontier between cons-
cious and unconscious, culture and nature, world and earth, has
been atomized and distributed. The frontier is everywhere and no-
where, and wherever it is, is the war. What wilderness yet remains,
exists by the grace of world, in sanctuaries, in parks; and all the ani-
mals on earth are, rightly speaking, in the zoo. If this vision is a little
futuristic, it is all too easy to see it quickly coming true.

The question posed by *Savage Fields* is: is there any escape? Deep
behind its argument lies George Grant's *Technology and Empire*, a
study of the intellectual and moral bankruptcy of western liberal-
ism, and of the inability of Canada to withdraw from that moral in-
solvency even were Canadians sane enough to wish to. Grant had
foreseen no escape, though he had a notion where to look for it. In
an essay 'In Defence of North America' he had written:

When we go into the Rockies we may have the sense that gods
are there. But if so, they cannot manifest themselves to us as
ours. They are the gods of another race, and we cannot know
them because of what we are, and what we did. There can be
nothing immemorial for us except the environment as object.

Couched in these terms, the prophecy is self-fulfilling. But the
proper question is a different one. It is: *can we manifest ourselves to
them as theirs?*

This is a question *Savage Fields* tries to pose. It is a question which
The Death of Harold Ladoo and *The Gods* attempt to answer.

The values the book gropes toward are what matter, of course, and not the book. *Savage Fields* is a work in progress, a treatise-in-draft to which the author has already published (in an article entitled 'Reading *Savage Fields*') a first set of emendations. But there is something to be learned by watching the book-as-it-is struggle to be what it may become. In its current form, it names no escape; it merely keeps asking how there can be one. Why does it find no escape from the strife of world with earth? Not 'for the excellent reason that there is no place else to go'. That discovery actually would be a kind of escape, or the beginning of one. And not for the reason that none exists.

The reason the book finds no escape is simply stated, but only in the language of the book itself: only in words which, outside its covers, may always look strange and arcane. This is a book about earth and world, in which world is conscious and deaf, while earth is unconscious and blind. It is nevertheless a book of analytical prose. It is written in the world's language, thinking the thoughts of the world. Though it names the earth, it cannot hear it. So the book, though it speaks to us of earth and world, is trapped inside the worldview of world. It is the world hunting its murdered mother: world hunting the one thing to which it refuses permission to be.

The escape exists by means of a condition which Heidegger describes, in a sentence Lee quotes and then dismisses. The sentence is: 'The world grounds itself on the earth, and earth juts through the world'. *Erde durchragt die Welt:* Earth pierces, punctures the world. But the book as it stands cannot think this. It can encounter the thought, yes, but it cannot hang on:

> Thinking proceeds by objectifying and mastering what is to be thought. The process is erratic and intuitive, yet the overall drive is towards a systematic clarity of idea which takes possession of the subject and wrings its structures from it, leaving behind the husk of one more object.

Or as Heidegger remarks in a pregnant phrase, *das Denken ein Handwerk ist:* thinking is work of the hand, a craft, a trade.

There is another kind of thinking. If we know what our feet are for, and know how to wear shoes, we can call it footwork thinking. If only our feet are in touch with the ground.

The author of *Savage Fields* is a poet, but the book is as he has valiantly struggled to make it: self-consistent and locked into the posture of analytical prose thinking. For this reason, its attempt (chapter v.4) to think about the implications of neurobiology in the voice of earth as well as of world collapses before it begins. World strives to prevent earth's jutting through it. World patches its pavements and climbs.

Savage Fields proper ends at the end of its eighth chapter. There, with this sentence, its circle concludes: 'It is hard to see how world can escape itself successfully, unless it has already escaped itself'. What follows is an epilogue, made up of jottings, called 'Entries'. It is hard to resist the suggestion that 'Exits' might have been as apt a name.

There in the epilogue, where the expository form of the book breaks down, another voice at last begins to sound. And I do not say this lightly, but I say it: perhaps we shall find that we must follow the same paradigm. Perhaps as the system, which claims so earnestly to have room within it for everything, finally disintegrates, another voice, which has been there always, will become audible to us all for the first time.

Until this difficult rediscovery is forced upon us, if we are so fortunate as to have it forced upon us, we can ponder a moral question, answered already at the end of *Savage Fields*:

Clear thought is an achievement of difficult beauty. I covet it. Yet it cannot finally be good to go on thinking within the models that rule our civilization, even though they take my breath away . . . .

How then shall we think? The epilogue, from which I continue to quote, poses the question. 'Can a man think his earth-belonging without merely possessing it conceptually?'

We have the testimony of the poems of Dennis Lee that some men can.

'To think sanely must be to think . . . more deeply than thought.'

Which is to bring the world to ground. Where what is and what isn't breathe one breath, the earth juts through, and men might even, by ones and twos, though it is a lot to ask, come to their claimed selves and live here. At home. On the earth. In the difficult world.

Polyphony

Enacting a Meditation

Dennis Lee

Author's Headnote To 'Polyphony'

This meditation will eventually appear in a collection of pieces on the same subject. In isolation, it may be hard to enter; I hope these notes will reduce the difficulty.

1 'Polyphony' assumes familiarity with another essay, 'Cadence, Country, Silence: writing in colonial space'. (Cited in the bibliography on page 244.) Some of the shorthand here is more accessible in light of the earlier essay.

2 'Polyphony' is also a re-draft of a previous piece, 'Enacting a Meditation'. (Cited on page 245.) On reconsideration, I found the parent piece verbose; I began wanting a more compact, generalizing approach, that uncovered some first principles of voice and cadence and then shut up. If the result is too compact for comfort, however, there's a more expansive approach in 'Enacting a Meditation'.

3 The parent essay anchored its points in the specific procedure of given poems. But the poem it turned to most often was one of my own, *The Death of Harold Ladoo;* I came to feel that this bespoke a level of egotism which even I found indecent. . . . That said, I'm not convinced that the strategy of this version — to cite no poems at all — is entirely preferable. But the discussion of monophonic and polyphonic voice does derive from the practice of actual poems.

IT IS TIME to speak more carefully of cadence, and the way it shapes a meditation. But it is hard to see where to begin — both because everything depends on everything else, and because cadence itself is the source of speech about cadence.

Bear with this beginning. It is spare, compressed, even somewhat airless. But it is not meant as a series of definitions, handed down from a lectern at the beginning of the first class. It is an attempt — slightly over-determined, I'm afraid — to concentrate on the few nuclear hunches from which the subject radiates. A mistake at the start will set the whole enquiry askew.

And since we are talking about things that matter, they should not be domesticated too hastily within familiar categories of thought, if that distorts their shape and nature.

1

A meditative poem exists because something has wooed it to be.

And it exists because the poem is wooing that something in return, seeking to mime its gestures of being.

The something is cadence.

* * *

It is all but impossible to speak nakedly of cadence. What one can do is show how a poem participates in its active life.

2

The medium in which a poem exists is voice.

Any voice embodies a particular timbre of being. It mediates one of the specific resonances, in which what-is *is*.

To hear a poem's voice on its own wave-length is to enter the poem's audition of cadence.

* * *

Specific inflections of voice are created by a battery of variables: line-lengths; timing of line-breaks; length of syntactic units; level(s) of diction; sound-colouring; interweaving of imagery and direct statement and irony and . . . ; stance of the 'I'; and on and on.

But technique is not our concern here. The nature of voice, as the fundamental medium of poetry, is.

3

An authentic inflection of voice must *embody*.

* * *

Much more common is the inflection which merely *states*. 'Recalling how you betrayed me, I feel angry.'

What does that voice convey? A discursive equanimity, which reports on its feelings (and on everything else) with arm's-length de-

83

tachment. The feelings themselves have no reality in the poem, since they never achieve embodiment within the controlled, declarative tone.

The poem no more 'feels angry' than it feels pink. The voice gives the lie to its own utterance.

* * *

If the poem is to ring true, let it *recall* the actual details of betrayal — and let it *recall them angrily.*

'Anger' need never be mentioned by name. It must be embodied in the movement & texture & pitch of the recollecting voice.

This calls for passionate vocal tact. As do inflections of playfulness, ecstasy, musing, despair. As does any authentic inflection.

* * *

The discursive voice embodies one narrow human strain, of editorializing urbanity, and excludes all other currents in the speaker's makeup.

But it is not just the speaker's personal nature which is straitened by this voice. People and wars and trees and daily multifarious aspirations all go de-selved, within a vocal range that cannot embody their indigenous tonalities. The whole world is shrunk down to a single repertorial wave-length — which is a far more drastic, claustrophobic limitation.

4

Most contemporary poems are *monophonic*, written in a single voice. (The main exception, poetry deriving from Pound, must be discussed in a different context.)

* * *

When it is prolonged throughout a poem, the discursive tone of 'I feel angry' is monophonic. The same is true of any unbroken inflection, of course. But the voice which states — clipped, descriptive, distanced from what it observes — is the most common monotone in contemporary poetry.

To mediate a very narrow range of being human, this is a decorous single voice. Anything deeper, more vibrant, more epochally alive, it minifies.

84

5

Most readers can read monophonically; most poets oblige. Polyphony has fewer denizens.

But a poem may modulate the inflection of its voice five times in thirty lines. It can rage, state, noodle, cavort, then shudder with grief.

* * *

Polyphony is the art of orchestrating more than one voice across a work.

The polyphonic shift from inflection to inflection, the clash and resonance of vocal timbres from one moment to the next, is what traces out the trajectory of a meditation.

6

That is, an authentic meditation must *enact*.

It does so by living its way from one inflection to another.

For it to be a meditation at all, a poem must embody in voice the way its experience is initially focussed — then proceed to envoice another focussing, and then another. To live its way to deeper and deeper knowing, which is what a meditation does, it must modulate from one vocal embodiment to another.

* * *

Otherwise it hasn't budged an inch — no matter how much the content may change. It is just a series of statements whose matter has been colonized in a single voice: a thesis, a lament, a tirade.

* * *

The plot of a meditation is enacted by the shifting inflections of the meditative voice.

7

To write polyphonically is to contest 'poetry' as it is now written. Perhaps even to repudiate it altogether; to walk off that field, and try to find the real one.

What have you got against a voice of calm statement, Mr. Lee? Or against orderly thinking?

Nothing at all. My point was different. We meditate with our whole lives: with our passions and mind and flesh and our past and our deepest hungers. So in a meditation, the act of stating — stating an idea, let's say — has to arise as exactly that: one local act in the total process, no more important than any other. And it has to belong where it occurs; it has to well up when it does because the meditating consciousness is compelled to explore an idea — *this* idea, at *this* point — by the complex pressure of all that has come before. What's more, the idea has to find its own right voice in the flow; one time it might need to be shaggy and impassioned; again, dry and precise; another time it could be playful.

So the act of thinking must be vocally embodied — *as* an act. And that action must play a decorous part within the total enactment of meditating — not just issue in a string of propositions, which stand as 'the poem'.

None of these reservations makes it improper to state, reflect, declare, from time to time. But only if you do so as a full and variegated human being, who is meditating upon a complex world with everything he is. Thinking and remembering and grieving and raging and celebrating — they all have to be orchestrated. As they are in the *Symposium*.

But whose work are you objecting to so strenuously?

I'll give you an example. If you look at the meditative poetry of this century, Wallace Stevens is one of the masters. But his poems — gorgeous though they are — are too univocal. He doesn't just state ideas; he states images, too. But 'stating' is all that happens. Open your ear all the way, and that's still the only wave-length it will get nourished on. The stating doesn't have roots — at least not within the poem itself — in any deeper, richer human quest. Successive statements are supposed to stand as the whole quest in themselves. Which means that his poems seldom enact any form of meditation I can recognize first-hand. If they did, the inflections would be all over the map; they wouldn't be just a series of splendid variations in the one discursive voice.

Of course, I speak this way about Stevens because his monophonic voice matters; it has weight and body and high seriousness. There are hundreds of pipsqueaks, but why bother even quarrelling with them?

Fair enough, I suppose. But you still haven't said what you do *want.*

9

Sometimes one inflection will hold for twenty lines; sometimes there are three changes in two lines. With voices flickering or criss-crossing or interlaced. Till there are scores and scores of tonalities across the piece, kinetic, and the whole thing starts to sing across inside itself. Voice over voice — that harmony. And what the orchestration of voices begins to enact is the full gesture of cadence.

That's part of what I mean. It's a start. It still isn't right.

10

So far, we haven't considered the *content* of meditation. In one way the subject is tangential to an essay on polyphony. But in another it is not, for the meditative voice can scarcely proceed without meditating *on* something. There is hardly ever such a thing as content-free voice in a poem.

But that way of phrasing it already needs to be challenged. It's not just that the 'voice' of the poem has a certain 'content'. In fact, there are three things involved: the meditating consciousness; the content of its meditation; and the voice in which the two are embodied and enacted. Clarifying their relationship will tell us something about the nature of polyphony.

11

In one aspect, polyphony must be heard as the inflected trajectory of the poem's content (as it is held in the meditating consciousness).

That is: abstracting to an 'objective' pole, a meditation consists of a series of thematic movements. Each is a new stage in the argument of the poem; its content necessarily reconfigures the voice.

* * *

In another aspect, polyphony must be heard as the inflected trajectory of the poem's consciousness (as it attends to the content of its concern).

That is: abstracting to a 'subjective' pole, a meditation consists of a series of psychic move-ments. Each is a re-focussing of the meditative consciousness of the poem; its stance necessarily reconfigures the voice.

Both these abstractions are useful. Neither is anything more than an abstraction.

* * *

The originating unity, which is schematized and over-simplified in these abstractions, is the kinesis of polyphony itself — the concrete trajectory of voice which the meditation enacts. In it, consciousness and content are coextensive and inseparable. We divide them only after the fact.

In a mature meditation, then, what we differentiate as 'content' and 'consciousness' are complementary aspects of the same thing. And the 'same thing' is the many-inflectioned vocal process which affords the meditation its medium of being.

If the polyphony rings true, the meditation will be simultaneously 'subjective' and 'objective'. The polyphonic process will enact the trajectory of consciousness and of content at once. Even to think of them, in fact, will be to stylize and abstract from the kinetic living unity of the poem.

12

To read a meditation rightly — to follow its meditative quest — is a matter of hearing its larger vocal rhythms. The way you hear successive movements in a symphony: absorbing individual passages, but also discerning the large-scale progression from one movement to its successor.

This structural logic, which flows (or leaps, or ricochets) from one clearly-etched focus of content/consciousness to the next, furnishes the basic rhythm of the meditation. It is a series of polyphonic gestures, a trajectory of inflections.

13

Such a trajectory doesn't just follow a certain fixed itinerary, like checking in at pre-established points on a tour-map.

The poem has to live its way through a course of attending, and be changed by what it discovers at each stage. And the change may carry things anywhere.

The guide is what rings true in the voice.

* * *

So it's not as if you had a battery of portable styles, which you pull out and slather over whatever new mood or content comes up next. The voice gets generated — often for the first and only time — by the torque and the drift and tensions of each new place you move to in the meditation. You may have to sit down and spend days or weeks, months even, feeling around and trying to find how to mime or utter the new place it's entering, in a voice that rings true.

Just trying to find out what the new place *is* — which comes to the same thing. You only occupy it when you hit the voice that rings true for *this* moment of consciousness, focused by *this* burden of content. It works when they're seamless.

14

To follow the trajectory of a meditation you need to listen to the music of the space it's enacting — the musics, really, because it pounds *and* loops *and* shimmies *and* tumbles; I wish I could do them all at once — and hear how the voice flows with that grain, gets inflected by it.

* * *

The 'movements' are a series of improved recoils. Like body English out loud. They may come in off key with the one before, and the one before that, but then you realize they've got their own right pitch themselves. And you hear them getting changed by one another, and then a funny concord starts to orchestrate itself out of the clash and changes.

* * *

Say it's ticking along very quietly, just ticking over, and all of a sudden it spurts straight up for a bit — ka-*ching!* — till you realize there's a long slow roll coming in from the side now, it crests right across the spurt and carries the thing on out the other side for 20 lines maybe, with just a bit of a tremolo around the edges. Bit of lace. Or whatever.

15

Very pretty. Very poetic. But there's one thing I still don't understand. When I read a theoretical description of an 'open' poem, I can't see why anything has to occur precisely where it does. Or even, sometimes, why it has to be in the poem at all . . . . What governs all these erratic leapings-about that you've been describing?

Hunches. Trial and error. Hearing the music in your forearms, and trying not to muff it . . . . God knows, you spend enough time muffing it; exploring dead ends you finally have to abandon.

But that doesn't tell us anything. If you start with no pre-established plan, and content and form are both up for grabs, and you're just winging it, how can you tell when you've muffed it and when you haven't? . . . Whatever happened to the ideal of organic form? How can you do anything but set down clever bits and pieces, and then link them up arbitrarily? What does formal coherence even consist of, *in this kind of poetry?*

There's something deeper, but I can't get at it yet. Something is enforced on you. See, I know my stuff moves around a lot. But I try to —

It's true. There is nothing in what I've said that accounts for the emergence of satisfying form. Nor even for the practical leads you get — since with or without a guiding theory, you do discover an organic way ahead.

You're right. I haven't said anything about the source of coherence in polyphonic writing.

16

What I need to concentrate on is the way cadence is present for you, when you're actually writing.

* * *

It begins long before individual words have come clear; that's one thing. Before they can be any guide to what's getting born. Cadence impinges as a kind of magnetic din, a silent raucous multiform atmospheric tumult you move around in, very clean though; and *always* — when you perceive it, when you don't. I could write hymns to it, almost. And not to the poems: to what I *hear*.

What *is* it?

It's there, that's all. It's *here* . . . . Not just to sponsor poems; that much I'm sure of. And I know: if you could somehow screen out the literal meaning of words in the finished poem, their polyphony would still enact the gestures of cadence. The sheer dance of voices. On its own.

Of course, you can't separate the play of inflections in the final poem from the literal meaning of words. But the music does exist at that pre-signifying level. And sensing it echoes the way the spurt and shimmy and hover and lunge first came at you — which was, they came tumbling through you long before there were stable words to flesh them out. You were galvanized by cadence, not yet knowing what its content was — let alone the shape of that content.

And what you need, miming that summons, is an utterly supple medium: polyphony, a voice that can metamorphose endlessly from inflection to inflection. Under the press of the necessities of the cadence it's born in. And borne in. Gradually at times. Or abruptly: but with no sense of the gears being ground. Nor of it being stage-managed in its changes. Like a field of luminous force, knotted and folding and stalling and skittering back, perpetual live energy, at home in itself. But not rarified, not removed, it's not Ideal; this worries me, almost — does it mean worshipping whatever is, good and evil like goulash? Because it's always just there, thudding like somebody breathing, magisterial, right now we're in it . . . . Oink . . . . Selah . . . . I barely know.

What *is* it?

17

And see, I *know* my stuff moves around a lot. But I go in the straightest line I can. I hate obscurity, I hate gussied-up decoration. There's just the one clean trajectory of attending; you hew to the grain. But in the space of cadence, what people generally see as direct or 'straight' lines — standard logical associations, received emotional, literary, even tonal ones — may bear no relation to the energy, the actual currents of meaning in that space. So if you go in a conventional straight line, you mostly falsify the grain of how things go about being themselves. Which means, you falsify the grain of the texture of the necessities they're thrown in, and configured by.

18

What moves around is voice. Content-and-consciousness, embodied in voice.

19

It's like the way — to use a limited geometrical analogy — it's like the way 'straight' lines on the surface of the earth are also curved. They don't exist in a flat plane to begin with. If you took a perfectly 'straight' line from Toronto to Madrid, you'd end up tunnelling through millions of tons of the planet. You wouldn't be respecting the curved grain of the plane you're moving in.

But that curvature governs what 'the shortest distance between two points' means at all, when you travel on the surface of the globe.

And 'travelling on the surface of the globe' is what we do every time we take a step. Going in a Euclidean straight line is an imaginary activity for us, albeit a useful one to picture at times. But we don't exist in two dimensions; we were confused for much too long, we thought we lived in Euclid's mind.

91

20

That's the kind of recognition you reach, listening in cadence. The grain of that space is no more 'straight' than the grain of our motion around the globe.

But the analogy is too limited, for cadential space curves much more unpredictably than does the surface of the earth — and more than that, it eddies and throbs and hiccups and loops and tumbles. It is not simply a question of recognizing that natural lines of motion curve regularly in three dimensions, instead of extending flat in two. Rather, you discover that the space of cadence keeps changing its texture continuously, and with all sorts of unexpected mutations.

Hence the fundamental ground-rules of 'straightness', of direct utterance, keep changing as well.

For a spell, cadential space may extend monophonically — as though in two dimensions. Then it may curve off regularly into three. Then it may suddenly pucker, bunch, recoil, explode, go becalmed.

You have to feel out that changing grain as you go. And the voice has to enact its changing texture from point to point, as the meditation progresses. That is what meditation consists of.

21

I speak of 'cadential space', and that may imply that a poem is a static map or picture which reproduces the space of cadence by describing it. But it's not like that. A meditation is itself the act of moving *through* textured space; it's wholly kinetic. And the words on the page are the track of its going. Their changing voices mime the changing configurations of the space through which the meditation moves. That's why polyphony at all.

A meditation doesn't describe a space; it enacts one. It is a finding-the-grain-of-meditative-space, and a following-it-through-in-voice.

22

And it's cadence that guides you. That is why a meditation must sense the gestures of cadence, and woo them and mime them.

You feel out how the grain flows, gradually, intuitively, in each new piece you start. And you let the poem flow with it. So the voice gets inflected by every whorl and spurt and flicker along the way; it embodies them locally, and then it enacts their changes.

That's moving straight. That's travelling direct, in the cosmos that cadence sponsors and makes manifest.

And you can feel the heft of the cells in your arms, your neck, your sexual centre — you feel your hopes and forebears straining to reach those articulate gestures of being. You can't compel them. But once you find the flow, once you enter the jostle and hover and rush of the right full carnal gesture in words there is such a de-kinking, such a deep sense of release into what is quick and still and implacably there, that it nourishes you utterly. And for a time, at least, you don't understand what other calling even makes sense.

23

It's a paradox.

In such a cosmos, polyphony is the craft of direct utterance. What is more complex, is simpler. Because a shifting tonality lets you hew to the grain directly, enact the rich multiform cadence of that space — with no short-cuts, and no frills. Just as a curve, the one right curve, turns out to be the straightest line from Toronto to Madrid.

* * *

I'm troubled, when people have difficulty hearing polyphony on the page. I guess they're not used to it. Because often they don't perceive how many shifts there are, how many tonalities are interlaced, till they hear it read out loud. They don't enter that cadential space at all; for them the real live poem, which is a many-voiced embodiment and a wooing, never begins to happen on the page.

What *were* they hearing, I wonder, if they didn't pick up that enacted space? Is it their ear or my music that was deficient?

* * *

I think I know how an 'open' poem can cohere, despite its bits and pieces. It's because, as the meditation moves through textured space, its changing configurations of voice are enacting what I've called an articulate gesture of being. A lived coherence.

The grain of the space you're travelling in — which includes your own motives, but they're only a minor part of it — already lives through such movements of being. If you learn to follow that grain in the meditation, you find the poem itself achieving a fundamental

93

gesture. Usually in spite of your preoccupations; sometimes against your will.

So you don't just wander around in the poem and stitch random pieces together. The cadence you're trying to mime already carries through a fundamental gesture in the kinetic vocabulary of what-is. You follow as best you can.

* * *

That's why meditative writing is also a letting be. You can't just whizz along in the pre-packaged grids and grooves we impose on things to organize them. Or if you do you violate, you man-handle, dismember, the torque and texture of the space you're writing in. You merely write a poem; you're a tourist, a small-time imperialist who imports his own right-angle inflections and tries to dig to China — instead of following the grain of local space and going the straight way round.

And that's why univocal poetry is so boring, and it feels like sacrilege. Even though it may be well-written too . . . a well-written minification of what-is. Most contemporary poetry *is* monophonic! Sure, the content changes from poem to poem. But all you carry away from any one of them is that single stating voice, buzzing in your ear without a modulation. And voice embodies being, and you hear the same monotonous news every time. The same reductive, claustrophobic blasphemy. And —

* * *

But I need to make distinctions. A good monophonic poem — and it's true, such a thing does exist — may mediate only one wavelength of what is. But it mimes it truly, and without trying to utter other wave-lengths which it cannot encompass.

What is unacceptable is the monophonic poem whose voice is badly cramped, and which still insists on reducing the whole variegated world to its single pygmy wave-length. It —

24

This is phoney, you know.

Phoney? What are you talking about?

I've been carrying on as if it was me who makes up the tumble and slide on the page. And sure, I write the poem; and that means hard work. But I don't *invent* the cadence I hear; I sit and play in the midst of it. Do you think I can boss it around? Most of the time I can't even keep up.

And don't you see? Those flexing voices — they *are* the poem. Without them there'd be nothing: no weight, no resonance, just a batch of strung-together words.

That's the point of everything I've been saying. But I've made a farce of it. I've been talking as if you can reduce a meditation, refer it all back to the technical moves of the writer. As if you can screen out that magisterial cadence, and ignore its sponsoring presence in the poem . . . . But that's a piece of shallow modern bafflegab!

I wasn't expecting . . . . I'm sorry, Dennis. But how else could we have gone at it?

That I don't know. But it's not just how you put a poem together; don't you see? That's only the outward part. The crucial thing is —

* * *

Cadence, and the mind-set of this era: they're incompatible. Cadence is something given, far greater than my own mind or craft, intimate, other, and which compels my awe. But the only analytic language for talking about it is the modern one — the poem as a product of technique, the 'creative' artist fashioning order from the raw material of the world or his own subconscious. All that stuff. I don't believe a word of it. Yet I'm a creature of modernity, and I still fall into the approach it's bred into us.

But it falsifies everything I know at the core. There has to be some way of talking about the two-way commerce between cadence and the poem, rather than just analyzing the poem as a kind of vocal engineering job.

25

The swivel and thrum I sense as perpetual, that I hear all the time like a sub-sonic throbbing, or the sea — even when I don't know I'm hearing it — I call 'cadence.'

It's what myself is turned toward, and homes to, even though I am so erratic I cringe to think about it.

In none of the senses I ever learned to use the word, I worship cadence.

* * *

I don't bow down before it. Partly because I can't locate an 'it' to bow down 'before'. And partly because I tried that stance earlier in my life, and I always blew it.

But I do worship cadence, because there is nothing else you can do with it.

I used to think that in worship you worked up a frenzy of will and devotion. But this is so meat-and-potatoes, it's not like that at all. It is sheer and simple attending, far beneath the threshhold of your awareness. It's awe, astonishment, delight, trepidation; knowing you're at home, knowing you're sullying it but that's your problem. But none of those things in a form you're even conscious of.

I worship so badly that it sounds absurd to use the word in the first place. But in an odd way, that's the point. Good, bad, or indifferent, the quality of my response does not determine the magisterial hereness of cadence. And that is already what is awesome.

* * *

Why call it 'worship'?

The response which cadence engenders is not curiosity; nor a desire to possess it (which would be ridiculous); nor to talk about it; nor to take it apart and see what makes it tick; nor any other inner, private motive. Instead, there is just impersonal stillness: the elemental acknowledgment that cadence *is*, here, perpetual yes and we're in it. (I don't understand what it *means* that 'Cadence is'; my head doesn't translate the knowing. But that doesn't matter, and nor does it bother me. If my head does its stuff with the fact some day, fine; if not, fine.)

So. Cadence evokes worship. And as a minor footnote, the quality of the worship it evokes in me is about .01 on a scale of 100. But that matters far less than the reality of cadence. If I worshipped better, cadence would be no more real for that.

26

I became aware of cadence in the ways I talked about in 'Cadence, Country, Silence'. When I was in my early or mid-twenties. I don't recall any single, sudden onset of it. I connected it first with writing. It doesn't seem to me either 'personal' or 'impersonal', though if I had to choose one term it would be the latter. Certainly I don't sit and talk to it; that's just not appropriate.

When the sense is strong, which for me isn't often, then you are so radically held — though there is almost no conscious excitement, nor even consciousness 'of' cadence — that you are utterly concentrated in it. Without passing out or anything. It's hard to describe.

It's not an 'extraordinary state'; I've had a few of those, and they're quite different.

I don't try to work up the experience of cadence, if it isn't happening. I try that with lots of things, but with this it just isn't appropriate. Cadence is going on always; I'm just more thinly attuned at times. But when it does take over, the attending — in which there's no choice; the only 'choice' would be *not* to attend, and barring an emergency in the house that would be ludicrous — the attending itself is what you're asked for. It feels like the first obedience that's enjoined on you; and it's scarcely 'obedience' at all. And you don't even feel 'enjoined' . . . . This is ridiculous.

27

There's also the writing. It is the fullest erotic response to cadence, for me at least. And a medium cadence chooses. And the practical thing it flows into, in your life.

When cadence sifts through you, the invitation has already occurred. 'Come and be part of me . . . . Sit still, and be me.'

What else can you do? You pick up some words, and you try to re-enact the inflections of that claim and courtship — which already sustains you, there's no question of your 'creating' it. Just of learning its indigenous gestures in your home medium.

Maybe that is the devotional discipline; I don't know. But again, it doesn't feel like the out-of-synch effort of will that comes with 'doing your duty', or what I thought 'worshipping God' meant when I used to try to do that. I'm clumsy when I mime the inflections of cadence in words; halting, at odds with what has to be done. But so what? The only thing you can even do is keep trying; it's not a matter of heroic dedication. You're lucky to get the chance. The problem isn't to make yourself do it, but to stop doing it long enough to lead the rest of your life.

28

And what about 'the rest of your life'? . . . It feels as if it is lived in the purview of cadence. There's nothing that isn't. But to my puzzlement, I don't find any great effect upon my day-to-day life. I don't trust that, since cadence seems so all-encompassing; but I have to report it. I don't think my everyday behaviour, which is scrappy and compulsive and out-of-focus much of the time, is modified by the presence of cadence in any way I can detect.

97

Maybe there is some connection between cadence and the ethical or socially responsible or religious dimensions of life. There must be. But at my kindergarden stage, I haven't discovered what it is. At least, not apart from the injunction I mentioned in the earlier essay, to find real words for the rich impossible space we live in.

That sets your vocation. And otherwise, you muddle along.

29

It comes to me somewhat — with less of the utter knowing that cadence *is* — whatever it is — you couldn't dissuade me of that short of lobotomizing me — it comes to me sporadically, but then with some measure of that central knowing — it's not just a bright idea, it's a recognition of a truth surfacing beneath your own resources — that what is proceeding in the quick of cadence is the life of cosmos.

Again, I don't know what that 'means'. And again, I'm not terribly exercised to find out. I guess I *am* more curious to 'find out' than I am with the basic presence of cadence. But essentially it seems like something that is so, and whether or not I learn what it means is immaterial.

30

Is it that the 'structure' of cosmos is given in the kinetic forms of cadence? . . . That sounds suspect, somehow.

Is it some 'process' in the universe — some process *of* the universe — that is resounding in cadence?

A process one has gotten tuned into somehow, like a fluke of reception on a short-wave radio.

I think it is. I think it's the process of be-ing. And if my use of the word is annoying, I'm sorry. It is not an abstraction; it's the most immediate word, it *refers* to the most immediate thing there is about things: that they are at all. Instead of not being.

That is what you hear, in cadence.

31

Cadence enacts the space of cosmos. 'Cosmos', as what is. And 'space', as the still and tumultuous process in which cosmos is perpetually recreated by the unspeakable energy of *be*-ing — of *being at all*. To be tuned by cadence is to vibrate with the calamitous resonance of being. And that is what is mimed in the polyphonic voice of meditation.

In this epoch, that is maybe how one speaks of it. In another, it would be different.

* * *

I don't think I could persuade a reader of anything about cadence, even if I wanted to.

My words for cadence are merely a gesture of salute.

32

All my poetry is a response to cadence. And maybe some of the strangeness of what I write will diminish if a reader perceives that. That would please me, of course. But it doesn't make the poetry any better or worse to say these things. Indeed, the poetry is finally by the bye from this perspective. It depends on cadence. But cadence doesn't depend on it.

Which is why I was mortified, to have spoken of polyphony as if it were a matter of vocal engineering. What polyphony mimes is what counts.

* * *

Cadence invites the poem to be, by being.

The poem reaches out to participate in those gestures of being-at-all.

Its polyphonic dance enacts the perpetual inflections of wooing, and being wooed by, the be-ing of what is.

99

The Prose Voice

Authenticity and Absence

Reflections on the Prose of Dennis Lee

E. D. Blodgett

Il n'y a pas de hors-texte.[1]

AN EPIGRAPH IS a sign, and for a long time I thought of choosing an apt quotation from Dennis Lee himself. But Lee's work is of such a various kind that it would be merely glib to bend him back against himself, to reflect by distorting. What is worse it would be an act of bad faith, for Lee, as both an intelligence and a moral presence in Canadian letters, bids us not to toy with him, no matter how tempting such an enterprise might be. Why I have chosen this epigraph, as superscript and statement, will become clear.

Incapable of finding a more appropriate word, I have chosen to call Lee's public statements 'prose'. It has been a mistake, I think, to consider *Savage Fields* literary criticism — Lee has denied that it is — and readers of his work have thus made serious errors in their efforts to understand it. Lee's fundamental concern is not the literary text but the problem of discourse itself. It is for this reason that he is so profoundly and ambiguously drawn toward the self-reflexive texts he discusses in *Savage Fields*, modernism repels him, and therefore teases him to speak, because such texts are concerned with the difficulties of discourse. Their self-reflexivity makes problematic both language itself as well as the largest implications of the work, the *hors-texte* — (that which is not the text, but is still bound in with it). Readers of such texts may become suddenly hortatory (in the manner of early Greek political elegists) and, with Lee, ask that

> *tremendum* rather,
> dimension of otherness, come clear
> in each familiar thing — in
> outcrop, harvest, hammer, beast and
> caught in that web of darkness
> we too endure & we
> worship. (G, p.32)

Significantly, because in such texts the 'we' also belongs to 'that web of darkness', even self becomes problematic. Thus, through language, self-reflexive texts generate their own self-enclosed worlds.

But Lee's fate is that, as he remarks in *The Gods,* 'I want/the world to be real and/it will not'. That the world is not real prevents self from achieving authenticity, and the lack — both that of the world and of the self — is that the language by which we would speak of 'gods' is gone. We speak holiness, the 'mysterium tremendum' as he calls it elsewhere,[2] and when words fail, we fail.

In the Introduction to *Savage Fields* Lee shows the reader how language generates the world, and thus how (the) world comes to be. Lee can do this, because, so far from being anti-modern, he is, in fact pre-modern. His perception of the world is at once theological — the referent is always the *mysterium tremendum* — and medieval. *Vox* (word) ought to correspond directly to *res* (its real referent). But, because he is also acutely aware that his 'dwelling' — a word borrowed from Heidegger and fraught with connotations of ontology — is the present moment, he knows that language has severed its connections with the 'gods'. It is always, then, in need of repair (from *repatriare,* to be brought back to its own country). As Lee observes elsewhere, his quest has continued 'till the/ words came real, that/ being here is home'.[3] Given the erotic context of the poem, the pun on 'came' cannot be missed, but the statement itself urges us to understand the degree to which words are for Lee real, and that he would refuse to be called a nominalist. He wants to be a Realist, one for whom language operates beyond mere meaning, for whom language participates in the problem of Being, and knows that, while such a desire is not illusory, words have a way of slipping back into problems of meaning.

So it is that when Lee opens his discussion on 'savage fields' he begins with a discussion of meaning. We are told that such a distinction as that which obtains between things and dictionaries is not only of long duration but also one that has seen many changes of meaning. Meaning, we are further told, is generated by situation, where, one is tempted to add, it dwells. Thus, 'A tree, for instance, has one cluster of meanings when it is located in the cosmos revealed by the medieval Christian faith, and a largely different cluster of meanings in the cosmos revealed by the physical sciences' (SF, p.3). Lee's sentence is itself revelatory, for it assumes that the reader will automatically blur the referential levels of the word 'tree'. Lee does not use quotation marks, for he wants the reader to move beyond concepts to things, to 'the real tree' which, it is deftly implied, is always brought into consciousness according to the kind of model that is employed. What does 'faith' do but invest a tree with symbolic value? What does 'science' do but transform a tree into a problem for organic chemistry? This question of language is the problem of

Savage Fields, and anyone who fails to make allowance for it will always be tempted to argue that Lee is a literary critic whose usefulness depends upon the degree to which we give assent to his model.

It could be asserted in Lee's defence that ordinary speech normally blurs distinctions between word, concept, and thing. But Lee is not using ordinary speech, and he is very aware of such distinctions. Lee is, in fact, developing a certain kind of discourse in order to make sense of a specific problem. 'One cannot speak,' he remarks, 'of the concepts "nature" and "civilisation" as though they had meant the same things throughout history . . .' (SF, p.3) But how to speak, which any essayist must face, is not the whole problem. What language can *do* is the core of Lee's enterprise. Hence he readily abandons such terms as 'nature' and 'civilisation' as no longer sufficient to the task. Instead he adapts two terms of broader range — 'world' and 'earth' — from Martin Heidegger's essay, 'The Origin of the Work of Art'. What is revealing about the manner of Lee's adaptation is that he is 'using the terms to say something substantially different' (SF, p.113) — as if terms could speak. It is revealing because they enter Lee's discourse as words and dwell there finally as signs for a 'cosmology' that is not elaborated in Heidegger, nor known before Lee. By the middle of the Introduction Lee can confidently declare: 'Each domain is coextensive with the whole of what is' (SF, p.8). Thus through 'world' and 'earth' Lee has created ontology. Although I think Lee would deny the truth of such a statement by saying that whatever is, is, no matter what words we use, it could be replied that without Lee's telling us we would not have perceived. And I think he is aware of this, for he begins with quotation marks to indicate that world and earth are merely terms; but once they are defined they become concepts, and finally, things. These changes happen so rapidly that one feels discourse is not only a problem for Lee, it is also an embarrassment — because it interferes with revelation. The pressure on discourse is thus obvious and Lee's impatience, his apparent belief that once language asserts, things are, would appear to be a kind of *hybris*.

Lee's ability to believe that (his) language creates (the) reality is the reason, simple as it may appear, why his readings of Ondaatje and Cohen have not received, for the most part, a sympathetic response. What is significant, as I suggested earlier, is the choice of these particular texts, both of which as self-conscious, 'post-modern' texts require precisely the kind of delicacy that Heidegger suggests is necessary to discover them as objects. No matter how much he might decry anyone who would bring this to his attention, Lee's patent unwillingness to allow, as Heidegger urges, the thing itself 'to remain in its self-containment', starkly underscores his impatience with language as a creative instrument. It cannot, Lee seems to imply, create *ex nihilo*, but must only be used in a referential manner, referring to something that must be there. Partial freedom, presumably, does not succumb to pure 'liberalism', the freedom of allowing signs to be merely signs. To succumb to liberalism would be, as Lee remarked in his reply to David Godfrey's reading of *Savage Fields*, tantamount to falling into the abyss of formalism and structuralism.[4] Should that happen, it would be necessary to face both the danger and the responsibility of being human, for then one would have to deal with both *homo faber* but also *homo loquens*, man the speaker. What else does Lee fear in *Beautiful Losers* but F., not so much because he is 'world' but because 'he goes on denying and affirming the Isis continuum, and the narrator's illumination . . .' (SF, p.85)? Inasmuch as I share Lee's fear — Dante's Ulysses always comes to mind as the exemplar of such use of language — I cannot help but want to give assent to it. But my reason remains unconvinced that F. is sufficient to the burden Lee lays upon him, nor is my reason convinced that Lee's argument has reckoned with all of its implications.

2

At the beginning of the gestation period that *Savage Fields* underwent, Lee was invited to speak at the first *Rencontre québécoise internationale des écrivains* where he gave the original version of 'Cadence, Country, Silence'. This was Lee's first major consideration of the themes that recur in *Savage Fields*, that is, technology and its evils, the planet and its fate, authenticity, ontology, nonbeing. The debt to George Grant is recognized and, therefore, the equation between technology and liberalism. What Grant showed Lee was the horror of unlimited freedom: 'Always we are totally free men, faced with a world which is raw material, a permanent incitement to technique' (CCS, p.44). Cohen's F. is such a free man who continually assaults earth with the technique of world. But Grant gave Lee even more. He taught Lee how 'to become articulate' (CCS, p.45) and this is the primary burden of his essay, in the same way as it is crucial to an understanding of *Savage Fields*. Words are loaded. They determine our authenticity, our being on earth, and the relationship we take to the country where we live.

What distinguishes Lee's use of discourse in this text, as opposed to *Savage Fields*, however, is his awareness that, as he puts it, 'civil nonbeing cannot be evaded' (CCS, p.52). Paradoxical as it may appear, this is the utterance of a poet made, one supposes, while his poem, *The Death of Harold Ladoo*, was in process, a statement that is prepared to admit the inauthentic into his imagination's dwelling. It concludes an essay whose point of departure deceptively announces a theme that would appear to have nothing to do with the themes we have already mentioned.

Lee begins by stating: 'Most of my life as a writer is spent listening . . .' (CCS, p.34). One is reminded of Rilke's first sonnet to Orpheus in which the animals, summoned by the poet's song, are given in his song a 'Tempel in Gehör', a temple made of hearing. Rilke knew that if language were any way a part of ontology (and in his third sonnet he was to say, laconically, 'Gesang ist Dasein', that is, song is Being), something must be heard, and this hearing constitutes the first gesture of the speech act that makes things be. At the conclusion of his essay, 'Language', Heidegger simply asserts:

Language speaks.
Man speaks in that he responds to language. This responding is a hearing. It hears because it listens to the command of stillness.[5]

For Lee the command is a goad which comes as a kind of cadence. There — and how accurate Lee's description is! — is where it all begins, the poem's origin. Then comes language and the discovery that, while cadence might be personal, language is not. Because language is social, cultural, and worse, ideological, the rift between origin and the oppression of discourse can be unbearable. 'Words arrive', he notes, 'but words have also gone dead' (CCS, p.36). Words rest on Being and Nonbeing.

The core, then, of this essay reflects the core of Lee's life as a poet. The problem for the poet is to find one's own *parole* or, as some would say, one's 'true voice'. For Lee, voice issues 'in part from civil space' (CCS, p.37), but civil space, at least in Canada, is not charged with authentic speech. So it is that one cannot speak as poets used to speak when they 'spoke of earth and heaven. There were no symbols' (CE, p.38). The space that has opened between word and referent can only be imperfectly intimated by the formulation of the symbol. How, then, when all civil relationships have become mediated, can men 'complete/their origins' ? (CE, p.35.) They cannot, and so 'alienation in that space will enter and undercut our writing, make it recoil upon itself, become a problem to itself' (CCS, 37). Such writing is precisely that of Ondaatje and Cohen, writing that Lee chooses to call 'colonial' to distinguish it, presumably, from 'imperial', that is, liberal, technological, and value-free. There is, of course, a truth in

Lee's diagnosis that has been argued already at length in Louis-Jean Calvet's study, *Linguistique et colonialisme: petit traité de glottophagie* (Paris: Payot, 1974). Central to Calvet's proposition is that bilingual policies are not only designed to destroy the economically weaker language, but also to create the right conditions for exploitation. In such a light, Lee's anguish for English-Canada may be distinguished from the anguish of Québec and other colonies whose native language is not English. For if language authenticates, how imperceptibly one loses a sense of authentic being in this country. For him the native becomes foreign, home is always abroad, one's origin is elsewhere.

Most readers of 'Cadence, Country, Silence', not to speak of Lee himself whose *Savage Fields* may be considered his own reading of it, have been detained by its nationalism and its consequent emphasis on ideological difference.[6] Such readings miss, not to say cover over, the greater value of the essay: Lee's sense that that writing is inextricably part of a writer's alienation and that for Canadians discourse is not only rooted in nationalism but produces ideology. Such a contention is borne out by Lee's overture to the problem of cadence. But what is cadence? It is not simply 'the cadence of the poems I have written,' Lee explains, for there is some deeper cadence that the poem 'tunes out' (CCS, p.35). This deeper cadence can only be reflected in the poem, and the cadence that is sensed 'as presence' is gradually lost as the poem takes shape. Its final shape shadows forth that deeper cadence in its own arriving (*cadentia*: a falling):

> A poem enacts in words the presence of what we live among. It arises from the tough, delicate, heartbreaking rooting of what-is in its own nonbeing. Out of our participation in that rooting, there rises an elemental movement of being — of celebration, of desire, of grief, of anger, of play, of dying. That movement is always particular, speaking the things which are. It does not issue just from what is outside us, nor just from what is inside us. A poem enacts that moving cadence of being. (CCS, p.53)

Cadence, then, takes its departure from Being. The act of the authentic poem is to preserve 'presence'. Cadence becomes obstructed when the space of the writer becomes colonized. Space is perceived as colonized when discourse no longer proceeds from within, but when language is seen as external to the speaker.

Without the presence of cadence, words are no more than signs. As signs, they are prevented from participating in the act by which we are known and by which Being is known. That act is a kind of listening, an acute state of attentiveness, that can only be responded to by speech, if one is a poet. But if there are no words 'within to hear', then one can only respond, if one chooses to remain authentic, by falling mute. It is this dialectic of speech and silence that governs the essay's thought. Hence the impressive role of illumination that George Grant plays in Lee's notion of discourse, for Grant is, in one sense, the author of Lee's text. Through Grant he recovered *parole* and, as he remarks, 'That first gift of speech is a staggering achievement' (CCS, p.45). The recovery of words, to hear what happens 'in "love", "inhabit", "fail", "earth", "house" ' (CCS, p.47), is not simply the acquisition of speech, but the overcoming of 'an *absolute* problem' (CCS, p.46; emphasis added). To recover speech is, as Heidegger asserts, 'To preserve the four-fold', which means 'to save the earth, to receive the sky, to await the divinities, to escort mortals — this four-fold preserving is the simple nature, the presencing, of dwelling'.[7] This 'presencing', this calling back things to themselves, remains problematic from the moment it is brought to consciousness. Thus, while the absolute problem of discourse is mastered, speech only becomes possible when its 'impasse becomes its own subject'. This would mean that 'to be authentic, the voice of being alive here and now must include the inauthenticity of our lives here and now' (CCS, p.49).

If authentic speech arises from where one dwells, from presence, what is the inauthentic that it must absorb? Lee distinguishes these two modes of speech that constitute the problematic of discourse in his poem, *The Gods*:

> For a man no longer moves
>   through coiled ejaculations of
>   meaning;
>   we dwell within
> taxonomies, equations, paradigms
>   which deaden the world and now in our
>   heads, though less in our inconsistent lives,
>   the tickle of cosmos is gone. (G, p.29)

The opposition is clear enough between 'ejaculations' and 'equations': one springs from the order of ontology; the other, as the poem later explains, is technology. That it is called 'technology' should not, however, deflect us from the core of Lee's concern. Nation, technology, dwelling, the self, the city, even George Grant, are only important to the degree that they impinge upon 'cadence' and the primal act of speech.

In their readings of *Savage Fields* most critics have been quick to point out that Lee's use of the terms 'world' and 'earth' implies a structuralist model whose oppositions are familiar. Lee dislikes structuralism as an outgrowth of a 'commitment to formalism', and he rejects 'its conviction that the ultimate use of reason is to map transformations between value-free structural grammars'. At the same time he notes that one of his key texts, *Beautiful Losers*, 'participates in the structuralist cast of mind' and that 'Earlier drafts of [*Savage Fields*] . . . explicated it almost *ad nauseaum*'.[8] Part of the problem, as Lee admits, is the traces *Savage Fields* retains of the several drafts it went through. Perhaps this accounts for why the central model of his project is so often perceived as a structuralist opposition; perhaps (and here I can only speculate) Lee does not want to abandon the structuralism of his earlier thinking, but should we continue to argue that Lee is, in fact, a structuralist? Has he, rather, ventured where he did not intend to go, and would this explain why the free-play of thought so clearly in evidence throughout 'Cadence, Country, Silence' is so much under control in *Savage Fields*?

The text itself of *Savage Fields* forecloses any need one might feel to speculate on Dennis Lee's intention. As a reading of 'Cadence, Country, Silence', it is already a refusal of that essay's implication of play and possibility. Its postulation of a 'cosmos', a self-regulating economy, is in fact a 'closure of being' (sf, p.48). The virtually inarticulate conclusion of *Savage Fields* may already appear forecasted in the earlier essay where he asserts that 'to dissent from liberal modernity is necessarily to fall silent' (ccs, p.44), but there are other reasons for the silence of thought, itself a rhetorical gesture, with which the book ends. Can anyone hope to resolve all the issues raised in *Savage Fields*? For 'liberal modernity' is not only American imperialism; it is also a rubric designed to cover a host of issues perceived as philosophical, religious, scientific, ethical, and literary. The villain of the piece is the Cartesian *Cogito*, the consciousness that created the division of subject and object, value and fact which is the ground of liberal thinking. The modern dilemma begins here, and Lee's book is a response to that dilemma. Against the 'structural' opposition of 'nature' and 'civilisation' Lee poses the model of 'earth' and 'world'. Their opposition is not binary, however, for they are mediated by 'planet', a proposal that, so far from being radical, appears merely to tinker with the system: 'The cosmology of savage fields inherits the structural categories of liberalism, but recasts and partially transcends them' (sf, p.118). The difference is that 'liberalism' perceives its categories as separate; Lee views them as simultaneous and coextensive, mutual aspects of 'planet'.

The oppositions that Lee would overcome are, of course, not so young as those of Levi-Strauss, or Saussaure, or even Descartes. He is arguing against a habit of mind that, for the purposes of this brief essay, may be said to be as old as our Western habit of thought. Inchoate as it may appear, Lee appears to announce the end of an era whose origins are 'Platonic' and whose structures of thought are metaphysical. His enterprise is not, therefore, greatly assisted by its occasional but crucial reliance on the ontology of Heidegger (who, in a fit of pique, is almost dismissed at the end of *Savage Fields* for his 'teutonic grandiloquence'). For ontology, not to speak of the metaphysics of presence, is the structure that governs Lee's thought. It is a structure, however, that is always shadowed by Nonbeing and absence. It is a structure that requires, according to its own logic, oppositions and, therefore, dualisms. Hence, it is a kind of mystification to assert that 'savage fields figure planet as "dual", but not as "dichotomous"' (SF, p.56). For such an assertion to be persuasive, logic must yield to rhetoric. And what is the impetus of Lee's rhetoric but to situate the reader theologically, which is precisely how he puts it:

> The apparent irrationality, then, of having two incommensurable accounts of every entity, both true, both exclusivist, dissolves when one perceives that the anomaly is not local, but rather the expression of a condition of being, and hence itself a principle of rationality. (SF, p.59)

Nothing in the logocentric view of the cosmos has changed and the Platonic era has not really ended. This is perhaps the 'logical flaw' that Godfrey tries vainly to bring to Lee's attention.[9]

Lee has proved himself more equal to exposing the limits of *Savage Fields* than his critics. One may draw several conclusions from this. I restrict myself to one, which I have already suggested, that Lee is repressed by his own ontology and the oppositions to which it belongs. He appears to wish the world were 'pre-Cartesian' — whatever ideal time that might have been — or, failing that, capable of the recovery that Cohen's 'I' pursues until all hope of recovery is destroyed by F.

* * *

Lee's notion in 'Cadence, Country, Silence' of a relationship be-

111

tween speech and writing — which on the one hand, would support the priority of speech but, on the other hand, would contradict it — begins to resemble structuralist Jacques Derrida's concepts. The priority of the spoken word, Derrida argues in *De la grammatologie* possesses such immediacy that the distinction between signifier and signified is effaced. The spoken word is thus ontologically grounded. Writing, by contrast, encourages loss of memory, and makes all notions of origin, consciousness, and Being itself problematic. Writing calls into question the fundamental structure of the sign as a figure of thought, for the sign is dual, always implying something signified. Derrida's uncovery of writing as the hidden monster in Western thinking not only encourages such doubt, but also radically calls into question the ontological centre that gives it order.[10] Lee comes to a similar conclusion about the state of Western language. He believes that speech gives voice to authenticity without which words die and one loses a sense of centre. But he does not distinguish so firmly the roles of speech and writing ' we live in space which is radically in question for us, that makes our barest speaking a problem to itself. For voice does issue in part from civil space. And alienation in that space will enter and undercut our writing, make it recoil upon itself, become a problem to itself' (ccs, p.154). Speech is permitted, apparently, to drift into writing for both are ultimately governed by cadence.

Prior, then, to speech or writing and the related problem of authenticity and presence is *cadence* whose description leaves Lee 'baffled'. It deserves scrutiny, for Lee's notion of cadence is surprisingly close to Derrida's notion of the trace — the 'beginning', before the opposition of nature and culture (and, one wants to add, before earth and world), and the ending therefore of the metaphysics of presence. '*The trace*,' writes Derrida, '*is effectively the absolute origin of sense in general*'. Which amounts to saying . . .'that there is no absolute origin of sense in general'.[11] Elsewhere he speaks of it as a 'blow' ('coup') or spur, whatever it is that precedes, continually opening sense and deferring fulfillment. Is it this that Lee the poet hears 'both as goad and grace and as something I experience almost as mockery' (sf, p.153)? Is it this to which he refers when he observes: 'You can't "write" a poem, in fact: you can only help it stand free in the torrent of cadence' ?

So certain is Lee of the priority of cadence that he can assert that 'finally, I believe, cadence chooses to issue in the articulate gestures of being human'. Such is the power of cadence for Lee that it is given a kind of will — 'cadence chooses' — so that the opening gesture of signification, which might have moved into a zone of free-play, is inhibited from the start. And so close he was to granting cadence a freedom which 'finally' is taken away! For cadence, before choosing, was 'a teeming process which overflows every prior canon of form (or is prepared to, and can when it chooses)'. But finally cadence is asked to mask itself in ontology, and 'the cadence of what is abounds only when we meet it in its fullest grounding in nonbeing' (CCS, p.52).

And so Dennis Lee, having stood beside the post-structural 'abyme', drew back before the freedom that he glimpsed there ('cadence teems') was released. But not before raising its spectre once again in *Savage Fields*, this time as neurobiology. Neurobiology is the science that has effectively destroyed 'The liberal cosmology [which] consists in precisely this bifurcation of the universe into objective facts and subjects who know, value, and will' (SF, p.51). By destroying the 'subject', that is, 'mind' or 'consciousness', neurobiology has dissolved the dichotomy of 'liberal' metaphysics. But it is one thing to use neurobiology to declare the old dichotomy dead, quite another to situate it into the model of 'savage fields.' 'We will not have situated the neurobiological phenomenon adequately', Lee remarks, 'until we have de-composed its strife-bound be-ing into its world-mode and its earth-mode' (SF, p.58). No, we will not, but the re-emergence of consciousness as 'world' so mystifies neurobiology that one can only accept its use as the destroyer of the old metaphysics, not to assist in the birth of a new one.

What must be preserved is the model within which Being may hide. Now that neurobiology has eliminated the subject, 'any attempt to wedge it back into the still blank spaces of research will be as futile as earlier attempts to cram God into the gaps in evolutionary theory' (SF, pp.52-3). But when Lee asserts, as an over-arching conclusion, that 'now the most difficult, unacceptable, wholly subversive thought is joy, the good resonance of being' (SF, p.109), one is tempted to ask, who is doing the thinking? What subject, and what 'being' is being thought? Within the model hides Being, ontology, consciousness, and oppositions as ancient as *physis* and *nomos*, nature and civilisation. The model, furthermore, as Lee is at pains to tell us, is forged (a forgery of?) by discourse, a privileged power of language by which naming calls into being. This is why, as I stated at the outset, Lee's project is essentially a project of language, for it is only through language that we become who we are. Hence the debt to George Grant is one of a catechumen, instinct with religious awe.

A text, then, for Lee is in fact a palimpsest, a text within which another hides. Discourse itself, as we know from 'Cadence, Country, Silence', is 'heterotextual' burdened with the Other. As Lee learned in his period of silence, the Other is inauthenticity. But it is that very inauthenticity that must be preserved, for it is grounded in Nonbeing; and 'To accept nonbeing at home in what is, to accept what-is at home in nonbeing, is perhaps the essential act of being human. Certainly it is the beginning of art' (CCS, p.52). What is more felicitous than 'nonbeing' — since it only needs to be uncovered for its opposite to be revealed? For how can non-being not but be related to Being? Thus it was discovered that the problem of writing contained its own solution, and the solution had to be one that both generated and reconciled opposition. Its name was 'cadence,' a word intimately related to music, as well as to the sound and inflection of discourse. 'I sense this cadence,' Lee writes, 'as presence' (CCS, p.35). Without it, without presence, how would one perceive Being, the authentic, one's self (the subject)?

4

Hidden more deeply in Lee's text, more deeply than Being, is the unwillingness to free cadence from its anthropomorphically divine bondage. We must accept that cadence is personified. It needs no demonstration. But to take a partial vocabulary from Heidegger, a brief conclusion from neurobiology (to name only two 'sources') without allowing the full implications of these two contradictory 'texts' to enter his own text, would seem disingenuous were it not for the notion of 'colonial space' that provides the focus for Lee's enterprise. Colonial space is infiltrated space, space that harbours the inauthentic. It is defined by the presence of Nonbeing, the presence of absence. So it is, perhaps, that Lee abandons the notion of 'colonial' while drafting *Savage Fields*, for he began to perceive that he was in fact discussing 'human' space. It would be more precise to say that Lee's subject was the mythology of that space, a white one, which he continually charges with words of a familiar kind.[12] As Lee knows only too well, we colonize with language. We allow it to 'master' us. We do this particularly through systems of belief (models) that we continually exchange with others. We do this fundamentally through the reification of our modes of origination (cadence).

But I had assumed for a moment that Lee was desirous of dwelling elsewhere than in colonial, white space. The obverse of colonial, however, is imperial (American), and to abandon white mythology would be to give up the assurance that Nonbeing always implies its opposite. The blame, for example, that Lee attaches to Cohen's *Beautiful Losers* results from 'the attempt of the governing consciousness to imagine an escape from the ontological condition of the world' (SF, p.102). Ondaatje's *The Collected Works of Billy the Kid* is privileged, by contrast, for its acceptance of these conditions. Both works together constitute a structural opposition, implying that further examples are unnecessary to demonstrate the truth of the argument. And what does such acceptance mean? It means that Ondaatje's fiction is 'paradigmatic': 'What does not change . . . is the recurrent conjunction of world and earth' (SF, p.32). Ondaatje's strategy is such that it 'allows each thing the freedom on the page to respond as it does in the savage field — now as earth, now as world, now as both; yet it also articulates a shapely order in the flux through the recurrent paradigms' (SF, p.33). The text of Lee's Ondaatje is a *pas de deux*. Thus to accept 'the ontological condition of the world' is to see it as dance. It means, despite Lee's disapproval of Heidegger's 'a-historical account' (SF, p.112), his own analysis has no recourse to history either. It merely posits: 'the cosmology of savage fields makes sense of the terrible era of modernity' (SF, p.11). Here we are, then, as if we simply fell here (*cadentia*); we have no choice but to accept.

The savage fields, then, are static, and one can well imagine that, had they not existed, they would require invention, man being what he is. And so they were invented, as a kind of Hobbesian necessity. Escape is forbidden, freedom is forbidden, the play of mind is forbidden. Lee's model, as closed as any other cosmos, is totalitarian. To live within it is to be condemned. Any model other than the static field (is this why the metaphor of the electromagnetic field is chosen to illustrate the concept? [SF, p.10]) is exiled from consideration. Only those texts that contain a certain duplicity are admissible as characteristic of our era. But for the model to be operative neither world nor earth can gain superiority over the other. To borrow Hubert Aquin's term, relationships can only be understood as analogous to an *antiphonary*. The very hint of such a brilliant conclusion as that of Timothy Findley's *The Wars*, in which Robert Ross seems transmogrified elementally into earth, would be forbidden.

The last, perhaps the ultimate, problem with Lee's model is that while it purports to speak for 'our' era, its synchronic character forbids it validity. Unless, of course, it is a model for apocalypse, which, I suppose, Lee would have us believe. There is only one 'now' for ontology, and that is outside time and history. Thus it comes as somewhat of a surprise to learn from Lee that for Cohen 'History is static, then, in the sense that it turns out to have been unreal to begin with' (*Beautiful Losers*, p. 74). Perhaps Lee is being ironic, for where is history in his own text? He is referring, of course, to what he calls the 'Isis continuum,' the ontology that opposes that of 'savage fields'. The failure of Cohen's project is that he allows, according to Lee, F. to deconstruct the Isis myth and, as a consequence, the ontology of savage fields. F. is mere consciousness, capable of continual making and unmaking. For Lee, this is sheer villainy. But cannot F. be read ironically to demonstrate the very fragility of system? For the same system that generates the eternal presence and absence of the Isis myth generates other oppositions as well. Osiris includes the cycle of life and death, Being and Nonbeing, and F.'s role is both to inscribe the myth into the text and to delete it. This is tantamount to telling us that the myth is at once real and not real. His villainy is to reveal myth as discourse, for then discourse becomes myth. If ontology hides in discourse, ontology might, then, only be a structure of words. The 'savage fields' might be the same. Discourse, then, must be controlled, for if it were not, ontology might escape. It might escape into time, and then time would no longer have a referent. Thus it is more prudent to turn against the Isis continuum, as well as against F., in order to keep one ontology intact.

The victim of ontology is history, and what is left is *aporia*, impasse, raised to the level of a metaphysical principle.[13] One is tempted to say that occasionally it seems as if Lee were sharing his mask of critic with someone else, that behind the mask came the voice of Mackenzie King ordering our era into stasis. It is only a somewhat fanciful analogy, for as well as sharing a teleology of impasse, they both seem to prefer closed systems where only the inscrutable, finally, leaks in. Each, furthermore, has the same predilection for the often opaque, contradictory text. They do appear to differ in their attitude toward conflict, but how far is King's tendency to reconcile from Lee's assertion that 'Everything that is, is world; everything that is, is earth' (SF, p.8)? How fundamental is the difference between the benevolent repression of conflict and the belief that ontology is unresolved conflict? Lee's model, in particular, raises the specificities of conflict to Wagnerian proportions and foresees for the plant nothing but a sustained *Götterdämmerung*, a stay of execution.

The problem is that all these ontologies, Beings, myths are only human (all-too-human), after all. Who is to say whether earth, whatever it is, 'cannot tolerate that which is not earth' (SF, p.9)? Should it 'care'? Earth is, indeed, as Lee is fond of saying, inscrutable. Under what circumstances are we to draw it into the horizon of the human? Why, in fact, close the horizon at all in the name of *aporia*? Why, finally, surround ourselves with human oppositions? For that is one of the fundamental failures of Western (white) thought, its human closure. As if rock were human. As if rock supported 'the great chain of being'. But in saying this I am reaching the limits of humanism, as well as the peripheries of Lee's horizon. It is also the limit of human discourse, the core of Lee's meditation, beyond which words will not reach.

[1] 'There are no "plates" '. An *hors-texte* is literally that part of a book not included in the signatures, but still bound into the text. Hence, there is nothing outside the text. See Jacques Derrida, *De la grammatologie* (Paris: Les éditions de Minuit, 1967). p.227.

[2] *Saturday Night*, 87, no. 9 (Sept., 1972), p.33.

[3] 'Song', in *The Gods*, p.24.

[4] 'Reading *Savage Fields*', *Canadian Journal of Political and Social Theory*, 3, no. 2 (Spring/Summer, 1979), p.176.

[5] See Martin Heidegger, *Poetry, Language, Thought*, trans. Albert Hoffstadter (New York: Harper & Row, 1971), p.176.

[6] See especially D.G. Jones, 'In Search of Canada: Dennis Lee's Ironic Vision,' *Arc*, no. 1 (Spring, 1978), pp.23-8.

[7] Heidegger, pp.158-9.

[8] 'Reading *Savage Fields*', p.176.

[9] 'On *Savage Fields* and the Act of Criticism,' *Canadian Journal of Political and Social Theory*, 3, no. 2 (Spring/Summer, 1979), pp.152-9.

[10] A useful introduction to Jacques Derrida's writing may be found in Frank Lentricchia, *After the New Criticism* (Chicago: The University of Chicago Press, 1980), pp.163-90.

[11] *De la grammatologie*, p.95. (My translation)

[12] On 'white', see Jacques Derrida, 'White Mythology: Metaphor in the Text of Philosophy', *New Literary History*, 6, no. 1 (Autumn, 1974).

[13] 'Impasse' appears as the climax of 'Cadence': 'the impasse of writing that is problematic to itself is transcended only when the impasse become its own subject' (p.165): and it is raised as a question and issue again at the end of *Savage Fields*, p.108. It appears inevitable.

The Role of the Poet

'The Poet as Shepherd of Being'

Sean Kane

'. . . by thinking our way soberly into what his poetry says, to come to learn what is unspoken. That is the course of the history of Being. If we reach and enter that course, it will lead thinking into a dialogue with Poetry, a dialogue that is the history of Being.'

—Martin Heidegger,
'What Are Poets For?'

'. . . THE HALT AND STAMMER, the wry self-deprecation, the rush of celebratory elan and the vastness of the still unspoken surround . . .' (CCS): these shifting intensities of being human in the northern half of America, which Dennis Lee hears in the best Canadian writing, have in the ten years since *Civil Elegies* become inflections of his own poetic voice. Of course, we had already heard these inflections in Purdy, from *Cariboo Horses* on, and in Margaret Laurence's narrators who speak and breathe and remain silent as nobody but a Canadian could. But in Lee we may be more comprehensively, more acutely aware of the particular life-resonance which these inflections express. He is the one writer who has inquired philosphically into the nature of writing in Canada as an act of authentic being. And he has carried a stubborn authenticity into a number of deeply typifying Canadian preoccupations that sustain the artist's realization of a true self in the world: a devotion to the spiritual sources of awe and wonder, an absorption in confessional, meditative experience, a commitment to writing as a discipline of remembrance, a service to culture lived almost as a religious obligation.

However we generalize these essentially nineteenth-century concerns — they were characterized in one reviewer's remark that 'Lee is a kind of Canadian Matthew Arnold' — it is obvious that Lee embodies something permanent and rooted in Canadian life and letters. That something contrasts cleanly with what Lee himself referred to in an interview as the 'trash-with-flash' of secular modernity, all 'liberal convenience and trendy disposable gratifications' (Twigg, *For Openers*, 1981, p.248). This isn't to say that Lee is a romantic nostalgist — rather, that by acts of discipline and faith he has carried expression forward in this country by writing against the grain of the modernist assumptions about literature and life. To this extent, he represents an alternative way of thinking and responding that exists as a suppressed strain in our culture. It is important, therefore, to try to talk about the authenticity of response that holds the separate voices of the editor, the essayist, the philosopher, the citizen — even the writer of nonsense verse — together in this poet. I will call the unifying power among these voices *Voice* — using the initial capital to distinguish that integrity of saying, which can hold together an immense variety of response, from a lesser poet's search for a noticeable tune. It is the deep strength that has made Lee the poet's poet in Canada.

It seems at once innovative and old-fashioned to be talking about Voice in poetry. There is reason to feel like a stranger to the term. Twentieth-century writers have generally shied away from personal expression, preferring instead to discover meaning ironically in the hard-edged juxtapositions of tone, content, persona or image. The modern author retreats in a Joycean ideal of detachment behind the screen of a craft that is rhetorically polished yet emotionally incomplete. Why did this retreat from Voice come about? The short answer is to see literary modernism simply as a reaction against the excesses of Romantic spontaneity, particularly as it found its ideal in what Hugh Kenner has called 'the poet as force of nature', who lays 'streams of little poems like cod's eggs' (*The Sacred Book of the Arts*, 1958). The more patient answer, however, is to be found in the crisis of naming which underlies all expression in our time.

For the deepest understanding of Lee, who says, 'I'm taking my particular moment as the last few centuries' (*For Openers*, p.247), it is necessary to see the history of this crisis as the history of modernism itself. The modern attitude to experience has many false starts, but it is really inaugurated by the Italian philosopher Vico's remark that 'what man recognizes as true, and what he has himself made, are one and the same' (*The New Science*, 1725). This statement has huge consequences for the way man regards language. In the sacramental world-view that prevailed up to Vico's time, words did not seem to be an independent source of meaning. Words were invisible except as the very things they re-presented, as the things which spoke through them and to which words were mysteriously and indelibly tied. But with the breakup of a uniform Christian-Classical world-view with its belief in a reality alive with God-given value, words came to be regarded as arbitrary devices for building worlds out of ourselves: all origin and value now had its centre in the creative power of man, imposing the form of his will upon a value-free world by bringing it into the magic circle of language. For modern man all meaning resides in the imagination of the alienated perceiver; what he believes to be true is ultimately the projection of his own language. Words have therefore become tools by which man fashions reality for himself.

In the face of this alienation of words from things, which had already become a crucial problem to poets in the nineteenth century, many modernist writers of stature took the obvious fork in the road. They explored the act of naming as the arbitrary meanings that re-echoed when words were flung out against a meaning-free world. For Mallarmé, the great prophet of modernist aesthetics, words were like dice thrown by the poet against the blank space of the page. Already in the novel the aesthetic had been broached in Flaubert's preoccupation with an ideal 'book about nothing, a book dependent on nothing external, which would be held together by the strength of its style, just as the earth, suspended in the void, depends on nothing external for its support' (tran. Francis Stegmuller, *Selected Letters*, 1953, p.127-8). This experimentalism underlies the sheer word-magic of much contemporary poetry which, as Kenner says of modernism generally, renders 'a universe of independent words, obeying their chemical affinities, with no restraint from things' (*Dublin's Joyce* 1956, p.303).

Within this characterization of literary modernism one must recognize a tradition of poets who rebel against the arbitrariness of such language. These are the writers from Rimbaud to Rilke and Yeats who have sought meaning in the dark energies which tie the unconscious, through symbol, to the primal world. In almost every art-form the attempt has been made to break the alienation of the self in a neutral world by revitalizing expression in a hectic subjectivity. But in the Dionysic heat of the expressivists like Plath or Dylan Thomas, as in the Appolinian coolness of the artificers like Borges and Nabokov, the problem remains of an apparently neutral world distinct from the self. These two modes of artistic expression, which may be said to be the pathologies of Voice in the twentieth-century, were carried to their necessary respective outcomes: exhaustion of the self through immolation, exhaustion of art through parody. The outcomes were honestly enacted, following the logic of the crisis of naming, and it is not meant to belittle the achievements of fifty years of modernism to point out that the common path leads, not surprisingly, to a self-conscious dandyism, in which a writer, to be fashionable, turns away in suspicion from the more deeply felt sources of meaning, and engages instead in a nervous hunt for the sparkle and jolt of the new. This tendency, now boringly patent in advertising, is an extension of the modernist principle that language is no more than a code, an arbitrary convenience of society. In advertising, as in much experimental writing, the speaker is freed of responsibility for what he says, since it is not really himself, but 'language itself which speaks' (Barthes, *Writing Degree Zero*). Thus there is lost to poetry the power of the speaking voice, the marvellous experience of a human being speaking . . . and listening! (for 'speaking itself is a listening', Heidegger said), of a human being struggling to hear what Keats knew as 'the holiness of the heart's affections'. And on the larger scale, Voice itself, as the record of man's encounter and dialogue with the awe and mystery of 'what's out there', is also diminished, having been made subordinate to the sign or symbol in the modernist aesthetic. Accordingly, 'the poet's voice' is reduced to the status of another item in the decoding of puzzles that goes on in the classroom, often with the indifferent intensity of a computer game. How, against an aesthetic based on the Cartesian *cogito*, is one going to teach a poet who says: 'I write to find out what the poem wants to do' (*For Openers*, p.243)? Like most of Lee's remarks, this declaration of the essential living otherness of a poem violates modernist assumptions about the imposition of technique or subjectivity on an apparently neutral world. Lee is modern, then, because he seeks out the way man lives on the planet in the present age, but he is anti-modernist in his rejection of a fashionable aesthetic which in his view, debases language by ignoring its purpose — to disclose the gestures of being human in the world. To suggest the poet's task is anything less than to speak for and through the reality of our being here, is, for Lee, not only a debasing of language, but of man. That is why it has been necessary to belabour literary modernism in this way, since in its entirety (though not in several of its technical innovations) it is what Lee stands against:

> Master and Lord, there was a
> measure once.
> There was a time when men could say
> my life, my job, my home
> and still feel clean.
> The poets spoke of earth and heaven. There were no symbols. (CE 2)

2

To write against the grain of modernism is to be plunged into a terrifying dilemma. For the poet cannot go back to the innocent dream of a unity of word and being which Vico swept away. Since the earli-

124

est Greek poets, poetry had been conceived of as the expression of reality itself, with the poet participating in the cosmic rhythms of creation. Poets have always felt that poetry meant more than simply the production of a work of art; it meant the primordial act of naming by which the world is established for men and women in imitation of the original call into existence by God. The poet was therefore a member of the most ancient tradition of the magus which understood divinity in terms of the first creative Word that called forth the world, whose energy reverberates again in the poet's calling forth to that world. In a painfully tenuous way, Lee can claim whatever strength is provided in the twentieth century by that tradition of the poet-thinker which began with Heraclitus and Pindar and was still nourishing to the Romantic poets. 'The moment we conceive the divine energy', Coleridge writes in his *Notebooks*, 'that moment we co-conceive the *Logos*'. In Lee's thoughts about writing, there is a similar humility and awe in the presence of 'a field of luminous force, knotted and folded and stalling and skittering back, perpetual like energy . . . .'. He calls it 'Cadence'. 'All my poetry is a response to cadence', and 'Cadence enacts the space of cosmos. "Cosmos" as what is. And "space" as the still and tumultuous process in which cosmos is perpetually recreated in the unspeakable energy of be-ing — *being at all*. To be tuned by cadence is to vibrate with the calamitous resonance of being' ('Polyphony: Enacting a Meditation', 1982). This cadence, whatever Lee means by it exactly, is clearly the authority for his vocation as a poet. His observations on the phenomenon (mostly found in 'Cadence, Country, Silence', 1972/1982) are intensely careful not to reduce the source of inspiration to any kind of practical definition, and perhaps we should not try to do so either, beyond saying that Cadence marks the point of departure for all of Lee's writing and stands as the determining element of what I am calling Voice. Other poets in the tradition, most notably Coleridge in his *Shakespeare Lectures*, allow themselves to be more explicit about the Johannine Word which still resonates beneath 'the old antithesis of *Words* and *Things*', and I think it must be toward this undifferentiated wholeness of creativity-and-creation felt beneath the conscious mind that Lee is pointing in his statement of an ancient intuition. Poetry, according to this intuition, is the force that holds things together, naming the eternal experiences of friendship, community, earth and sky, and by doing so establishes a ground for human existence.

Yet to return to this role of articulating the universal song of being — even to contemplate in the abstract such a return — is to involve oneself in a paralyzing void that opens up around the act of naming, where alternatives call each other's projects into doubt. On the one hand, there is the tradition just described, the activity of Voice as existence itself speaking, now rendered dumb by the knowledge that while the primordial unity of the word and the world is an ideal to which poetry can aspire, it is no longer a reality that may be grasped. On the other hand, there is the modernist recognition that if meaning is merely man-made, then nature, earth, existence, God, are nothing more than words. As Heidegger says, 'The gods have fled'. In a poet who is honestly sceptical enough to be troubled by the crisis of value, this alternative also renders Voice inauthentic: 'Any statement of ideals by which we might bring our plight into perspective turns out to be either a hollow appeal to things we have no access to, or (more commonly) a restatement of the very liberal ideas that got us into the fix in the first place'(CCS).

And we cannot get on, no matter how we
rearrange our lives, and we cannot let go for
then there is nothing at all. (CE 2)

For anyone trapped in this crisis of meaning, it is comforting, and unnerving, and probably necessary to go to Friedrich Hölderlin (1770-1843) who felt the crisis so keenly that he spent the last decades of his life mad, 'received' as Heidegger says, 'into the protection of the night of lunacy'. Lee acknowledges an enormous debt to this 'master of poets' (LADOO, 1976/1979). This debt is seen in Lee's particular rekindling of Hölderlin's measure into anapaestic meditative surges; into long confident lines stalling suddenly, at line-end, with the plunging hesitancy of the unspeakable; verse paragraphs that remain stately even when shot through with the charged gaps and spaces of an awesome something that has already made syntax jump and tangle and snarl, as if words had been passed through a magnetic field. Even the choice of elegy and hymn, and the interpretation of these two ancient Greek conventions of Voice in one poem like *The Gods* (1978/79), shows Lee's discipleship through Hölderlin to an older tradition. As his translator Christopher Middleton describes it, Hölderlin's poetry is 'a field of vision crossed by whirlwinds of fire' (Friedrich Hölderlin Eduard Mörke, *Selected Poems*, 1972, p.xxii): To understand why his poetry is tormented in this particular way, one must imagine a young man brought up in the Orphic tradition of the poet as primordial namer, listening with dismay to the doctrine of pure value-ascribing subjectivity in lectures given by the philosopher Fichte, yet still finding in the world, especially in his beloved Susette Gontard, the very presence of divinity which the consequences of Kantian idealism had banished from the world. He must write, therefore, from the belief that in the field of words nature spontaneously reveals herself — reveals herself not in clear patterns of order but in something *heard*, a vibrancy of being. Hölderlin's favourite metaphors for this disclosure are musical: chord, vibration, resonance; in Rilke, too, there is the intimation that 'Song is existence' (*Sonnets to Orpheus*, III). The experience of the vibrancy of things in a force-field will be carried to a strange intensity by Lee, particularly when he announces that natural coherences do obtain, and that perhaps one may enter them and find adequate words being born.

How did I
miss it? that
haltingly, silently,
openly, home
each mortal being, hale or crippled or done,
announces the pitch of itself in
a piecemeal world. And
here! it was always here, the living coherence!
Not abstract harmonies but, rather, that
each thing gropes to be itself in time and what is lovely
is how, once brought to a pitch it holds & presides
in the hum of its own galvanic being.
And more: as it persists it picks up
everything that is, and neither in
yammer nor concord but half alive on
all those jumbled wave-lengths, inciting
a field of near-coherence
in the spacey surround.
(*Not Abstract Harmonies But*, 1974/79)

The event that chooses this moment to break into words is comparatively rare in Lee's experience. He has written only a few serious poems, revising them often in the struggle to hear cleanly. The explanation of this trial of authenticity lies in the dark night in which poetry must now be written — the dark night first entered by Hölderlin, who never returned. The spirits of a living universe, the gods who through the mediation of the poet bring language to the people, have become 'the absent ones' (*The Gods*). Until the universe becomes a sacrament for mankind again, it is a time of dearth. As Heidegger observes in his essay on Hölderlin, the poet 'has been cast out — out into the *Between*, between gods and men'. Lee's poems, *The Gods* and *The Death of Harold Ladoo* most explicitly, are compelled by this in-betweeness, which has become a more attenuated space in the modern century, where it is impossible even to tell if the gods 'are godhead or zilch or daily ones like before' (G), even as the intimation of their presence is still terrifyingly felt as something holy. Like Hölderlin before him, who declared: 'Near and/ Hard to grasp is the god', Lee can sense but not possess the numinous power without form:

> I scarcely comprehend,
> and least of all can I fathom . . . .
> how I am to salute you, nor how content with your being   (G)

And again, as Heidegger said of Hölderlin, he must 'hold the ground in the nothing of this night'. The poet, like Jacob, wrestles all through a dark night with the angel of being; but at dawn, it is the poet, not the angel, who must give to his adversary a blessing and a name, 'wrapping in song', as Hölderlin says, 'the divine gift to the people'. Hölderlin is one of the last poets to accept without question the Orphic role of primordial namer who opens out a dwelling-place for man in the world. But the isolation in which he carries out this role makes him 'the precursor of poets in a destitute time', as Heidegger recognized. Hölderlin knew the fate that waited for him:

> Yet it behooves us, under the storms of God
> Ye poets! with uncovered head to stand.
> With our own hands to grasp the very lightning-flash
> Paternal, and to pass, wrapping in song
> The divine gift to the people.   ('As, when on festive days')

Saying that 'he received more from the gods than he was able to digest', and standing alone in the night made mad by truth, Hölderlin is Lee's spiritual ancestor. The role of the poet as Orpheus envoicing creation becomes in modern Canada the task of enacting the cadence of civil and spiritual belonging in a colonized space that recognizes neither citizenship nor the sacred. *Civil Elegies* defines this struggle of Voice to bring men and women into community around the eternal metaphors of Earth as home. Beyond that, the Voice calls forth, in a second volume entitled *The Gods*, the hidden forms of its power.

128

3

Why is the artist's role made savage and impotent by modern life? Why, asks Lee in *The Death of Harold Ladoo*, is the artist the bringer of death? The difficult question can be faced by looking at the elegy on the writer, a friend of Lee's, who used art as a way of courting his own eventual murder, and so by extension enacted the death-wish of his century.

In Hölderlin's time a pre-scientific idealism provided some remaining ground for believing in the commensurability of words and things. But with the imperial rule of liberal modernity, from its base-camp in the Cartesian ego confronting a cosmos of raw material, words also became raw material, to be shaped by the artist's technique. If in this situation of meaninglessness you demand of a writer that he create, then you place him in the dilemma of Beckett's Molloy, for whom saying is merely inventing: 'it little matters what I say, this, this or that or any other thing. Saying is inventing. Wrong, very rightly wrong. You invent nothing, you think you are inventing, you think you are escaping and all you do is stammer out your lesson, the remnants of a pensum one day got by heart and long forgotten; life without tears, as it is wept. To hell with it anyway. Where was I?' (*Three Novels*, 1959, p.38). With objective existence unnamable, the self is also unnamable, having no foundation for its being except in the fictions it compulsively spins out as if to stave off the void or to confirm its alien principle of identity. Literary modernism, as we have already suggested, responds in two ways to the dilemma.

The first is the way of the impersonal artificer who, in Joyce's famous words, dwells 'within or behind or beyond or above his handiwork, invisible, refined out of existence, paring his fingernails'. Accepting the modernist dictum of the arbitrariness of words, and of the worlds they constitute, the artist is as free as a god to invent his own universe for himself. The aesthetic challenge, then, is to use parodic and recursive techniques to shine light on the very processes of invention, as Joyce does in *Finnegans Wake*, as if in fulfillment of Flaubert's ideal 'book about nothing'. Against this cool objectivity, the second way is that of impassioned meaning and fervent subjectivity. Originally the path taken by the symbolists from Rimbaud on, it includes in American experience poets writing in the tradition of Whitman's *Song of Myself* and Ginsberg's *Howl*, as well as a host of doomed artists in other media: William Burroughs, Charlie Parker, James Dean, Jimi Hendrix, Janis Joplin — to name a few. As long as Cartesian modernism exists there will be the daring ones who carry out kamikaze raids on the inarticulate even as the act requires the immolation of the conscious, purposeful self which is seen to repress the energies of life. In other words, the attempt to break out of the alienation of words from things by touching a white-hot, birth-pang expressivity is doomed to failure because it only acts out the Cartesian assumption that all meaning and value is embodied in the alienated subject. The assertion of a hectic subjectivity implicitly confirms the neutral objectivity of the world which that display has failed to awaken. And against the inventor of words, who dwells godlike above his artifice, this second tradition only reiterates the urge to make oneself the absent demi-god. Since this tradition of the doomed Romantic artist shows the pathology of Voice which the Orphic vocation takes when infected by Cartesian modernism, it is the tradition of greater concern to Lee, who sees it brought to its fatal conclusion in the life of Harold Ladoo:

> And mostly I believe the artists further
> the systematic murder of the real, and if their work does have
> the tang of authentic life
> it is one more sign that they are in business to kill.

But how, in this confrontation of the high demand of poetry with the impossibility of authentic speech, is one going to write about the death of a friend, especially if that friend was a living example of the artist as the systematic murderer of the real, and if the elegy itself might be just another systematic murder?

The answer is to be found in the pure enactment of Voice as the genuine rapprochement with the calm energies of what-is. For Lee this is an earned experience and not a simple solution to an artistic dilemma. The original earning of that experience between 1968 and 1972, and its culmination in the re-writing of *Civil Elegies* (1968/1972), will be described in the next part of the essay. But let us turn first to *The Death of Harold Ladoo*.

I have read this long poem often, in several drafts. Once I heard it read to a university audience. It is a wrenching experience, finally serene in its honesty. Somehow the poem manages to envoice modernity and a counter-stance to modernity without crumbling. It enacts and cancels the exploitative power of consciousness. Again and again through the course of the poem — it is, in fact, an emotionally exhausting meditation — the poet's mind is caught in the act of 'saying is inventing', as it spins out inadequate rationalizations of Ladoo and Lee as friends and artists. Even the high demands of the formal elegy itself turn out to be another of the ego's gratifications. The ideal of making the dead one 'legendary/in permanent regions of praise' conceals the exploitation of Ladoo for the sake of the ego's need to produce a good poem, and the whole exercise practically falters when it owns up to the fact that Lee is making rhetorical use of Ladoo as an exemption of the modernism Lee rejects. It would be pedantic to trace the movement of the poem through all the swerves and quarrels of this love-hate relationship to its mixed and tentative conclusion. What does need to be said is that the significance of the poem is not to be found exclusively in specific words or images or any other positivistic formulations of experience. Instead, meaning is to be heard in the way these inadequate formulations ring hollowly against the unsaid, in that 'deep unscheduled ground of caring' which surrounds the futility of sheer invention, where actions speak louder than words.

The *enactment* of a poem is, then, for Lee the only possible authentic response to the arbitrariness of language in our time. In the essay 'Polyphony: Enacting a Meditation', he describes enactment as this very sort of negative discourse in which the ego tries to intimidate Voice into assuming the role of an objective reporter of experience, and Voice responds by letting the full-bodied struggle to name overwhelm the ego's fears. To write against the dictatorship of the ego in this way is also to confront most contemporary poetry, with its 'univocal' range of expression, its 'discursive equanimity which reports on its feelings with arm's-length detachment'. A fuller, more emotionally honest expression will enact the monotonal language of the self within the process of a meditation 'living its way from one inflection to another'. No emotion can be merely named during this process; labelling a feeling always falsifies it. Instead, emotion 'must be embodied in the movement & texture & pitch of the recalling voice', even if the action that results is unpredictable. The Ladoo elegy practically rejoices in this unpredictability. It breaks all the rules of rhetorical composition. The poem flows from one resolution to another as each of the vantage-points of still-inadequate naming is rejected by feeling, which then swirls and eddies in its hunt for a truer expression. 'The poem must live its way through a course of attending, and be charged by what it discovers at each stage,' Lee says. Emerging in this alteration of form and process is an integration of knowing with the least accessible levels of consciousness, those levels that express themselves only in the innocence of pure enactment. But what is the principle that makes the enactment consistent with itself, and not merely another haphazard effort at invention?

We return to Cadence as that mysterious Voice of existences in their distinctiveness and difference from each other. It is this poly-phony of Being which the poem enacts, even as 'Cadence woos the poem into being' (ccs). Lee cannot be more explicit about this mystery, except to say that its presence is a startling intrusion of the real into the false consciousness of modernism and into the uses which modernism forces upon words. In fact, the indeterminacy, or rather, poly-determinacy, of Cadence is what disintegrates the act of conscious purpose that would give it meaning — just as it sabotages the writing of any poem that attempts to report from a pre-estab-lished plan or model of experience. For this intimation of the in-transitivity of things in a mysterious moment before speech, the analogy to Beckett is revealing. Though Lee's honesty is of a totally different kind from the satirical rigour of Beckett, there is in the great dramatist of language the same preoccupation as Lee's with what his *Texts for Nothing* denominate as 'for ever the same murmur, flowing unbroken, like a single, endless word and therefore mean-ingless, for it's the end gives the meaning to words' (1967, p.111). To write against the grain of structured speech is to approach this meaningless void in which words theoretically stand free of the de-vices of human control; to go with the grain of speech is to cover up the void with invented words into whose meaning the speaker disap-pears.

In these terms, Ladoo's fate is seen to be a 'vanishing into words'. This is not to render the hero of the elegy insignificant — Lee's atti-tude to him is rather like Marlowe's to Kurtz:

> You pushed it past the limit, further than any of us and also you died of it.

But the admiration is tempered by the acknowledgement that La-doo was living out the agony of his century in 'a fresh explosion/of that lethal paradigm' of the artist who immolates himself in words, hoping thereby to render them numinous. In the Cartesian night all things are idols of the mind rather than sources of Being. Indeed, the very gods are 'mutants'. The only authentic path left open to the poet is to name this condition, though by an enactment which at its least self-indulgent will not carry the artist himself headlong into the gratifying madness, for:

> A world that denies
> the gods, the gods
> make mad.

132

How Lee achieved the special poise of being that allows Voice to speak the truth in a terrible age is a complicated story. As Lee did, we will have to take the long way round, and go back to the period before his good writing when the problem of naming presented itself to him as an absolute dilemma.

4

In the modern century the role of the poet as primordial namer is even more tenuous because, a Heidegger said of Rilke, 'even the trace of the holy has become unrecognizable'. ('What Are Poets For?') Yet the *act* of singing remains. It remains as an absurd, glorious possibility, the possibility of Rilke's *Duino Elegies* and *Sonnets to Orpheus* (1912-1922). This is the posture entered into clumsily and mocked by the 43 sonnet variations that make up Lee's first book, *Kingdom of Absence* (1967), and it is worth looking at these poems because they demonstrate the abyss into which much good expression falls when the poet performs self-consciously on the high-wire, carrying a load of *Angst*.

Essentially, the poems report the frustration of naming for a poet who desperately wants to give meaning to that country whose national asset is nothingness. The path taken is self-mockery and a playful exercise in the self-refuting substitutability of words, enlivened not by the illusion of freedom but by an awareness of the nonsense of it all. (This will be the source of his later children's verse, for it also comes out of the predicament of language: the nonsense of words against the need to name a country). But for now, *Kingdom of Absence* registers futility about the modernist role of the poet:

> Oh Rilke, work your lovely fraud
> for we who are your music must applaud.   (KA XI)

The futility is augmented by a dismay with modernist contemporaries in Toronto who, abandoning the sacred altogether, resort to 'improvising lives' (XVII) by relying on 'the sleek and shifty mind' (XXII). Coming between these two alternatives, a statement that faces the issue directly — 'my subject is the absence of the real/In time' (XXXIV) — confidently asserts what it cannot enact. In these sonnets, Voice is paralyzed by the double bind that inheres in the authentic use of speech in an inauthentic era.

The first edition of *Civil Elegies* in 1968 promised a vocal breakthrough of sorts. But until 1972, when Lee recognized the ampli-

133

tude of expression pent up in the elegies and revised them considerably for the 1972 edition, he was caught in a situation that he could not assess. The result was an utter silencing of his writing. It may be said that the situation became all the more difficult in these four years by being forced into a tidily logical dilemma. Lee often relies on pairs of opposing terms in his thinking (see the conclusion to *Savage Fields*, for example); the hard-and-fast dichotomy gives an imaginary symmetrical elegance to a real issue, freezing it into the condition of paradoxy. This reification is, I imagine, the occupational hazard of as heady and internalizing a thinker as Lee, and we should look at the idealized form of the question more closely because Lee embodies so much that is both real and merely imaginary in Canadian experience.

In its idealized form, the complicated character of naming emerges in Lee's writing as a paradox of unreconcilable opposites. The opposites are unreconcilable because each term is defined simultaneously at the expense of the other which it excludes. Whether the terms are 'concrete monotone' *versus* 'blue muskoka' (as in *Kingdom of Absence*), or 'World' *versus* 'Earth' (*Savage Fields*), or 'civilization' *versus* 'the land' (in a 1972 article, 'Running and Dwelling: Homage to Al Purdy'), the issue in question has been polarized into an antagonism of opposites. This 'double bind' (I am using Gregory Bateson's original term for the phenomenon: *Steps to an Ecology of Mind*, 1972) is a form of retreat: it gives an ideal simplicity to a complex problem by reducing it to an 'either/or' dilemma, but one from which there is really no escape since any choice will lead the mind back to a dead-end in the manner of the classic paradox. Anthony Wilden calls the phenomenon 'symmetrization' (*The Imaginary Canadian*, 1980), suggesting that modern culture is riddled with these false 'either/or' choices accepted in place of the real contexts they distort: success 'as opposed to' (*'versus'*) failure; salvation *'versus'* sin; man *'versus'* woman represent similar paralyzing retreats from complexity. In his study of schizophrenia Bateson points out that in the face of such a paradoxical language, a language unmediated by other contexts that might give the terms more concrete substance, a common response of the subject is to reject the use of language altogether. Once this threat to speech is appreciated it is easy to see why a poet, whose very calling is speech, would find refuge for a while in silence.

It probably comes as no surprise to see that Lee's attempt to define the condition of modernism by using the metaphor of opposing elements only bedevils him further. For the metaphor of equivalent opposition issues from a peculiarly modernist compulsion to divide a problem up into artificial polarities in order to command it more efficiently. In relying on such a root-metaphor Lee is subject to the modernism he decries. The act of distinguishing 'this' from 'that' is a natural human reflex, not to be confused with the modernist habit of defining a 'this' prejudicially as the pure *opposite* of a 'that'. Wilden sees this adversarial metaphor as the formula for exploitation because it indulges in a tactic of divide-and-rule. According to the tactic, a preferred value gains substance and definition by being divided from, then set against, a disparaged single 'opposite' to which it is actually more intricately related. The real complexity of the relationship then becomes effaced in the imaginary polarization of two absolutes, each essential to the other's meaning. The disparaged term can then be imagined to sustain the privileged term in the way colony serves empire (in the code of colonization), nonwhite serves white (in racism), woman serves man (in sexism). Unless mediated by the recognition that reality is organized ecologically in interlocking and inclusive patterns of activity, the human impulse to draw boundaries becomes deformed into an urge to state antinomies: distinctions are hardened into absolute dualisms. While the idealization of polarity (and the paradoxes that ensue) is encouraged by an economic system that treats all things and values as commodities, it has its locus in the single-minded tendency after Descartes to define the self as opposed to something projected as other to the self. This liberal cosmology (which is the cosmology mapped from within itself in *Savage Fields*) depends upon a separation, then an identity, of self and other — however that 'other' is defined, whether as body, woman, land, or spirit. Having projected an imaginary dualism of this sort, the psychological impulse is to seek meaning by immersing the self in the excluded opposite upon which the self is predicated and to which it is fatally attracted for its completion. As soon as the self is defined paradoxically in terms of some opposing other by which it is sustained, the self must survive by seeking its identity in competition with imaginary 'others.' Accordingly, Hegel maintains that 'Man exists insofar as he is opposed'. In this fondness of the enlightenment mind for symmetry, terms become tangled about each other in states of pure antagonism, when the issue is always more complex than the mind is prepared to accept.

It is not meant to belittle the magnitude of the problem of naming to say that it becomes even more of a problem to itself when it is restated, paradoxically, in the modern way by the mind seeking to sustain its control. Lee himself has said that modernism distorts everything, including even the attempt to clearly name its own condition.

The problem swallows the problem. Therefore it is testimony to the integrity of Voice which finally broke this condition to notice the iron hand of symmetrization in Lee's early writing. The oscillation in *Kingdom of Absence* between sanctity looked at through the eyes of the secular sceptic, and scepticism looked at through the eyes of the seeker of the sacred, is one instance of a tendency toward symmetrization in Lee's work. It is strongly present in his 'Running and Dwelling' article in the form of the classic idealization that fed Canadian nationalism in literature and politics in the early seventies. In contrast to the Americans ('this country' *as opposed to* 'that country'), Lee remarks, 'we belong to the land — it does not belong to us' (*Saturday Night,* July 1972, p.14). Whichever side of the civilization/wilderness symmetry one supports — whether one supports the values of this something called 'the land' against aggressive civilization, or civilization against 'the land,' one is plunged promptly into Cartesian speech with its alternating scepticism and reverence for the shadowy other imagined to lie outside the self. One cannot remove exploitation simply by inverting the terms in its formula, since that sleight-of-hand only preserves the artificial division intact (e.g., woman 'as opposed to' man). Instead, what must be dissolved is the language of exploitation itself, the speech of the empire of the self in its solitude, into which so many questions fall to be paralyzed beyond recognition. How easy to avoid enacting a condition by seeking refuge in the 'Abstract Harmonies' of mind! The escape is especially alluring to a mind attracted to the Teutonic polarities of Heideggerian existentialism, and to the black-and-white demands of a mysticism in which the alienated self yearns for its necessary completion in the imaginary Other of a spiritual wholeness achieved beyond some void. Yet the fear that made Lee retreat into the masochistic comfort of mental deadlock is very real. For the alternative, as he found in the writing of *Civil Elegies*, was a complete 'letting-go' of the language of the self, including the whole possibility of using speech at all.

5

The period of utter strangulation of Voice between 1968 and 1972 is recounted in 'Cadence, Country, Silence':

> Everywhere around me — in England, America, even in Canada — writers opened their mouths and words spilled out like crazy. But increasingly when I opened mine I simply gagged; finally, the words no longer came. For about four years at the end of the sixties I tore up everything I wrote — twenty words

on a page were enough to set me boggling at their palpable inauthenticity. And looking back at my previous writing, I felt as if I had been fishing pretty beads out of a vat of crank-case oil and stringing them together. The words weren't limber or alive or even mine.

But out of this stalemate came a displaced energy of service. Perhaps it was compensatory. Anansi Press was founded in this period, and Lee helped many of the Toronto writers of the seventies come to words, though he could not find words in himself.

However, in this period another man was talking clearly about liberal modernity. This was George Grant, whose 'Canadian Fate and Imperialism' (1967; republished in *Technology and Empire*, 1969) gave words to Lee's dilemma. It showed how the act of the poet who 'holds the ground in the nothing of this night' was preeminently the authentic response of citizens of the world's largest colony — Canada. '. . . all languages of good', Grant writes, 'except the language of the drive to freedom have disintegrated, so it is just to pass some antique wind to speak of goods that belong to man as man. Yet the answer is always the same: if we cannot so speak, then we can either only celebrate or stand in silence before that drive. Only in listening to the intimations of deprival can we live critically in the dynamo' (p.141). This suggested a political as well as a spiritual response out of which authentic expression might come. If the writer could not write against the grain of modernism without participating in that very mentality itself, he might at least find in silence the meanings which modernity concealed. But this was the path of greatest risk. What if there were no meanings after the entry into silence? This awesome letting-go is what compelled Lee's *Civil Elegies*.

The letting-go could be honest only if Lee let the experience of complete deprival direct both sides of the crisis of naming — what is God-given, what is man-made? — that he had been harbouring in himself. Any more assertive response would have reduced the experience to a theme, to another mental category, in the manner of *Kingdom of Absence*. He could not, therefore, even be assertive about absence. In other words, there was something like a Heideggerian 'turning' here. Instead of writing *about* the condition, Lee invited the condition to direct the writing, so that in this reversal of content and form, the experience of authentic speech and speechlessness, which is the experience of Voice itself, could become audible in English Canada. That is why it is important to see that the *Elegies* are written in two voices.

One is a citizen's voice. He is troubled by the issues of the day —

pollution, resource sellout, war — and the other anxieties which overwhelm any individual who stares fixedly at the goings-on of the world. The other is a religious voice; I will term it, somewhat inadequately, the 'private' voice, though I think Lee would want to regard this speaker as a citizen too, a citizen *sub specie aeternitatis*. He is entranced with the possibility of transcendence and release. These two are perhaps the articulators of (in Frye's terms) the myth of concern and the myth of detachment: whatever we call them, their confrontation extends only to the end of the 4th Elegy, and what might resemble initially a medieval dialogue of sense and soul is transformed as each voice pushes the other beyond its fears and cover-ups — its false heroisms, specious rationalizations and magniloquent *credos* — into a primal spiritual-and-civil space that is beyond words to name . . . though not beyond enactment.

Thus the first speaker, who dominates the 1st and 3rd Elegies, is the public voice, the voice of all that is man-made and 'World' (to use a key term from *Savage Fields*). Taking his cue from the quotation of George Grant's in the epigraph, this speaker oscillates between the full-bodied *Jeremiad* he really wants to write and the sudden explosions of meaninglessness he feels. At its most stentorian (the citizen is the better poet of the two), the voice might enunciate a memorable elegy on the defeatism of Canada, were it not defeated itself by the near-impossibility of describing any 'presence which is not sold out utterly to the modern' (CE 1). Nevertheless, while distrusting the verity of any constructive alternative, because it might turn out in the end to be another modernist project of 'improvising cosmos', the speaker resolutely sees in Toronto's new Civic Square the possibility of the resurrected body of mankind, 'a civil habitation that is / human, and our own'.

Beginning in the 2nd Elegy, the other voice answers with the strange mixture of patience, yearning and soul-ache of the religious self. But this voice never takes charge on its own terms, since it is the strangled voice of Orpheus, the song of 'Earth' lost in modern clamor. Its elegy is of a different quality because what this voice has lost is not civil belonging, but a belonging to the spiritual sources of the real which it feels it can meet only in mystical detachment. What seems to hold both speakers from abject muteness, and keeps them in conversation, is some intuition of a moment before speech in which things are sensed intransitively. This intimation of a deprived and subterranean 'resonance that held' is first heard in Moore's sculpture 'The Archer' in Toronto's central square (CE 3). Though the first expression of this intuition may be overstated by the speaker's overwhelming need for meaning, the speakers cannot help but be affected by this reverberation of something that Lee will later call 'Cadence', associating it with the gods to whom 'The Archer' stands as a talisman:

> . . . it moved in sterner space
> was shaped by earlier space and it ripples with
> wrenched stress, the bronze is flexed by
> blind aeonic throes
> that bred and met in slow enormous impact,
> and they are still at large for the force in the bronze churns
> through it, and lunges beyond and also the Archer declares
> that space is primal, raw, beyond control and drives toward a
> living stillness, its own.

But the public voice, whose perception this mostly is, fears such a perception of a judging ampler space as the void that undercuts all purposeful action, and caught between this intrusion of nothingness into the public domain and the compulsion to assert some structure of citizenship, the voice goes on to articulate a negative celebration of the dispossession of land as the ground of identity, rendered in poetic stretches of manic beauty that suddenly flounder on their own irony. This inability to name, *enacted* in the rhythms of elegiac manic depression, is the first sound of authentic Canadian Voice in the poem. It makes the 3rd Elegy feel like a homecoming, though with a strengthening and fading signal like that of a short-wave radio.

Within the movement of the ongoing meditation that comprises the nine Elegies, the fourth poem is the most thematically defining. It hovers at the brink of commitment to whatever surrounds the language of selfhood and control. The religious voice, which dominates the first and third sections of this four-part movement (there is an unmarked stanza break at the bottom of page 43), insists that if the political self would renounce civilization and its discontents, then this renunciation might betoken a loosening of the logic of control of space on which imperialism is founded. The public voice, in sections 2 and 4, is quick to label this as mere escapism, but beneath its sneer is a timidity in the face of the loss of the best of civilization, including 'the magisterial life of the mind'. The interweaving of the voices suggests by analogy the insight (it will reach its fullest articulation in the 8th Elegy) that the private voice fears something too, and beneath the spiritual impulse to detachment lies yet another fiction of the mind, that great idolater, in this case the idealization of absence itself as a comfort and a stay against oblivion. Hence both voices are flawed in this Elegy: the other-worldly voice by a self-conscious, hurt-seeking idolatry of nothingness ('is void our vocation?'), the worldly voice by the heroic melodrama of the individualistic last stand:

> Yet still they take the world full force on their nerve ends, leaving the bloody impress of their bodies face forward in time and I believe they will not go under until they have taken the measure of empire.

Ostensibly at loggerheads, the two voices really speak the same language of the self. And because they speak the language of the self, they speak the language of exploitation and control. The 4th Elegy is vital in setting the language of colonization into relief. The public self reacts against 'the imperial way of life' in the very code of mastery it has learned from its masters, and there is no assurance that once in control of its destiny the civil speaker would be more than another 'lonesome ego/ . . . dragging its lethal desires across the world' (CE 5). The private self, for its part in the symmetry, turns the language of aggression in upon itself like a weapon, making a martyrdom of its isolation. What both the sadistic and masochistic voices exclude from their behaviour at this point in the overall meditation is the very void that surrounds their selfhood. Fearing it, they hold it at arm's-length as a something 'out there', either to be mastered or surrendered to. Void, silence, nothingness is an internal condition of being that both selfhoods refuse to face, confronting it instead as an imaginary 'other' according to Cartesian logic. Only in the last Elegy when the speakers, now undivided from each other, can say 'void is not a place, nor/negation of place' is the logic of colonialization with all its divide-to-rule tactics finally broken. Broken with it is the attempt by the religious speaker to predicate spiritual plenitude on nothingness: 'void is not the high cessation of the lone self's burden'. And broken also is the similar yearning on the part of the civil voice to seek the missing half of nationalism in the same imaginary quality. The private, religious voice had earlier maintained paradoxically: 'nothing/belongs to us, and/only that nothing is home'. Now both voices can easily say with the Taoist sage 'We strive to build a house, but we live in the space, the nothingness, between the walls'.

The proper wisdom of it all is found in the way human beings treat each other. This is the concern of the 7th Elegy. The tangible centre of the code of mastery and control is the empire of one human being over another, and the subjection of one being to the other in the manner of a colony, in which 'they take on the crippled roles that each has singled the/other to partner'. The defeatist whom a Canadian habitually elects as his political leader is simply an extension of this existence 'on the go half out of his mind with the need to fail and be hurt'. It is a wistful elegy around whose margins breathes Rilke's beautiful wisdom about a lover as the guardian of the other's solitude. One feels in the poem a deepening of vision within the inevitable movement to the last two elegies.

In these, the idolatry of nothingness turns out to be the last either/or stand of the self. It is seen in retrospect to have been a neurotic spirituality, a counterfeit mode of high detachment that is specifically the failure of Saint-Denys Garneau, the 'master of emptiness' troubling the speaker in the 4th Elegy. A relationship is therefore implied between Cartesian enlightenment and the dark night of the Jansenist soul, its spiritual 'other'. The split being of modern man is a central concern of Lee's. One sees it in his preoccupation with the passionate idealism of 'F' in Cohen's *Beautiful Losers* and of William Bonney in Ondaatje's *Billy the Kid* (both studied assiduously in *Savage Fields*), in the figure of Harold Ladoo — and, perhaps to a degree, in Lee himself with his upbringing in 'the suburban United Church' (*For Openers*, p.248):

                    it was all
        detachment you hoped, it was
        exquisite penetration, it was
        fear of life, the mark of Canada   (CE 8)

Beyond this code of exploitation of self and other, a silence opens in the 9th Elegy. Into this opening a few things emerge, at the end of the *Elegies*, to speak themselves. But this is, or has to be, a blurry kind of recognition. In Lee, as in Heidegger, to speak without manipulation is not a 'letting it be' in the unilateral sense. The experience of truth is both a revealing and a concealing of the phenomenon, because the symbols of human belonging and deprival — 'water, copout, tower, body, land' — can never be truly given outside of whatever myth of control surrounds them. Yet while myths change, underneath, as Heidegger says, paraphrasing Hölderlin, 'Mankind is a conversation'.

The endless murmur of this 'one dialogue that we are' is part of the meaning of Lee's term Cadence. Beneath the alien language of modernity, and beneath the silence which that false language of the self creates, there may be heard the intimations of a more authentic speech — though one that remains unspeakable in its polyphony. It cannot express itself honestly in words, since all words now have been invested with the language of control. It cannot speak in silence. But Cadence might provide the impetus and the ground of an enactment which reveals the fragile words and gestures of being human in a space without authentic being or belonging. In such an enactment the alien language of the self, together with the speech of all that the self makes alien, might be held in a single expression struggling to take form. This authentic expression is Voice.

One can imagine that to discover Voice is to begin a historical and metaphysical meditation. Any vision of what is gained and lost by being human in the modernist era involves a recognition of the extent to which we are separated from each other, because we are separated within ourselves, by the ego's language of colonization, with its fear of the nothingness it imagines to underlie its tactics of control. This divide-and-rule condition explores its artistic consequences in the self-whipping hubristic soliloquy of the expressivist and the sadistically detached craftsmanship of the artificer. If Lee's poetry represents a movement beyond the modernist impasse, it advances by looking backward, revaluing the Romantic intuition of a pre-human ground of meaning, voicing that meaning in the Victorian confessional mode, and carrying confession into the full experience of modernism in its failure to name.

This experience of Voice, however, has an extra-historical dimension, even while the enactment of Voice is compelled by the special historical circumstance of our being in a colony. In 'Cadence, Country, Silence' Lee remarks that the vocation is at once forced on us and made easier for us in the colonial muteness of twentieth-century Canada, which makes things more able to be heard, elegiacally resonant in their domain of non-existence, as the perishable, suffering particulars they are. This special sensitivity is the call to a more authentic life, for 'To accept nonbeing at home in what is, to accept what is at home in nonbeing, is perhaps the essential act of being human'. So it is by a kind of peeling away of the language of the self that things come to name themselves in poetry. But it is by that naming of existences in the 'halt and stammer, the wry self-deprecation, the rush of celebratory elan and the vastness of the still unspoken surround' together with the other inflections of our deprival, that the poet continues in the face of modernity to be, in Heidegger's phrase, 'the shepherd of Being'.

Simultaneity in the Writings of Dennis Lee

Ann Munton

'EVERYTHING MATTERS', Dennis Lee has said, 'and / nothing matters'.[1] Everything is significant, the reader might respond, while nothing is still significant. Throughout Lee's writing there are numerous seeming opposites and apparent contradictions which are affirmed or experienced as simultaneous. Whether it be in subject matter, cosmological views, conditions of creativity, political or social programmes of action, or the actual form of his poetic meditations and 'enactments', Lee proposes a way out of paradoxes through a vision of simultaneity. Lee does not deny the existence of opposites as a monist might, claiming that there is ultimately only one substance, consistent and perfect, but neither does he accept the dualist division of a universe into diametric contraries — whether they be spirit and matter, mind and body, civilization and nature, or content and form. Instead he proposes a simultaneous duality.

In his poetry and critical work Lee often separates his subjects into related pairs, but instead of simply juxtaposing them for greater effect or polarizing them for greater contrast, he emphasizes differences while maintaining that a simultaneous perception is necessary for a better understanding of each and both. For example, in *Savage Fields* Lee translates the dichotomous pair — 'nature' and 'civilization' — into what he terms 'a dualism of simultaneity' with the new titles 'world' and 'earth'. The division of substances is made into two types, both irreducible, and thus Lee seems to be designating, albeit with new labels, yet another separation in the mainstream of dualist tradition. Where he diverges from the mainstream, however, is in his insistence that these categories must also and always be perceived as simultaneous. '*All* planet is world; *all* planet is simultaneously earth' (SF, p.56).[2] With the introduction of the term 'planet' to mean 'everything that is (including the rest of space), as it affects or can be known or imagined by inhabitants of our planet' (SF, p.9), Lee is not simply slipping into a monist stance. Planet, as he envisages it, is at once 'seamless' and perceivable in 'two exhaustive, contradictory models' (SF, p.9). 'Planet obliges us to see it as world and earth simultaneously' (SF, p.10), while it is also 'the field of interplay' between the two — a field characterized by strife. The savage strife within this simultaneous duality is both subject and title for Lee's book.

While *Savage Fields* provides one of the clearest and most sustained examples of Lee's vision of a simultaneous perception of existence, it is evident throughout both his critical and poetical writing. As he acknowledges in a letter, 'The notion of *simultaneity* is not all that easy to cozy up to, but it definitely is of great use in approaching my writing'.[3] Lee's influential essay, 'Cadence, Country, Silence', for instance, describes his personal experiences of creativity and introduces a specific simultaneous duality — cadence and silence — that governs his work. While cadence, for Lee, is rhythm or 'presence' — 'that press of meaning . . . teeming towards words' that gives poetry its wellspring — silence is the condition 'one must continually reenter before the words can be spoken at all'. The 'cadence of what is' must 'resound in its own silence', Lee says, emphasizing the symbiosis.

The particular 'problem' of silence Lee encounters is the impotence of words: 'Words arrive, but words have also gone dead'. Words can only live if they are authentically rooted in the here and now of the user. If words authentically reflect their particular location, they will naturally be universal in their appeal and intelligibility. For this reason, true nationalism is more universally accessible than false internationalism. Lee paints a picture of himself as an early poet who used American and British words, not authentically Canadian ones (by 'words' Lee means 'all the resources of the verbal imagination, from single words through verse forms, conventions about levels of style, characteristic versions of the hero, resonant structures of plot', [CCS, p.38]). After these early 'inauthentic' poems, Lee is silent for four years: during this time he is discovering the writings of George Grant, which help him to understand his personal silence by linking it to what he views as the larger silence of Canada's wordless, colonial space.

What is important is the problem of language-alienation in a colonial space, the correlation between Lee's personal and civil silences, and the correlation between these silences and his ability to write authentically in cadence: 'To explore the obstructions to cadence is, for a Canadian, to explore the nature of colonial space' (CCS, p.37). Articulation and silence are inextricably involved with the most important issues of existence:

> If we live in space which is radically in question for us, that makes our barest speaking a problem to itself. For voice does issue in part from civil space. And alienation in that space will enter and undercut our writing, make it recoil upon itself, become a problem to itself. (CCS, p.37)

Thus Lee now understands his muteness and links it to the voice-lessness of the Canadian colonial situation:

> To speak unreflectingly in a colony, then, is to use words that speak only alien space. To reflect is to fall silent, discovering that your authentic space does not have words. And to reflect further is to recognize that you and your people do not in fact have a privileged authentic space just waiting for words; you are, among other things, the people who have made an alien inauthenticity their own. You are left chafing at the inarticulacy of a native space which may not exist. So you shut up.

* * *

> But perhaps — and here was the breakthrough — perhaps our job was not to fake a space of our own and write it up, but rather to find words for our spacelessness. Perhaps that *was* home. This dawned on me gradually. Instead of pushing against the grain of an external, uncharged language, perhaps we should finally come to writing *with* the grain. (CCS, p.47)

And for Lee 'writing *with* the grain' means starting with the very words and letting them 'surface in your own mute and native land', 'reappropriating them in this space-less civil space' (CCS, p.47). Learning about Canadian space for Lee means learning to articulate the muteness as well as allowing the mute and silent language to surface with new Canadian meanings.

Lee thus proposes the idea of the simultaneity of the cadence and the silence. He not only agrees with both descriptions of creativity presented at the conference for which his essay was originally written — 'a good piece of writing bespeaks encounter with emptiness as its first source; a good piece of writing bespeaks encounter with things, things most as they are, nothing but things alive with their own mode of thingness, as its first source' (CCS, p.51) — but Lee also thinks that both must be true *simultaneously* for a work to have any real worth. Silence not only surrounds language, but silence and language only fully exist when they both exist at once. And so with all persons or things: 'Each stands forth as what it is most fully, and most preciously, because the emptiness in which it rests declares itself so overpoweringly' (CCS, p.51). This coincidence of being and non-being is crucial to an understanding of Lee, and it is poetically explored in *Civil Elegies* and in *The Death of Harold Ladoo*. Cadence declares being, while silence declares non-being, and both are necessary simultaneously for Lee. He recognizes the primacy of civil silence to identify civil being for himself, as well as linking civil silence to creative silence:

> For some of us at least, the cadence of what-is abounds only when we meet it in its fullest grounding in non-being. Then each thing comes to resound in its own silence. And the inauthenticity of our civil space is one such grounding . . . it is only one mode among many; I am certain that the silence I go into is more than civil, and that men in many countries enter it in their proper terms. But to write in colonial space is to have that civil silence laid irrefutably upon you; whatever else overtakes you, civil non-being cannot be evaded. (CCS, p.52)

Our Canadian wordlessness is, thus, for Lee, one silence to be entered before reaching the creative possibilities of the being-ness of cadence. Civil silence is the most easily describable silence for him, and the 'loudest' of his silences. Linked with cadence, however, silence also allows poetry to exist for Lee, which is the very essence of 'being human':

> A poem enacts in words the presence of what we live among. It arises from the tough, delicate, heartbreaking rooting of what is in its own non-being. Out of our participation in that rooting, there rises an elemental movement of being — of celebration, of desire, of grief, of anger, of play, of dying. That movement is always particular, speaking the things which are. It does not issue just from what is outside us, nor just from what is inside us. A poem enacts that moving cadence of being.
>
> To be human is to live through such movements of being.
>
> Quick in its own silence, cadence seeks to issue in the articulate gestures of being human here. (CSS, p.53)

Lee's self-awareness as a writer, exhibited in 'Cadence, Country, Silence', is also present in his first book, *Kingdom of Absence* (1967), a series of forty-three consecutively numbered sonnet variations, variations divided into seven sections. The title indicates Lee's central concern in the book: the primacy of the void in modern life and the problems of alienation that it engenders. Each of the sections explores a type of 'absence', and all concur in their condemnation of the dehumanization of city life. Although there is no redemption or transcendence reached, Lee does express some faith in a shadowy 'secular purgation' (KA XXXVIII) and in the communication of love.

146

Lee later criticized this early work as 'labored, tortured',[4] and 'artificial' (CCS, p.49); certainly the poetry is uneven and self-conscious. Where 'Cadence, Country, Silence' details Lee's search for an appropriate poetic style, *Kingdom of Absence* acknowledges that he is 'hung between styles' (KA XXI); for even while writing these poems, he knew he had not yet found the words for his condition. Still, in this first book Lee does employ in embryonic form the ironic wit and elegiac tone he perfects in his later work, as well as the form of the extended meditation. Although Lee has repudiated much of the conceptual framework of *Kingdom of Absence*, its ideas and logic have not so much been jettisoned as they have been modified. His particular concern with absolutes and the need to acknowledge apparent opposition in *Kingdom of Absence* are the constructs out of which his later philosophy developed. Even in his first collection, his attraction to opposites is clearly present: 'I make the song of the lively extremes' (KA XXXV). The division between city and country is expressed both in the book's structure and in its vision, and although this division does become less distinct in the poet's consciousness by poem's end, still no complete coalescence is achieved in this early work. As Lee himself now acknowledges, 'I don't believe I had fully accepted the a-logical nature of my hunches at that point.'[5]

In spite of the tentative nature of the work, *Kingdom of Absence* does nevertheless begin the development of *silence* as a central concept in Lee's writing. Given the emphasis of this early volume, it is not surprising that silence is most often an image of dissension and broken communication, and is rarely associated with cadence — let alone perceived as its necessary counterbalance. The book, by beginning and ending with images of rural Muskoka, is framed by scenes of natural silence. Between these boundaries are sections on the city and on its silence, which become an existential void embraced by the poet. The movement within the collection is thus clearly symbolized by the poet's relation to silence, and his dilemma is the pull he feels between these opposing silences.

Two of the central sections, 'Cities of the Mind Interred' and 'Annex Elegiac', present a damning view of the city and the void it represents. 'Cities of the Mind Interred' condemns what in *Savage Fields* Lee calls the liberal cosmology, and provides an historical and philosophical explanation for our present existence in limbo, while 'Annex Elegiac' explores the specific horrors of a contemporary Canadian city. The mechanized life of modernity, with the systematic silencing of imagination, is the disease, and those infected are 'strung up' (KA VI) in the terrifying silence of the void. As the silence of God is agonizing, men 'are combing the holy mountains, freelance, foraging, / out for logos' (KA VII), but they find only emptiness, longing, and more silence.

This silence is the opposite of the peaceful silence of the first section ('Muskoka Elegiac'), which describes a secular sacrament in which the poet's Lady, who seems strangely out of time, gathers silence and light around her and, in doing so, provides a 'baptism'. In contrast, the second poem of 'Annex Elegiac' (even the titles are parallel), describes a mock eucharist. Again the participants are surrounded by silence, but they are now all too mortal:

> Now they come silently
> the hung ones, the cool.
> Mortal presences, I drink your blood; I
> drink your blood. (KA XVIII)

In the Annex the silent recipients are actually victims of modernity, estranged and cut off, far from understanding the link between cadence, silence, being, and belonging.

> Toronto the Good is dead, and Revell's luminous towers
> look down on yankee heaven: chrome under smog.
> Hung between styles.
> . . . . . I am Canadian. (KA XXI)

Lee is here only obscurely aware of the link between the personal and the civil condition (later so central to *Civil Elegies*), for this is as yet only a 'log-jammed attempt' (CCS, p.49) to find the right words and cadence. Though he realizes that silence is both his *and* the Canadian condition in this transitional stage, he does not yet fully associate it with cadence.

Two poems in the section called 'Cities of the Mind Interred' describe Rainer Maria Rilke's way of handling silence. For Rilke as for Lee, the modern cosmology has brought about a devaluation of objects, so one task of the poet is to reverse this process by renaming the universe and giving it new substance. Lee finds this approach attractive, for he is still paradoxically part of Rilke's music and 'must applaud', yet he must also call it a 'lovely fraud' (KA XI). Rilke's 'Ninth Elegy' sets forth his scheme for 'the redemption of language', which is to 'start with the simplest linguistic act: the naming of things'. This reduction of language is also a cleansing, and for Rilke it provided a way of approaching silence without embracing it. Lee's problem is similar to Rilke's, in that they are both trying to write using a language that has become blunted and obscured. They both

148

must begin again by naming their universes. Despite their similarities, however, Lee still cannot accept Rilke's solution totally:

We explicate the trees but they go sorrowing
mutely beyond us, botched in our dimension.
Rilke, master of ripeness, and the things'
celebrant, rapt, be near to us in limbo. (KA XI)

While Rilke renames 'with an eye to "humanizing" things', Lee's renaming must confirm the inhumanity of the Canadian condition. He must go over the horrors and desperation of modernity. More vividly aware of the problem of language and his method of handling it by the time he writes 'Cadence, Country, Silence' and revises *Civil Elegies*, Lee concludes that 'the impasse of writing that is problematic to itself is transcended only when the impasse becomes its own subject, when writing accepts and enters and names its own condition as it is naming the world' (CCS, p.49). Lee is feeling his way in *Kingdom of Absence*, and his introduction of Rilke in this manner points to his later attempts at repossessing his language. The start he makes in this poem is the metaphorically described embracing of the void and its silence in the 'Kingdom of Absence' section. The start he makes in his creative life is his actual silence of four years. Susan Sontag describes the necessary preliminaries: 'A tremendous spiritual preparation . . . is required for this deceptively simple act of naming. It is nothing less than the scouring and harmonious sharpening of the senses . . .'[6] Lee does this in actuality during his years of creative impotence, having foreshadowed it poetically in the section 'Kingdom of Absence'. His description of the void there was a necessary step to his own embracing of it and of its silence.

When in *Kingdom of Absence* disintegration is complete, and the poet embraces the void of absolute silence, Lee chooses for this total letting-go into absence the particularly apt image of a ride on an ice-floe across a silent expanse of sea. The final two poems of this section express Lee's desire for 'utter' and 'distilled' absence. He wishes absolutely to embrace the abyss and thus to reach the bottom of the silence, for only then does he expect any growth. The only 'birth' for which he asks is 'by these zero / calms' (KA XXVIII). Silence, at this point, becomes his very topic: 'My subject is / . . . the deprivations of the tongue' (KA XXXIV). Speech can only come from a confrontation with the silence of the void, for a poet 'cannot speak what is, unless his words / be uttered by the darkness where it rides' (KA XXXIV). The image of getting to the bottom of silence before creation or expression is possible is an early and incomplete image for Lee, one that precedes the later ideal of the simultaneity of cadence and silence. It is important to note, however, that the image *is* found even here, in poems that he later criticizes both for their manner and for their belief in an absolute. If the way is later found to be wanting, at least the image is well-wrought. Apprentice works tend to present concepts more baldly than do more mature works, so the centrality of certain ideas and images can often be ascertained by their appearance in early efforts.

The final two sections of *Kingdom of Absence* return to love and the natural world in an attempt to reconcile the two opposing views of silence found in the book. The poet's previous gladness for his Lady's 'sweet body' was mistaken in that it 'left out the world' (KA xxxv). Having once acknowledged the primacy of the abyss, love is altered. Still rooted in the natural world, love is no longer a 'sacrament'. The poet and his Lady come together, and blossoms swell from their intertwined growth out of 'stony ground'. In his search for truths the poet has been led to explore absence, 'in extremis / an awe went out of me' (KA xxxv), and this is the difference. This loss of awe is more clearly catalogued later in *The Death of Harold Ladoo*, while here Lee simply acknowledges his vocation as a nominalist ('My subject is the absence of the real / in time . . .' [KA xxxiv]). Afterwards he will modify this absolute stance, but for now he 'will celebrate void' (KA xxxv). Again, he is fumbling with faint truths that will in time clarify for him. While in 'Cadence, Country, Silence' Lee clearly explains 'this grounding of what is in its own non-being' (CCS, p.51), in *Kingdom of Absence* he gives precedence only to the darker side of the later simultaneity.

The inventory-taking of his world becomes, in the absence of God, a 'secular purgation, / the way of unmeaning' (KA xxxviii). Even though words do not have any 'real' sense, the nominalistic process of naming his personal and civil condition is still purgative. The poet can still 'honour now' the 'beauty of the renascent will' (KA xlii), which, while nearly destroyed by the void, continues to record the struggle. Language is reduced and approaches silence, but the attempt and achievement of poetry are worthwhile:

Song I thirst for grunts like prose; among the flimsy
    fables of the real I want
a factive, brute and palpable abyss.
    And therefore I demolish what I am
or long to be, pure dark incarnate outcry,
    and I make my city's mawkish human cries. (KA xliii)

Kingdom of Absence thus concludes with the poet nearly reduced to silence — but not completely. He retains the need to create, to name — even in the possibility that his act is specious. His poetry may be but 'mawkish human cries', but it remains a song, the song of the city. This urban lament continued to be Lee's form in his next two long poems, the two versions of *Civil Elegies* (1968; revised 1972). Between the publication of the two, Lee moved from the nihilism that dominated *Kingdom of Absence* to his doctrine of simultaneous duality.

Both versions of *Civil Elegies* are clearer explorations of many ideas first raised in *Kingdom of Absence*, but they extend beyond the philosophy of Lee's first book. If the first version of *Civil Elegies* is good, the second is excellent. Many of the changes are artistic polishings and refinements, and many are also a sharpening of former insights. Most of the stylistic changes are for the better: the elimination of false or self-conscious lines, the tightening of syntax, and the addition of passages to clarify and concentrate the purpose. Lee also expanded the book-length poem from seven to nine elegies and rearranged the original order. Some of the elegies are altered hardly at all, others moderately, and still others, notably the concluding one, are rewritten almost entirely. The result is a much more powerful and carefully composed version of the poem. Under these technical changes are philosophical ones as well, perhaps most clearly manifested by the overall alteration from a somewhat rhetorical monologue to a carefully conceived dialectic of two voices — his civil voice and his more personal, religious one.

As the title of *Civil Elegies* indicates, Lee's poem is a meditation mourning Canada's colonial condition. The consciousness of the poet is centred on Toronto's Nathan Phillips Square in front of the new City Hall. Centrally located, the square is a place in which to hold demonstrations, meet friends, or contemplate alone by the pool. Near the centre of the square Henry Moore's *Archer* rises up and exists for the poet as a reference point,[7] while the graceful, crescent-shaped towers of civic government loom above, and the concrete and glass buildings of business stand opposite. Nathan Phillips Square is an appropriate location in which for Lee to set his meditation, because as the economic and cultural capital of English Canada, Toronto is the obvious target for his anti-colonial attack, and this square in particular is the heart of the city. Perhaps more than any other urban centre in Canada, Toronto, for Lee, symbolizes continentalism: its architecture, that of a technological society, is the home of international companies, and, as the centre of English Canada's communications networks and the headquarters of most of the major publishing firms, it receives and disseminates ideas without regard to origin or destination. Nathan Phillips Square itself stands in front of the seat of civic government and at the head of Bay Street, Canada's major financial district. From this location *Civil Elegies* issues.

The major silence found in both versions of *Civil Elegies* is civil silence; and both versions, therefore, explore minutely the inauthenticity of the civil situation in which Lee finds himself. By cataloguing the civil non-being of his colonial condition, he continues his aesthetic of silence. The revised *Civil Elegies* more clearly emphasizes the association of civil and personal non-being and silence, however, and describes the possible solution of reclaiming space by reclaiming language. The primary simultaneity which shapes *Civil Elegies* (and is emphasized in the revised version) is the necessary coincidence of being and non-being in order that either may have any true meaning. Echoing 'Cadence, Country, Silence', Lee poetically explains that only through an exploration of silence and nonbeing can cadence and creativity be achieved in either personal or civil terms: the poet must have the courage to name his own emptiness or 'non-being'.

The 1st Elegy immediately locates the poet in Nathan Phillips Square 'haunted by / unlived presence' of what Canadians might have been, compared to the ugly reality of modern society in Toronto, its 'yankee visions' and its aridity. Thick smog chokes the air, while soaring buildings block out even a fitful sun. Concrete, chrome, and corruption fill the city, as developers bribe politicians, and parking lots and high-rises replace homes. In the first stanza Lee has a vision of the teeming smog, swarming with 'airborne shapes' flowing across the square to smother him. Lee imagines these shapes as ancestors dragging with them all of their unrealized, possible futures, and so, Janus-like, the image faces two ways in time. As he describes them in 'Cadence, Country, Silence', they are both 'ex-Canadians' because of American dominance and, more hopefully, they are also 'not-yet-Canadians' (CCS, p.45). Accusatory figures in *Civil Elegies*, these ancestors symbolize the promise of the past that has not yet been realized in the present of Canadian urban life. They thus embody Grant's view of our Loyalist forebears,[8] whose natural inclinations were opposed to the American liberal ideal of the pursuit of liberty and happiness. Lee thus pictures Canada as haunted by 'the conservative impulse, in which Grant sees the future we almost used to have' (CCS, p.44). Lee's ancestors 'died truncated, stunted, never at / home in native space' (CE 1). In Grant's scheme this conservative impulse was diminished through the invasion of liberal ideals from America, and therefore the direction of growth the ancestors had a right to expect is not yet realized. The very world view from which they were trying to escape has overtaken them, and all Grant can say now of this conservative impulse is that 'it can sense "intimations of deprival"' (ccs, pp.44-45). In *Civil Elegies* Lee says 'Canada . . . / specialized in this deprivation' (ce 1), while in 'Cadence, Country, Silence' he acknowledges that the conservative impulse can sense these intimations 'only in waiting and silence' (ccs, p.45). Silence can thus have positive aspects: while it is the condition of Canada's colonialism, silence is also the way to a better understanding of that condition and its expression.

Hoping to recapture the impulse for good from the past, in the second stanza the poet begins to fantasize a glorious heritage — a spirited suppression by the Loyalists of Mackenzie's rebellion. Unable to maintain the fictional history, however, he destroys it with a harsh picture of fleeing rebel and loyalist alike. Ironically, he describes it as 'the first / spontaneous mutual retreat in the history of warfare. / Canadians, in flight' (ce 1). In contrast to this actual, inglorious past, Lee evokes a vision of what Canada might still be if Canadians could only 'accept [our] flawed inheritance', reject the American dreams, link the city to the country, and therefore give a new civil meaning to our existence.

In stanzas added to the revised edition Lee emphasizes the coincident duality of the situation — the past unlived lives which are also our 'destiny', 'still / demanding whether Canada will be' (ce 1). All time sequences converge in the present: what might have been may yet be, but for now the past is 'still dead weight'. The nothingness and non-being of the poem's present may yet allow the 'being' of a nation-space in time. The non-being must first be recognized, however; the muteness and silence must be acknowledged so that the cadence can be tapped and the authentic words can flow. The progression of this meditation is thus first to denounce angrily our ancestors for failing to leave us a clear heritage, design, and progress, and next to introduce private emptiness into the civil emptiness. Foundering marriages and a lack of communication are the consequences of modernity. The void is both a private emptiness of personal discord, loneliness, and creative sterility and a vision of civil horror — concrete, steel, and polluted sterility. This association also signals Lee's hope for the future, in which 'men complete / their origins' (ce 1), for the solution in both cases is reunification. By jamming the present progress of modernity and clearing a space to be in, Lee here sees the hope for the future in which the people may grow:

And the people accept a flawed inheritance
and they give it a place in their midst, forfeiting progress, forfeiting
dollars, forfeiting yankee visions of cities that in time it might grow
whole at last in their lives, they might
belong once more to their forebears, becoming their own men. (CE 1)

Lee here envisages what Grant seems to think is impossible — a re-
jection of progress and continentalism, with a return to the conser-
vative beginnings of the country and a concomitant elevation of the
common good over individual freedom. Lee does not reveal how his
political vision, with its inherent possibilities for nationhood, is to be
achieved, except in an idealized union of city and country. As such it
would be an example of flawed and idealistic political vision, but it is
only a vision. The 1st Elegy is thus not only a direct denunciation of
Canada's inauthentic civil space, but also a literary solution, a
'grounding in nonbeing', as Lee says at the end of 'Cadence, Coun-
try, Silence', in which only 'the cadence of what is [can] abound';
'Then each thing comes to resound in its own silence' (CCS, p.52).

The silences which Lee chooses to elucidate in the 2nd Elegy —
an entirely new section added to the revised edition — are the si-
lences of an absentee Deity and the silence of His belief-bereft con-
gregation. Lee mourns the loss of religious faith and a valued exist-
ence and clearly associates the civil, religious, and personal silences
(as he continues to do in his later works). All these silences have
their source in modernity and the technological civilization which
homogenizes all countries and religions.[9] According to Grant, 'We
no longer consider ourselves as part of a natural order and as subor-
dinate to divine law. We see ourselves rather as the makers of histo-
ry, the makers of our own laws.'[10] As interpreted by Lee, these mis-
givings about modernity become a moving account of individuals
desirous of faith, while simultaneously living in a secularized society.

The 2nd Elegy opens with an anguished question: 'Master and
Lord, where / are you?' But no God is evident, and the questioner is
forced to agree with society: 'they all give way and declare your real
absence'. Caught in an uneasy silence, the speaker realizes that even
the absence can be a grounding for today: 'It is a homecoming, as
men once knew / their lives took place in you'. The being-non-being
reflex definition has hold of us. No longer are there values in our
universe; no longer do words have absolute meanings; and there is
no longer 'a measure' for our world and our actions. Although poets
were once namers of real substance — 'The poets spoke of earth
and heaven' — today's writer must be a special sort of nominalist: he
must talk of non-being to talk of being and translate silence to create

154

cadence. He must take an inventory of his own devalued existence, as Lee ably does in the next Elegy. The revised version's 2nd Elegy thus sets up a positive function to embracing the void: out of nothingness the poet creates substance. He produces a spontaneous awareness of being and non-being.

The 3rd Elegy (the 2nd Elegy of the original version) is a catalogue of inauthenticity. It begins with the complaisance of the summer sun-eased square and the malaise of the people who come to share their lunches by the pool, but the poet, beneath the noon sun, discovers a visitation of cadence appropriate to the Canadian situation as he views it. His body reacts to the negative 'space of the square', while everything seems out of place except the great Moore sculpture: 'the only resonance that held was in the Archer'. This is an important sensation for Lee, for it records his recognition of the commonality of cadence in the Archer and his own authentic work. Suddenly in Nathan Phillips Square nothing but Moore's Archer holds any meaning for him. Only the Archer is 'adequate in the aimless expanse', and he feels an answering cadence in his own body: 'the / clangor in my forearms found its outlet'. This is the bodily feeling Lee describes as often accompanying cadence, the sensation in his 'forearms', 'gut', or 'head' (ccs, p.35). The Archer dominates both the square and a 'sterner space'; it at once dominates its surroundings and is more than them. The cadence in the sculpture 'churns / through it, and lunges beyond and also the Archer declares / that space is primal, raw, beyond control and drives toward a / living stillness, its own', so that again we have the paradox of simultaneous movement and stillness, cadence and silence. The Archer and Lee's answering poetic moment 'churn' and resound with their cascading inner cadence; both also move towards and contain a point of stillness, a cadence-defining silence. As an addition to the original Elegy, this passage is significant. It phrases poetically the ideas about cadence and silence that Lee expresses in 'Cadence, Country, Silence'. As he says there, his understanding of cadence and silence developed more fully between the writing of the first and second versions of *Civil Elegies*: this added passage emphasizes the growth of that understanding.

This 3rd Elegy moves from the square and the poet's recognition of primal power in the Archer to a reflection on the Canadian Shield, and finally concludes with a return to the square and a fuller appreciation of both the sculpture and the Canadian 'space'. In the second version of this Elegy, the poet is at first intellectually unaware of why exactly the Archer arrests him, but intuitively he compares the huge 'bronze [which] is flexed by / blind aeonic throes' to the vast Canadian Shield, so similarly birthed. Lee describes the geologic aging of the Canadian Shield in all its mythic dimensions: the volcanic conception, glacial combat, and first contacts with man. He reflects on 'the inability of the early settlers to assimilate the claim which [the Shield's] austere demands made on them'[11] and the continued betrayal of Canadians who have plundered their land without ever understanding it and turned it over to Americans for their use. Canadians are thus 'traducing the immemorial pacts of men and earth'. Both the form and sense of the 3rd Elegy are contained in 'the resonance between the "space" of the Archer and the space of the Shield'. In a letter Lee explains that the Canadian Shield is literally a vast manifestation of primitive energy, while the Archer artistically construes 'just such a massive configuration of earth-energies':

> So the Archer judges the square by recalling us to our deeper vocation in Canada, of coming to terms with the most primordial processes of earth — with which we really have to live (or fail to live), in that we inhabit a country in which the Shield occupies so much space. (LETTER)

Although Lee concludes the revised version of this Elegy in much the same way that he did the first — Canadians must recognize their bankrupt culture, they must 'honour the void' — the new Elegy as a whole suggests an energy that such a resignation will yield.

The 4th Elegy, added in 1972, is an unrelenting meditation on the disease of our time. Structurally, it is an unresolved debate (Lee calls it 'a dialogue of self and soul') between that poet's two voices, as already articulated in the first three Elegies. While the 1st and 3rd Elegies are spoken by the civil consciousness, and the second by the religious consciousness, the fourth is a dialectic of both voices, reflecting the larger process of the entire collection. In the 4th Elegy each voice presents its own view of silence, with primacy given to neither.

> [For the] musing religious consciousness . . . it is a serious possibility that the experience of nothingness, including the civil void that is Canada, serves the function of freeing men from their furious attachments, their desire to *own* what is given to them . . . , [while for] the civil consciousness . . . any such intuition is a sell-out, since it appears to encourage a passive, quietist acquiescence in the country's dismemberment. (LETTER)

Although seemingly contradictory, *both* views are valid within this poem and emphasize the notion of poetic enacting of the movement from one voice — which embodies a particular stance or condition — to another, as the poem develops a progression of thoughts. This idea of the poem presenting the development of a meditation leads to the possibility of coincident beliefs, as well as of growth. Although both voices lament the diminished condition of life now in this country, the conclusions they draw are somewhat different. On the one hand, once the religious consciousness recognizes the very absences as reality for Canadians — 'only that nothing is home' — objects 'move at last in the clearness of open space, within the / emptiness they move very cleanly in the vehement enjoyment of their bodies'. This is again the recognition of non-being as a necessary condition to the re-definition of being, for if one faces the silence, whether the private inner silence of word-impotence or the civil wordless state of Canada, eventually the cadence will be reached and creativity or reclaimed civil space will appear. On the other hand, the civil consciousness condemns the mercenary behaviour that has made a Cain of all Canadians: we have sold our birthright, natural resource by precious natural resource, before it even became our own. Articulation becomes necessity — because silence can also imply complicity — and it buys men the dignity of self-recognition — 'they will not go under until they have taken the measure of empire'. In this stanza the poet affirms the reflexive nature of non-being and being, while at the same time justifying his brutal strategy of naming the void.

The next three Elegies continue and further the dialogue. The 5th Elegy (originally the third) condemns Canada's growing tradition of quiet diplomacy and non-interventionist policies. What raises it above the level of prosaic propaganda are its brilliantly linking images of city-squares and children. The pell-mell children in Toronto's civic square recall children in other and distant squares, distant in time as well as in place, and they play under the urban pollution, an apt image for the encroaching American presence. For Lee, even if someone is sitting satisfied in Toronto's civic square enjoying the children at play, he is as guilty as if he had himself napalmed a Vietnamese child. The children, in their terrible significance, link us with the crime; the polluted air of American takeover is heavy with the stench of 'burning bodies'; and the silence of our colonial position seals our complicity. Only a short thirteen lines, the 6th Elegy, which follows, continues this condemnation of technopolis newly armed with napalm, while the 7th Elegy associates private silences and insufficiencies with these civil ones.

The remaining two Elegies conclude the dialogue and successfully balance the tensions between the individual man and the mass. The 8th section, moderately altered from its original version, concentrates on the French-Canadian poet Hector de Saint-Denys-Garneau and the ninth one, substantially revised in the 1972 *Civil Elegies*, focuses on Lee himself. Both Elegies specifically return to Nathan Phillips Square, the 8th at the end of the day, the 9th at the end of the year, and from these Lee describes the confusions and cross-pressures of living in the modern world. Some balance is necessary, and some surface tension is needed to offset the emptiness, void, and total silence of the 'lonely inward procession' (CE 8). Few survive a complete abnegation of world for the inner exploration — the study 'of the lore of emptiness' (CE 8). By way of terrible example in the 8th Elegy, Lee turns to Garneau, who 'came this way and made poems out of [his] body, / out of the palpable void that opened / between the bones of [his] spine'. Garneau is one who increasingly withdrew from the world and embraced solitude. Lee emphasizes the link between the private silence of Garneau and the civil silence of Canada by describing Garneau's terrible, excessive shyness as 'fear of life, the mark of Canada'. Again, the fault lies not so much with the search for solitude or inner contemplation, but with the turning of the search into an absolute: the fatal flaw is in not recognizing the possibilities of a simultaneous vision. Garneau, according to Lee, followed the negative mystic, John of the Cross, 'patron of void' to the point that his self-abnegation became almost self-idolatry. This fascination with Garneau arises from Lee's recognition of his own image, exaggerated and reflected in the French-Canadian poet. Lee realizes the error in his early 'wrong start' of embracing the void, of making a presence of absence. He must now 'keep [his] distance [from Garneau] and praise'. This is not complete rejection, but a tempering of a former absolute:

And I will not enter void until I come to myself
nor silence the world till I know its lovely syllables,
the brimful square and the dusk and the war and the crowds in motion at
    evening, waiting to be construed
for they are fragile, and the tongue must be sure.

Again, Lee juxtaposes silence and language. To silence the babbling horror of modernity, he must verbalize it. Paradoxically, his words also combat the silence of a wordless, colonial space and reclaim it, and thus once again Lee accepts his poetic role, his aesthetic of silence, a namer of nothingness in order to reveal its hidden sub-

stance. The world out there is 'waiting to be construed', to be cata-
logued and revealed. The task is not easy, for all things 'are fragile'
— contain their own non-being — 'and the tongue must be sure'.
The words must be precise that confront the silence.

And those of the last Elegy in the second edition are precise in-
deed. Of all the revised sections it is the most altered, with approxi-
mately one quarter of the original length excluded. More than any
of the other Elegies, the ninth is a poetic correlative of 'Cadence,
Country, Silence', for in it Lee reviews his former, inauthentic poet-
ry, the embracing of the void, the silence of the inability to write,
and finally the recognition that for him the appropriate poetic is one
that clearly enunciates the condition of his society:

But when the void became void I did
let go, though derelict for months
and I was easy, no longer held by its negative presence
as I was earlier disabused of many things in the world
including Canada, and came to know I still had access to them,
and I promised to honour each one of my country's failures of
     nerve and its sellouts. (CE 9)

Perception of the void is validated by recording that perception. In-
stead of abnegating the self in pursuance of the negative space, the
recorder can and should restore his self through his creative actions.
In this view good and evil cease to be a question of congruence, as
negative and positive forces converge.

Having established that Canada is 'a conquered nation' (CE 9), Lee
sees in this last Elegy only two options open to Canadians: either
choose to accept imperial status or fight it 'with motherwit and guts,
sustained / by bloody-minded reverence among the things which
are, / and the long will to be in Canada'. Part of this dream is re-
claiming the language and giving new meanings to words out of the
silence of word-withdrawal. The redemptive, creative journey which
results in a poem is not possible until the civil condition is faced, and
the redemptive journey of re-entry into civil space is carried out.
Again, two seeming opposites are experienced as simultaneous,
inextricably bound together for Lee:

The storm-wracked crossing, the nervous descent, the barren wintry land,
and clearing a life in the place where I belong, re-entry
to bare familiar streets, . . .
finding a place among the ones who live

on earth somehow, sustained in fits and starts
by the deep ache and presence and sometimes the joy of what is.

Echoing the conclusions of 'Cadence, Country, Silence', the revised
Elegy comes to an acknowledgement of the void which 'must / re-in-
still itself in the texture of our *being here*'; (emphasis added). Lee
clearly articulates the important literary solution of reclaiming
words in the face of an inauthentic, and therefore for Canadians, si-
lenced, imperial language:

And though we have seen our most precious words
withdraw, like smudges of wind from a widening water-calm
though they will not be charged with presence again in our lifetime
    that is
well, for now we have access to new nouns —
as water, copout, tower, body, land.

The few building words are thus reaffirmed.
Reaffirmation and a confirmation that for Lee truth lies at the
confluence of perceptions — so ends *Civil Elegies*. If Lee, then, is the
totality of his beliefs, so his poem is the totality of its expressions, for
'the whole truth of the poem consists of the whole poem itself, not
the position it reaches at any one point' (LETTER). The closing stanza
acknowledges some of the seeming opposites and reemphasizes the
necessity of a simultaneous understanding:

Earth, you nearest allow me.
Green of the earth and civil grey:
within me, without me and moment by
moment allow me for to
be here is enough and earth you
strangest, you nearest, be home.

The ongoing enactment of a dialectical meditation continues with
even more force in Lee's next major poem, *The Death of Harold
Ladoo*. Ostensibly an elegy to a friend and fellow-writer who was
murdered in his native Trinidad in 1973, *Ladoo* is this and much
more: it is a coming to terms with Lee's feelings about Ladoo, about
himself, and their friends, and creativity in general with its rapture
and responsibilities. Lee, who comments on *Ladoo* extensively in the
essay-interview 'Enacting a Meditation', says: 'The large rhythms are
those of progressively grieving, accusing, cherishing, pondering'.
And the progressive aspect of the poem is enhanced by 'enacting',

by making shifts in the voice that proposes each new stage. Any one voice does not contradict another, for again it is the synthesis that is real.

In *Ladoo* Lee continues and refines the image of silence as raised in 'Cadence, Country, Silence' and *Civil Elegies*. Reviewing both Lee's and Ladoo's common past in the first half, the poem concentrates on the political and personal silences generated by Canada's civil condition, as construed by Lee. This includes, for Lee, the inauthentic nature of the country and his response of silence, broken only by his conscious decision to resume writing and reclaim a language suitable to the situation. In the second half, the poem concentrates on an aspect of modernity only tentatively raised in *Civil Elegies* in the new 2nd Elegy — that is, the secularization of society in response to technology. Often difficult in diction, Lee again coins a term to express his dis-ease and his country's disease — 'desacramentalization'. In *Savage Fields* he describes this process as being 'one of the most striking features of the liberal cosmology':

> Before the rise of the liberal cosmology, the universe was not thought to be value-free. As a result, each new positive science has had to de-mystify and objectify the phenomena it sought to regulate: to expel the angels, demons and qualities which had previously quickened those phenomena. Thus in the change from a sacramental to a neutral universe, an entire valuative dimension was stripped away from the external world, revealing the 'true' cosmos of the objective fact. And eventually these deracinated qualities and presences, now epiphenomenal in the objective world, were assigned a new home — in the consciousness of the subject. They became part of its 'value-system'. (SF, p.50)

Here Lee is describing the loss of belief in divinity: the old assumption of a universe composed of man, nature and an all-present God who subsumes the other two is no longer available to modern society. However, Lee seems in his work to long for the religious underpinning in which he can no longer believe. The second half of *Ladoo* depicts the results of the 'liberal cosmology': a world without the divine voice. For Lee, such a condition silences language in the same way as does civil inauthenticity. In a desacramentalized society the poet must renew words and practise an aesthetic of silence in order to restore language.

Although in actuality the poem took over four years to reach its present form (it first appeared in 1976 and was published again, substantially revised, in 1979), it employs the conceit of being written in one long night of the soul, the night of the summer solstice, 1975. The poem opens with the poet addressing Ladoo, acknowledging that he has finally come to face the 'old compulsion, come at last / to wrestle with your death' (G, p.39). In other words, the poet must articulate his feelings, and by necessity frame words out of his inner cadence, while surrounded by the silence of his inhibitions which had so far restrained words.

In Part One Lee constructs his words out of 'the tension' between the attempt to write a traditional elegy and the natural urge 'to honour all the incomplete, confused parts of one's psychic anatomy'.[12] The first impulse tends to formalize experience in words, while the other continually reappraises and criticizes. 'Ladoo . . . does enact the process of living within this tension', and at points the tension is resolved, when 'the two impulses coincide temporarily'. The meditative process finds expression in several different voices as Lee reappraises Ladoo, their friends, and past. He sentimentalizes, accuses, grieves, rages, and reveres. And each of the various emotions is as valid as the next: 'I think that's how we do come to terms with things . . . Not leaving anything behind en route, but letting each of these vehement partial truths collide with others, and get tempered and re-aligned as they stay suspended within the whole that's developing' ('Enacting a Meditation', pp.50-53). Thus, in Part One, Lee's notion of simultaneity breaks free of severe dualistic pairing and gives way to a multiplicity of contradictory but simultaneous positions.

In Part Two Lee goes beyond his personal loss and the project of writing: 'the private grief eventually finds the condition of our whole civilization to be its real subject'. He focuses on two strains of social decay. Like the eminent twentieth-century social and literary philosopher George Steiner, and like fellow Canadian poets Eli Mandel and A.M. Klein, Lee recognizes that language has been severely weakened if not co-opted in our contemporary society. At the same time, like political philosophers Jacques Ellul and Leo Strauss, and like fellow Canadian George Grant, Lee remains convinced that the loss of a religious structure has sweeping ramifications in modern culture. However, unlike either group of thinkers, Lee *links* the lines of thought, connecting the decline of language and a loss of belief in a divine pattern.

In order to depict graphically the chaos and terror which he feels inherent in modern, technological society, Lee focuses on its 'desacramentalization'. In *Ladoo* the banished gods, angels, and demons, which, according to Lee, were exorcised from our world in order to objectify it, seem to have returned to haunt us in fiendish form. The monstrous spectacle of modernity itself produces these warped, deviant divinities:

> Gone from the kingdom of reason they surface
> in hellish politics, in towering minds
> entranced by pure technique, and in an art refined by
> carnage and impotence, where only form is real.
> And thus we re-enact
> the fierce irrational presencing we denied them — only warped,
> grown monstrous in our lives. (G, p.53)

The role of the poet in this impoverished time concerns Lee deeply, and he thus explores the poet's possible complicity in the evils he records. Remembering Holderlin's question 'What good are poets in a time of dearth?' (G, p.52), Lee shows that the messiah-myth of transcendence through writing, like that of epiphanies through poetry, is a trap, albeit an attractive one. Ladoo 'pushed it past the limit, . . . / and also . . . died of it,' while others 'toppled headlong' (G, p.55) into it. Lee would go back to this hypnotic myth himself, but he can no longer believe in it as an absolute. (The harm is not necessarily in the position, for the ideas may be valid, but the evil is in the action of making it absolute and following it to the exclusion of all others.) The gifts of the warped age, if one chooses an absolute role, are 'redemptive lunacy, . . . bush league paranoia, / fame as a useable freak, depression, and silence' (G, p.53). This negative silence is the ultimate punishment for the poet, as it means a cessation of his art and not the positive silence of a resonant surrounding for his words. This silence is neither to be dallied with nor courted. Lee, even while recognizing that the role of nominalist is the only one open for him now, sees it as simultaneously implicated in the meaninglessness and destruction as well:

> For a world without numinous being is
> intolerable, and it is his gorgeous vocation
> to bludgeon the corpse for signs of life, achieving
> impossible feats of resuscitation, returning, pronouncing it
> dead again. Opening
> fever paths in the death heaps of a civilization.
> And he names the disease, again and again he makes great
> art of it, squandering
> what little heritage of health and meaning remain,
> although his diagnoses are true, they are

truly part of the disease
and they worsen it, leaving
less of life than they found; yet in our time
an art that does not go that route
is deaf and blind, a coward's pastorale,
unless there be grace in words. (G, pp.53-54)

The poet is part of the 'desacramentalized' society and must continue naming the disease and cataloguing the symptoms. This is his only route, even though he becomes involved in the destruction himself. The simultaneity of two energized forces, here articulation and destruction, is negative but unavoidable — 'unless there be grace in words'. Grace in words would allow the necessary and positive simultaneity of seeming opposites, as Lee once again charts a difficult and demanding course: one must attempt to articulate the disease without furthering the destruction; one must heed the gods but not accept the role of poet as messiah; and one must embrace the silence without giving in to it utterly. The ideal would be if 'he [could] articulate without simultaneously destroying'. In an unpublished interview Lee stated that this is a 'deep longing' that he expresses without knowing if it will ever 'occur in time'.[13]

In this interview, Lee also agreed that such simultaneity is linked with the simultaneity of 'Cadence, Country, Silence', that cadence and silence therefore define and ground each other, but that neither of them is enough on its own. 'That I suppose is very much like the being-non-being [relationship] . . . That everything comes to be the most fully when it is most fully not.' The route of simultaneity is a difficult one:

'Everything matters, and
              nothing matters.'
It is harder to live by that on earth and stubborn than to
         rise, full-fledged and abstract,
              and snag apocalypse. (G, p.57)

This realization is harder than Lee's first polarities, the abyss or apocalypse, absence or messianic role. Silence defines the cadence and the poem is produced — no other way is possible. A complete acceptance of silence or the abyss denies poetry and cuts off creativity, but at the same time a complete immersion in cadence is self-indulgent and dangerous. As Lee says in 'Cadence, Country, Silence', the silence in relationship with the cadence has a beneficent power to stop up easy words, and Ladoo is an example of the fatal nature of the messianic poetic role. He totally indulged himself in the mythic, apocalyptic view of poetry and, in part, this led to his death. The other poetic pathway, complete silence, exemplified by Lee's depiction of Garneau in the 8th Elegy of the revised *Civil Elegies*, is equally destructive. 'Real silence' in the face of the evils of 'this season of dearth' would be a silence of complicity, and must be resisted. 'Though how to live . . . and still / resist real evil, how to keep from / quietist fadeouts, that I / scarcely know' (G, p.57). It is difficult not to view the evil and be struck dumb by it, but Lee recognizes that this condemnable silence must be resisted. Lee is caught in the dilemma between viewing himself as a poetic messiah and embracing a complete, existential silence that would imply complicity. He is attracted to both and sees part of himself in each: his coincident balance is difficult, but simultaneity must be sought:

> We must withstand the gods awhile, the mutants . . .
> But to live with a measure, resisting their terrible inroads:
> I hope this is enough.
> And, to let the beings be.
> And also to honour the gods in their former selves,
> albeit obscurely, at a distance, unable
> to speak the older tongue; and to wait
> till their fury is spent and they call on us again
> for passionate awe in our lives, and a high clean style. (G, p.59)

Once again, in this conclusion, Lee echoes Grant, but, whereas Grant focuses on the philosophical aspects of the problem, Lee focuses on the literary ones. Grant also desires the reintegration of awe in our lives, but he locates the dilemma in 'the dialectic between antiquity and modernity':

> To what extent is nature to be contemplated as the limit of a Creator God? To what extent is nature to be conquered by humans who believe in a God of Redemption? The first question, first posed by the ancients, calls for awe and reverence. The second, first posed by the moderns, calls for action and mastery.[14]

Although Grant has ultimately been unable to maintain a vision of nature contemplated and dominated coincidentally, Lee does continue to suggest simultaneity as the only possible solution.

The final poem of note here, *The Gods*, is, as the title suggests, a continuation of the meditation in the second half of *Ladoo* and as such emphasizes that the place at which the poet can engage in a battle with modernity is still at the literary level:

> ... faced with an alien
> reality it [the imagination]
> stammers, it races & churns
> for want of a common syntax and
> lacking a possible language
> who, now, can speak of gods? (G, p.29)

'Desacramentalization' is reflected for Lee in today's weakened, debilitated language, one which is even deficient in terms of describing past beliefs. If creativity is possible, it takes place in the few isolated occasions in which 'god-force', as Lee calls it, still visits the poet in this silenced and diminished time. This inspiration sounds suspiciously like a visitation of cadence to the silenced poet as described in 'Cadence, Country, Silence', and *Civil Elegies*:

> dense air clogged with its roaring and
> ripples of power fork through us:
> hair gone electric   quick
>   pricklish glissando, the
>   skin   mind skidding, balking is
>   HAIL (G, p.30)

The final page *The Gods* summarizes much of what Lee has been saying up to this point. Criticizing modernity, he links it to the 'desacramentalization' of the world, which in turn, and in conjunction with the colonial condition of Canada, has led to a reduction in language's power. He then affirms his faith in a literary aesthetic of silence, the simultaneity of cadence and silence in his society as he experiences it:

> I do say gods.
> But that was time ago, technology
>   happened and what has been withdrawn
> I do not understand, the absent ones . . .
> how I am to salute you, nor how contend with your being
> for I do not aim to make prize-hungry words (and stay back!) I want
>   the world to be real and
>   it will not,
> for to secular men there is not given the glory of tongues, yet it is
> better to speak in silence than squeak in the gab of the age
>   (G, p.32)

Lee's vision of simultaneity, then, goes beyond contemporary patterns of logic. While it describes his own manner and mode of creativity as a poet in the latter part of the twentieth century in Canada, it also helps him to deal with the crisis of modernity in the larger society of our whole planet. The literary solution of nominalism is, for Lee, the only hope of revitalizing a diminished civilization. While he questions in *Savage Fields* whether the delineation of modernity may not in fact 'acquiesce in the crisis of being which it is laying bare' (SF, p.42), in his poetry he proposes the simultaneous perception of 'what surrounds us' as a protection: at one and the same time we must 'loathe it and cherish it' (G, p.19).

Lee acknowledges but dismisses the problems inherent in such a view of existence. With regard to the 'solution' of simultaneity that he proposes in *Ladoo*, for instance, Lee says, 'If that violates logic, or bends the speaker's nervous system into dismayingly uncomfortable postures, so much the worse for logic and his nervous system.'[15] Although simultaneity may be a difficult means of perception, for Lee and for an understanding of his work it is fundamental and necessary.

[1] *The Death of Harold Ladoo*, p.57.

[2] In a footnote to *Savage Fields* Lee explains his divergence from liberalism:

> The cosmology of savage fields inherits the structural categories of liberalism, but recasts and partially transcends them. It accepts that 'consciousness' and 'the objects of consciousness' are the two primal structural units of planet. But it envisions those domains as simultaneous, rather than separate. In taking over those categories, it reveals its origin in liberalism; in insisting on their simultaneity, it goes beyond. (SF, p.118).

[3] Personal letter to the author, 6 Feb. 1982.

[4] In Adele Freedman, 'Separating Dennis Lee's Psyches', *The Globe and Mail*, 23 Nov. 1977, p.11.

[5] Letter from Lee to Munton, 6 Feb. 1982.

[6] 'The Aesthetics of Silence', *Styles of Radical Will* (New York: Farrar, Strauss, and Giroux, 1969). My discussion of Rilke's Ninth Elegy owes much to Sontag, and her perceptive discussion of Rilke's recognition of

the problem of language and his near approach to 'the horizon of si-lence' helps to clarify these poems by Lee. Sontag speaks of 'redemption of language' by which she means 'the redemption of the world through its interiorization in consciousness'. Sontag equates this 'naming of things' with nominalism and makes a distinction between 'the benign nominalism proposed by Rilke . . . [and] the brutal nominalism adopted by other artists'. Lee's naming is certainly of the second type.

[7] Lee emphasizes his bond with Moore, in the opening pages of 'Cadence, Country, Silence', where he twice mentions his recognition of the presence of a sympathetic cadence in Moore's sculpture.

[8] Lee argues that Grant distinguishes between the attempt of our Loyalist ancestors to respond 'to the demands of the good' (CCS, p.42) and the actuality of the American, liberal pursuit of personal liberty and happiness. 'What the Loyalists were refusing was the doctrine of essential human freedom, which in an argument of inspired simplicity, Grant sees as the point of generation of technical civilization' (CCS, p.43). Both *Civil Elegies* and *Savage Fields* vigorously attack American domination of Canada, the liberal ideal, and 'technological civilization'. Another very fundamental link between Lee and Grant is their desire to idealize the Loyalist position, while clearly recognizing its failings. One is forcefully reminded of *Civil Elegies* in this description of Grant by Lee: 'This undercutting of a past he would have liked to make exemplary is a characteristic moment in Grant's thought, and it reveals the central strength and contradiction of his work. He withdraws from the contemporary world, and judges it with passionate lucidity, by standing on a "fixed point" which he then reveals to be no longer there' (CCS, p.43). This is a technique Lee himself seems to employ, most notably perhaps in *Savage Fields*.

[9] According to George Grant, *à la* Leo Strauss, via Dennis Lee.

[10] *Philosophy in the Mass Age* (Toronto: Copp Clark, 1966), p.42.

[11] Letter, 6 Feb. 1982. Lee's comments on *Civil Elegies* subsequently cited are from this letter.

[12] In *Twelve Voices: Interviews with Canadian Poets*, ed. Jon Pearce (Ottawa: Borealis Press, 1980), pp.44-59. In my discussion of *Ladoo* Lee's comments have been drawn from this essay. Lee's statements on *Ladoo* subsequently cited are from this article.

[13] Munton, interview with Dennis Lee, 20 Oct. 1977.

[14] Frank K. Flinn, 'George Parkin Grant: a Bibliographical Introduction', *George Grant in Process*, p.196.

[15] Letter, 6 Feb. 1982.

On Civil Elegies

Stan Dragland

1 An *I* in Nathan Phillips Square

> This undercutting of a past he would have liked to make exemplary is a characteristic moment in Grant's thought, and it reveals the central strength and contradiction of his work. He withdraws from the contemporary world and judges it with passionate lucidity, by standing on a 'fixed point' which he then reveals to be no longer there. (CCS, p.36)

TWO SORTS OF CENTRE draw in to themselves and focus the heterogeneous matter of *Civil Elegies*. One is the speaker of the poem, a persona whom I will call 'Dennis Lee', though I know he speaks in a voice quite different from that of Dennis Lee in his essays, or his letters, or over the phone. The other centre is the setting, Nathan Phillips Square, with the ordinary activities that go on there. In the square are Viljo Revell's City Hall architecture and Henry Moore's sculpted Archer, and within these Lee unsettlingly locates opposite impulses (say World and Earth, to borrow terms from *Savage Fields*). The square, then, along with the *I* whose mind ranges a long way out from Toronto, east and west and north and south, as well as backwards and forwards in time, becomes a container as well as a core for the whole poem. 'It's hard to stay at the centre when you're losing it one more time', Lee says about the Canadian will to fail, but, as we will see, what he is explicitly saying and what he is doing very often contradict or qualify each other, so it is clear that technique as well as thought is something he shares with George Grant. Nathan Phillips Square, for example, is so vividly, if cumulatively, realized, in a poem that usually seems to be talking about loss and unreality, that it becomes permanently fixed in a reader's mind, and in consequence turns out to be very hard to lose. Of course, neither the Square and its contents nor the man who speaks from this 'place of meeting' are static. Both sorts of centre change in the dialectic of the poem, because of the need to register how comforting and treacherous both the mundane and momentous in life may be.

The Square is a public place in which Lee sits or stands, apparently always at noon, a temporary refuge from the work force, from the jobs which he so often links with kids and home, endangered decencies in the poem. As a middle-class presence, he is concerned with finding out how to maintain the simplest continuities of ordinary life, but at the same time he also explores regions miles from that ordinariness — with an intensity not normally attributed to the average citizen. Thus a tension is established: this *I* is an ordinary citizen and also a person apart who articulates what the average person cannot, one who undertakes the probing and naming of the disease ('fear of life, the mark of Canada') that is generally submerged in all our unexamined lives.

The Square is frequented not only by kids racing about, lunchers, and idlers, but also by a swarm of 'furies', unrooted ancestors who haunt the place, loading a weight of responsibility upon the man who sees them. These ghosts will not be laid until their descendants find a way through their fear of life to occupy the land in more than body. Meanwhile

> the dead persist in
> buildings, by-laws, porticos — the city I live in
> is clogged with their presence; they
> dawdle about in our lives and form a destiny, still
> incomplete, still dead weight, still
> demanding whether Canada will be. (CE 1)

For a people in desperate need to get moving into authentic lives, these spectres contribute to the inertia of daily 'miscellaneous clobber', of 'friends and lacerations' suffering and failing in their relationships, and of the vortex of American empire sucking us south: 'every year attaches itself behind and we have more to drag'.

But the Square's ordinariness, with its continuity and serenity, relieves the weight of responsibility at times. Sometimes Lee is caught up in its 'placid continuance', its 'blessed humdrum'. In spring (1), summer (3 and 5) and fall (9) much occasional feeling of well-being is provided by the noon-time sun which warms everything. The dailiest sources of satisfaction may turn sour, however, and so does the peaceful, sunlit Square in the 5th Elegy. This passage lulls the reader into expecting a more comforting analogy than he gets:

> In Germany, the civic square in many little towns is
> hallowed for people. Laid out just so, with
> flowers and fountains and during the war you could come and
> relax for an hour, catch a parade or just

get away from the interminable racket of trains,
   clattering through the
outskirts with their lousy expendable cargo.
Little cafes often, fronting the square. Beer and a chance to relax.
And except for the children it's peaceful here
too, under the sun's warm sedation.

The irony of 'lousy expendable cargo' is not so pronounced (one hardly notices having slipped into a Nazi mind) as to undercut totally the portrait of German civic squares: they *are* attractive; perhaps they need not have been avoided ('Does the sun in summer pour its light into the Square / for us to ignore?'), even by a people who were being undermind by atrocities done in their name. Indeed, the seventh line of the passage seems almost to let us off the hook, by acting with the fifth to sandwich the 'lousy expendable cargo' between two thoughts about the pleasantness of civic squares. Two lines later, however, the poem bites again, in 'sun's sedation': the innocent sun, like the placid square, can be a drug to conscience. And Lee shows us we had no cause for complacency here, either, because Canada's 'clean hands' were making napalm to fry Vietnamese. If that era of American imperialism has now passed, the relevance of *Civil Elegies* has not, and will not as long as the U.S. extends its single-minded power all over the world (unless — but how? — we disentangle our affairs from theirs). 'Sun's sedation' therefore recalls the ambiguity of the 1st Elegy in which the square 'takes us in' (both 'gathers' *and* 'fools us') and looks ahead to the word 'cop-out' in the 9th Elegy.

Less ambiguous than the sunny square which is both enjoyed and resisted are Revell's towers, though the Archer undermines what they represent. These City Hall towers are 'luminous' and beautiful. With the humdrum of the square, they provide relief: this 'spare vertical glory of right proportions' has a calming effect, creating a respite from desolation. The towers are a

                              sign, that not
   one countryman has learned, that
   men and women live that
   they may make that
   life worth dying. (CE 1)

'Revell's sign' thus becomes an achievement that reproaches the general rule of botched city architecture, maps jammed 'with asphalt panaceas', 'banks of dreary high-rise', which urban men make

172

out of the domination of number and the profit motive. Like Moriyama's Metropolitan Toronto Library, it says that people meet more wholly in beautiful surroundings, that mere functionality does nothing to feed the spirit, which must be fed.

Revell's towers are the urban at its best and are associated with the human spirit making models for life as it might be lived harmoniously. Moore's Archer does something else. Revell the Finn and Moore the Englishman have together expressed one of the major contradictions of Canada. Moore's Archer matches those Apollonian towers with its own chthonic reminder of the untouched nature whose power the pioneers felt and which can still be felt not very far north in any part of the country. The Archer

> Was shaped by earlier space and it ripples with
> wrenched stress, the bronze is flexed by
> blind aeonic throes
> that bred and met in slow enormous impact,
> and they are still at large for the force in the bronze churns
> through it, and lunges beyond and also The Archer declares
> that space is primal, raw, beyond control and drives toward a
> living stillness, its own. (CE 3)

The energy of the verbs helps to create an impression which is opposite to the serenity in square and towers. It is a feat of concentration to find in the Archer, located *in* downtown Toronto, the primal wilderness of Canada, the Shield that Lee links with the urban setting to express his sense of Canada, the barbaric land that broke so many settlers: 'Despotic land, inhuman yet / our *own*' (ours, and yet completely independent of us). Like Pratt's Laurentian dragon in *Towards the Last Spike*, and his more ominous 'paleolithic iceberg' in 'The Titanic', the Archer occupies a space 'which violates our lives, and reminds us, and has no mercy upon us'. The presence of the Archer is so powerfully established, in the 3rd Elegy, with its primitive refutation of the beautiful or botched civilization that formed our settlements, towns, and cities, that it declares to the gut how complicated a matter it is to claim this country as a whole. So Lee brings into his urban poem a northern reality which generates all those works like Atwood's 'Progressive Insanities of a Pioneer' or Birney's 'Bushed' that arise out of the confrontation of civilized man with primitive nature.

Technological man, given to conquest of the alien, can triumph in such confrontations; *Civil Elegies* acknowledges what is more fully mapped out in Grant's *Technology and Empire* and in Lee's own

Savage Fields. It takes time to create even an uneasy bond with 'brute surroundings' made of time, and it can be done only by accepting what we can of the land's own terms — but time is not one of our luxuries. Not only is the country 'pelting very fast downhill' in a decline that makes Lee think of Rome, but the resources torn from the north race 'toward us on asphalt across the Shield' to be 'shipped and / divvied abroad . . . .' The country is being sold out from under us in so many ways that the determination to claim it is undercut before it is even seized. And something *can* be claimed from the wilderness. Lee ranges out from his centre in the square to show us how Tom Thomson did it.

Thomson claimed the north before it claimed him — drowned him — by becoming 'part of the bush' and making art of it. He showed that wilderness could be captured with respect, just as Revell showed that urban architecture could transcend its function. In the 3rd Elegy the unity of Thomson's art with its subject, the landscape, is expressed in the image of a painting of sunrise. This image is powerful because the continuous sentence which contains it makes nothing of a great leap from wilderness into art:

<blockquote>

Often when night
came down in a subtle rush and the scorched scrub still
ached for miles from the fires he paddled direct through
the palpable dark, hearing only the push and
drip of the blade for hours and then very suddenly the radiance of the
renewed land broke over his canvas.

</blockquote>

The word 'renewed' is significant — beyond the redemption of the land from darkness by light — because such acts as Thomson's merging with the bush and making art of that are the sort that claim the land for us, and therefore for the truncated ancestors who failed to claim it. No such act, however, roots us once and for all. 'We cannot malinger / in the bygone acts of grace', Lee says. *Civil Elegies* is therefore an act of sustaining and extending what Thomson and others did, making the art that grows out of one's personal search a basis to claim his country.

If the main axis of this poem which centres on Nathan Phillips Square extends north to the wilderness and south to the u.s., Lee also makes a gesture west in the 1st Elegy ('the prairies, the foothills'). He later reaches east into Quebec by introducing the figure of Saint-Denys-Garneau, moving 'across / two decades and two nations' to locate another of the defining tensions of Canadian life. Lee characteristically both recognizes the cultural integrity of Quebec and claims Garneau (and implicitly Quebec) for Canada by calling him '*our* one patrician maker' (my emphasis).

A great deal of Canada is present in Nathan Phillips Square, then, and in the *I* who meditates from that centre, even though the further east and west Lee moves from home ground, as one might expect, the thinner the country appears. Garneau can hardly bring with him the whole texture of Quebec because he spent much of his life weaning himself from that. Still, if not exactly writing *a mari usque ad mare*, Lee is claiming a large chunk of the country (taking it by giving to it), partly by reaffirming the local and regional basis of Canadian identity. This reaffirmation is consistent with his lament in the 6th Elegy over 'the continental drift to barbarian / normalcy,' because the assertion of a presence alternative to that of the u.s. in North America, 'a presence which is not sold out utterly to the modern', would mean very little if it were uniform from coast to coast. Part of our dilemma thus is that while we could much more easily resist the downhill continental slide if we were anchored in a unified front of native normalcy, resistance to homogenizing is much of the alternative we have to offer.

2   Void

For always standing within us
A man not to be beaten down
Erect within us, turning his back
                    to where our looks are turned
Erect in his bones, eyes fixed on the void
In a fearful dogged facing and defiance.
                              (Saint-Denys-Garneau)[1]

All the details of the poem — the cumulative portrait of Nathan Phillips Square; the particularized portraits of, or scenes involving, 'exemplars' like Thomson, Garneau, Chartier, MacKenzie and even Paul Martin; the shifting orientation of the speaker within the dramatic moments that focus his experience (those moments that appear in the 1st, 3rd, 5th and 8th Elegies, usually announced by the word 'once') — are there to celebrate the integrity of specific things and people. But the mass of detail also grounds the generalizations about Canada and its problems, and helps to ground the most mysterious aspect of the poem, the encounter with void (absence, emptiness, silence, non-being) which makes a continuous thread through the poem. Void is difficult to catch partly because it is as unapproachable a ground of being, or measure of existence, as God, for whose absent governance void supplies to Lee a kind of alternative. But void is also elusive because, like so much else, it is protean within the poem. 'We do not encounter Void', Lee says in 'Cadence, Country, Silence', 'we encounter this void and that' (CCS, p.52). Void takes on various identities in *Civil Elegies* as Lee makes it as palpable as possible.

Void is least ambiguous when it is identified with the evil done in the name of empire; it is both attractive and dangerous in its pervasive form as the context of being. In approaching it, Lee approaches the edge of the abyss, pushed by the complex of negatives embodied in Canada. Before he turns back, he follows Garneau a good distance into his void with the hope of sacrificing attachment to things that they might live more fully in their own being. When he subsequently turns back to this world, it is not that he has escaped the inescapable void, but that he has managed to reorient himself to life and the emptiness that surrounds it all by finding a difficult but possible way to live in the world as a Canadian. He has availed himself of the 'lore of void' to honour void, and has returned from his 'lonely inward procession' with the promise to himself that he will 'honour each one of my country's failures of nerve and its sellouts'. Thus he reaffirms a truth about identity that everyone has to learn for himself, the one expressed by James Reaney in *Colours in the Dark*: 'things you've lost are inside things you don't like'. [2] Lee does not renounce void as the dominant pull on him until the 8th Elegy, which is thus the turning point of the poem. The 9th Elegy is the dénouement, and works like the consolation of a traditional elegy.

There is no better place than 'Cadence, Country, Silence' to go for a gloss on what void means to Lee (unless it is to the end of the first section of the elegy for Harold Ladoo, where Lee movingly clarifies what it means to die by reckoning up the wonder of 'all that / sweet and cross-hatched bitter noble aching sold-out / thrash of life'. In the essay Lee reflects on an epiphany which simultaneously undercuts life and gives it value:

> There is a moment in which I experience other people, or things, or situations, as standing forth with a clarity and a preciousness which makes me want to cry and to celebrate physically at the same time. I imagine many people have felt it.
>
> It is the moment in which something becomes overwhelmingly real in two lights at once. An old man or woman whose will to live and whose mortality reach one at the same instant. A child who is coursed through with the lovely energies of its body, and yet who is totally fragile before the coming decades

of its life. A social movement charged at the same time with passion for decent lives and with the pettiness, ego-tripping and lack of stamina that will debase it. A table, at once a well-worn companion and a disregarded adjunct.

Each stands forth as what it is most fully, and most precious-ly, because the emptiness in which it rests declares itself so overpoweringly. We realize that this thing or person, this phrase, this event, *need not be*. And at that moment, as if for the first time, it reveals its vivacious being as though it had just be-gun to be for the first time. (CCS, p.51)

If it were possible to crawl into the empty surround of being, free-ing other people, things, situations, to burn more brightly and con-tinuously as themselves, that would be one way to 'clear a space' in which everything presently cut off might take root again. Every-thing, that is, but the martyr to void who made it possible. Lee comes to realize that what the space is cleared *of*, by pushing to-wards void, is oneself. He does manage a qualified clearing by the end of *Civil Elegies*, but he turns away from the 'barren route' to void for a less narrow one that permits simultaneous being and let-ting be.

Although the word 'void' does not appear in *Civil Elegies* until the 3rd Elegy, the 1st and 2nd Elegies lament emptiness left by the loss of civil and divine presence — the latter lost, and the former never completely found. Void gets its most complete treatment only retro-spectively, in the 9th Elegy after the escape from its domination. By then it has been defined and re-defined in the context of each par-ticular elegy, so that it is seen to lurk everywhere. After the ironies about a Canada that scarcely exists (in the 1st Elegy) and the plain-tive lament of the disappearance of a 'Master and Lord' who sup-plied a measure to all things (in the 2nd Elegy), the conclusion of the 3rd Elegy begins an active exploration of void:

> We have spent the bankroll; here, in this place,
> it is time to honour the void.

These lines announce a determination to deal with void rather than passively being dealt with by it, and the 4th Elegy begins to ex-plore one of two possible sources of action. Perhaps void is 'our vo-cation', perhaps there are regenerative possibilities in it:

> Dwelling among the
> bruised and infinitely binding world

177

are we not meant to
relinquish it all, to begin at last
the one abundant psalm of letting be? (CE 4)

This is a question, not a statement of certainty. But what might happen if we took up this possible vocation, as people once undertook to serve God? (The association is made not only in the image of 'vocation', but in 'psalm' — and later in 'beatitude' as well.) Perhaps we might be acting on the spirit of reverence for everything that aches through the passage I quoted earlier from 'Cadence, Country, Silence':

free to cherish the world which has been stripped away by stages,
    and with no
reason the things are renewed: the people, Toronto, the elms
still greening in their blighted silhouettes — some dead some
burgeoning but none our property, and now they
move at last in the clearness of open space, within the
emptiness they move very cleanly in the vehement enjoyment
    of their bodies. (CE 4)

The model of detachment is Saint-Denys-Garneau, 'master of emptiness'. We get a fuller and more critical view of his example in the 8th Elegy, but for now it seems plausible to follow him into the ground of every thing, 'oblivion'.

Even while he is expressing his attraction to Garneau's way, Lee never suggests that it would be easy to let go one's purchase on life. And he does not ignore the complication that might well render a successful quest for void useless. How should Canadians

        clutch and fumble after beatitude, crouching for
years till emptiness renews an elm-tree,
and meanwhile the country is gone? (CE 4)

What good is a 'psalm of letting be' if it is sung with the head in the sand? Thus the 4th Elegy invites a regenerative void and then undercuts it with an evil — empire (explicitly called void in the last section of the 6th Elegy) — after Canadian complicity in the Vietnam War has been starkly established: 'And this is void, to participate in an / abomination larger than yourself . . . to fashion / other men's napalm and know it'. Here is a void that must be actively resisted, even if in another aspect it might be worth moving into. The void of empire must be confronted, if there is to be any basis for resolve to fight it.

178

These two movements — toward regenerative void and away from void as abomination — come together in the 9th Elegy, still contradicting each other but held together in uneasy tension:

To rail and flail at a dying civilization,
to rage in imperial space, condemning
soviet bombers, american bombers — to go on saying
no to history is good.
And yet a man does well to leave that game behind, and go and find
some saner version of integrity,
although he will not reach it where he longs to, in the
vacant spaces of his mind — they are so
occupied. Better however to try.

The poem does not let go, even as it reaches its most affirmative stage. Activist raging is good, though one rages to improve what is doomed; it is good to look inward for what is impossible to find.

While in the 2nd Elegy the familiar and reverent address is to the 'Master and Lord' of an obsolete order, still the allure of that order is made palpable at the same time as attachment to it is rejected as crippling nostalgia. Might a new order rest on void? Meeting the emptiness, Lee says to God,

is a homecoming, as men once knew
their lives took place in you. (CE 2)

Both unreachable absolutes, God and void, are parallel if opposed. If the void is to serve the same function as God, it must be without the comfort of anthropomorphism, without a personification like 'Master and Lord'. And it does not take centuries to come to mistrust the reliability of void as home. 'What if the void that compels us is only / a mood gone absolute?' Lee asks in the 9th Elegy, where again we meet the analogy between God and void. There neither is denied a continuing influence; instead both are naturalized. Rather than inhabiting 'the realm above our heads' God 'must grow up on earth,' and at the same time the void must 're-instill itself in the texture of our being here'. Given the quite natural human thirst for absolute measure, it is not very reassuring to conclude that what can be discerned of this is diffused throughout existence and recognized only fitfully. But the poem sets out to win what reassurance it can without glossing over the obstacles in its way; one would not expect the weight Lee has been carrying to suddenly and finally fall away, like the burden from Christian's back in *Pilgrim's Progress* or the albatross from the Ancient Mariner's neck. Nevertheless the mood of the 9th Elegy is celebratory. Taking his 'right to be from nothingness', but 'no longer held by its negative presence', Lee has found that the clearing away of illusions still leaves him access to 'many things in the world / including Canada.'

Since at one point in the 8th Elegy Lee says 'I will not speak of where I have not been', and that would seem to include void, one important thing remains to be said about that. Not much is made of the fact that Lee appears to enter void, perhaps so that his public poem does not get usurped by his private Dark Night of the Soul (St. John of the Cross is here called the 'patron saint of void'), but the 9th Elegy mentions that 'when the void became void I did / let go,' 'derelict for months'. This reference to an emotional nadir, paradoxically the point of release that makes him finally 'easy', is I think the experience dramatized in the 3rd Elegy in a scene that adds to our understanding of what the Archer represents. Lee normally comes to the square to be soothed by placid continuance, calmed by the beauty of the towers.

But once at noon I felt my body's pulse contract and
balk in the space of the square, it puckered and jammed till nothing
worked, and casting back and forth
the only resonance that held was in the Archer.

Lee describes a few lines later how one may easily stray into void in the 'brute surroundings' of the hinterland, where 'men who had worked their farms for a lifetime / could snap in a month from simple cessation of will,' but void may also yawn its abyss in the city as well. Fortunately the Archer, shaped by primal space quite other than man, saves Lee from being pushed in Nathan Phillips Square:

Great bronze simplicity, that muscled form
was adequate in the aimless expanse — it held, and tense and
waiting to the south I stood until the
clangour in my forearms found its outlet.

And when it came I knew that stark heraldic form is not
great art, for it is real, great art is less than its necessity.
But it held, when the monumental space of the square
went slack, it moved in sterner space. (CE 3)

This is a thorny passage. What is 'stark heraldic form' that it could be more real than 'great art?' Is it that great art, art period, draws away from the chaos (void) that never ceases to be a fact of existence, making a human order profoundly satisfying *because* it distances the chaos? The Archer seems not to have been created by Henry Moore, but by the earth itself, like the Laurentian Shield; it has therefore somehow directly tapped energies almost always outside man's jurisdiction. Lee has mentioned this force elsewhere, in a generalization which should be helpful here.

> Canadian literature has long included an experience which the theologians call *mysterium tremendum* — the encounter with holy otherness, most commonly approached here through encounter with the land — to which an appropriate response is awe and terror. It is a very different thing from alienation.[3]

This is not the place to pursue the possibilities Lee opens up for a reinterpretation of the 'threat' of the wilderness, so I will just mention what good sense his comments make of a line which catches all that has seemed problematical about nature in Duncan Campbell Scott's 'At Gull Lake, August 1810': 'After the beauty of terror the beauty of peace'. Surely this is the double hook of *mysterium tremendum*. Glorious and dangerous, the Archer is of it. So it holds, and Lee holds on to it when everything else goes slack, a mysterious artifact of void.

3   Cadence[4]

> *Je vois ces emmêlements et ces noeuds du champ de l'existence dans notre continuum, et les rejoindre et les définir nécessitent que mes vers décalquent clairement et simplement ces remous, ces tourbillons et cette nodosité. Les vers et les mots servent à cela, et dans le cas où cela viole la syntaxe normale, pour moi, c'est que la syntaxe dite normale n'est pas à la hauteur de la trame de l'existence. Je ne vois aucune raison de démembrer et de sectionner l'être des choses pour le subjuguer à la syntaxe. Je ne cherche pas non plus à hacher et à démembrer la langue par pur fantaisie, mais pour la façonner jusqu'à ce qu'elle soit apte à exprimer ce que les choses sont. Si cela signifie que j'aurai parfois l'air excentrique dans ma langue et ma syntaxe, je suis bien prêt à cela.*[5]

So Lee writes in the afterword to *Élégies civiles* called 'Lee, poète du processus', in which he talks about the challenge of recording a reality 'très nébuleux et multiple'. Much of that reality as caught in *Civil Elegies* should be apparent by now. But the 'eccentricities' of its style demand a share of the attention for two reasons. For one thing, the style may well seem uneconomical and perhaps unnecessarily strained if it is not made clear how flexibly and purposefully it is manipulated. More importantly, all that I have said about the themes and structure of the poem also takes place in the style.

A poet of process is not a poet of content (if there is really any such thing), even if his product is as full of ideas as *Civil Elegies*. When we catch the eddies and undercurrents in its flow from line to line, we engage the poem on the level at which it most engaged Lee while he was writing. The language at work in the poem is one of the ways in which Lee roots the experience his poem presents. That style is an animal — a fox — instantly responsive, in its moves, to any situation, always *engaged*, totally at one with its environment.

Lee writes free verse, so he can be abrupt or hesitant (as in the 2nd Elegy) by utilizing short lines and frequent punctuation, but the characteristic line is a long one which creates a flow of thought and feeling, spilling across the page in an all-at-onceness that ignores conventions of grammar and syntax. Commas might conventionally separate clauses and phrases (though an ambiguity is sometimes created when one of those expected commas is missing) but a comma might also join complete sentences. Or punctuation might disappear entirely, as it does to create the tight-lipped jamming together of 'yank and gook and hogtown' in the 5th Elegy. So punctuation has more to do with pacing than with syntax.

The conjunction 'and' is omnipresent, often appearing at the beginning of new sentences. The frequent use of conjunction is one of the techniques that some might find annoying, though its function seems to arise out of Lee's vision of life as a continuum of contradictions. In a normal sentence 'and' links things; it gives elements equal value because it does not make one a modifier of another. So when Lee makes a verbal chain with 'ands' he implicitly asserts a relationship between often quite different grammatical units and their contents, while at the same time recognizing their integrity. He never bashes a sentence completely beyond recognition, though, so a reader can hear the normal punctuation shadowing what appears on the page. Two systems working at once keep a reader loose. Lee's syntax is not an inherited closed system; it responds to the nature of what it carries, no more a fixed measure than God is a fixed definer of identity or anchor of conscience.

Lee is inclined to work in lengthy, elastic, portmanteau units that, while they may begin with a capital and end with a full stop, contain a range of syntactical relationships in between. The internal structure of some of these units is tightened by the repetition of a word or phrase that moves, like the backward curl of a wave, in a direction contrary to that of the main thrust of a passage, enacting the internal tensions and contradictions that Lee wants to embody whole. For example, the phrase 'our own' is repeated three times with different emphasis in a passage about the land (in the 3rd Elegy), which mainly shows how the land is *not* our own. How can it be ours when it is our 'adversary' and when it is 'occupied' by empire, and when we have never fully claimed it? Well, it both is and is not, and that will always remain the case, even though the 9th Elegy clarifies the terms by which fuller possession may be taken.

Similarly the word 'goodbye' crops up twelve times in the passage in the 4th Elegy about the process of acting on the assumption that void is regenerative, and everything should therefore be let go. Yet each of these 'goodbyes' is contradicted by the gathering field of images they punctuate, images that firmly fix the tenacity of the flawed and precious things that are ostensibly being abandoned, so that the simultaneous effect is of letting go *and* holding on.

    If only
here and now were not fastened so
deep in the flesh and goodbye, but how should a man
alive and tied to the wreckage that surrounds him,
the poisoned air goodbye, goodbye the lakes,
the earth and precious habitat of species,
goodbye the grainy sense of place, worn down in
words and the local ways of peoples, goodbye the children returning
as strangers to their roots and generations,
and cities dying of concrete, city goodbye
    my city of passionate bickering
neighborhoods the corner stores
all ghosts among the high-rise, like bewildered nations after their
surrender as their boundaries
diminish to formalities on maps goodbye, so many
lives gone down the drain in the service of empire,
bombing its demon opponents though they bleed like men, goodbye
and not that all things die but that they die meanly, and
goodbye the lull of the sun in the square, goodbye and
goodbye the magisterial life of the mind,
    in the domination of number every
excellent workaday thing all spirited
men and women ceaselessly jammed at their breaking
points goodbye who have such little time on earth
    and constantly fastened
how should a man stop caring?

The 'goodbyes' supply the glue to this passage as it meanders designedly through much of the matter of the poem on its way back to where it began, in 'fastened', finally completing the framing question which has been suspended for nineteen lines. The 'goodbyes' are so variously placed in this shapely unit, sometimes with the sense of verbs, that they create surprise as well as continuity (which is true of the line-breaks as well). Because leave is taken not only of people but of the air, the city, the country, empire and so on, another sort of link is made between highly diverse things — the care for them all felt by the man who addresses them.

If the passage from the 4th Elegy is full of tender feeling, a very different effect of repetition occurs in the second section of the 5th Elegy, where Lee is again maintaining two things at once. Good men, honourable men, necessary men, who by proxy fry 'the skin of kids with burning jelly', are also criminals. One sentence will exemplify the basic — and repeated — structure: 'Even though he loves kids he is a criminal'. The passage is an accusation that begins in short-sentence bursts, then quickens and swells in an outraged rush, 'he is a criminal' hammering through it, before drawing back into shorter lines and irony about 'a nation's failure of nerve':

> And the consenting citizens of a minor and docile colony
> are cogs in a useful tool, though in no way
> necessary and scarcely
> criminal at all and their leaders are
> honorable men, as for example Paul Martin.

Lee fingers a decent man; he is perfectly serious about the bind that good men may find themselves in: service of an abomination dirties the hands. The end of the section reinforces the irony that began it, an irony rather slow to break and more devastating for that: 'In a bad time, people, from an outpost of empire I speak.' There may be visions of exiled Chinese poets raised by this; one may even think of poor Ovid sending elegy-letters to Rome from his place of exile on the Black Sea, but the irony here is that this outpost of empire is our home, a supposedly independent nation.

Such examples demonstrate the necessity of watching what the language of *Civil Elegies* does, because it gives muscle to what is being said. A beginning is all that can be made here, because the richness of the poem defeats the attempt, certainly in a foray no longer than this one, to catch more.

4 Home

It is not much to ask. A place, a making,
two towers, a teeming, a genesis, a city   (CE 1)

It is ironic that so much has to be gone through to gain even the
chance to begin accomplishing the very little asked for in *Civil
Elegies*. Never underestimating the barriers that block the way to
true independence, Lee deliberately sets his sights low. He begins a
passage of the 1st Elegy quite clogged with punctuation — commas,
semi-colons, periods and dashes — by saying 'In the city I long for,
green trees still / asphyxiate', and goes on to describe his yearned-
for city exactly as it is now — the breeding ground of emptiness —
before introducing what would make all the difference: 'but in the
city I long for men complete their origins':

      they clear a space in which
the full desires of those that begot them, great animating desires
that shrank and grew hectic as the land pre-empted their lives
might still take root, which eddy now and
drift in the square, being neither alive nor dead.

'Not much to ask.' So how much closer is Lee to getting what he
wants, after agonizing his way through all the problems to the 9th
Elegy? Given that what he longs for cannot be made by one man, or
a few men, he is light years away from achieving his minimal desire.
And yet there has been a kind of enharmonic change in his position,
because he has found his own shaky ground to stand firmly on, with
the will to reenter his home and greet the very coffee mugs of it as
though for the first time. This is good news for those miserable,
gawking, ancestral spectres of the 1st Elegy, because now in taking
up his own civil life, Lee takes on theirs and becomes pioneer and
explorer:

And I must learn to live it all again, depart again —
the storm-wracked crossing, the nervous descent, the barren wintry land,
and clearing a life in the place where I belong . . .
[find] a place among the ones who live
on earth somehow, sustained in fits and starts
by the deep ache and presence and sometimes the joy of what is.
                             (CE 9)

So the poem ends in the exhilaration of a new beginning, 'in the early years of a new civilization', and in the sort of prayer that would never pass the lips of those who believe that the way to take care of the devastation and alienation caused by technology, 'progress', is to lay on more technology. But it is the sort of prayer that would be understood by the swindled Indians of this country, because they had this kind of reverence for earth before its spoilage had begun:

> Earth, you nearest, allow me.
> Green of the earth and civil grey:
> within men, without me and moment by
> moment allow me for to
> be here is enough and earth you
> strangest, you nearest, be home. (CE 9)

5   Homage

A serious criticism of [*Lament for a Nation*] has been that to write in terms of inevitability (call it if you will fate) is to encourage the flaccid will which excuses the sin of despair in the name of necessity. By writing of the defeat of Canadian nationalism, one encourages in a small way the fulfillment of the prophecy. (George Grant)[6]

Of course Grant also writes that 'When a man truly despairs, he does not write; he commits suicide'.[7] But if Grant is to be reproached by readers of little heart who miss both his rhetoric and his passion, so is Al Purdy, writing in the introduction to his anti-American anthology *The New Romans* that he thinks it is too late to stop the sell-out of Canada.[8] This is the same Purdy whom Lee salutes as the most Canadian of poets, a man who gets bored with all the clamour about Canadian identity because he knows what it is without thinking about it. *Civil Elegies* must hit many Canadian readers hardest as it first hit me — with rubbing of the nose into something all too true and all too painful: the need to fail, at least the willingness to fail, that is so woven into the fabric of this country. This is one sort of bottom line that will not be erased simply by asserting what is also true, that there is a lot more to Canada than failure. At an early stage of thinking about this article, I considered detaching myself from Lee's vision of Canada, perhaps with the help of Al Purdy's 'Transient', which catches my instinctive feeling of belonging here, not in nor expecting a nation *accompli*, but in a process. But immersion in *Civil Elegies* yielded the realization that it

186

is nowhere imprisoned by the impotence that is part of its subject. So the poem does not perpetuate emasculation, not only because it moves through and beyond that, but also because it is always throwing up those curls of wave which contradict placelessness. The curls make a wave of their own that swells through the poem and crests in the 9th Elegy, confirming the attachment to home that is palpable, if often muted, everywhere in it. Lee might agree with Margaret Atwood that 'if we do choose [this country] we are still choosing a violent duality', but he would speak in terms of multiple dualities. The themes, the structure, the very cadence of *Civil Elegies* make these complexities inescapable, and thereby Lee earns his determination to be at home here in heart and body and mind. His poem is sinewy and sensuous, and a great innoculation of fibre into wills inclined to be flaccid.

1 *Complete Poems of Saint-Denys-Garneau*, John Glassco, trans. and ed. (Ottawa: Oberon, 1975), p.164.

2 James Reaney, *Colours in the Dark* (Vancouver: Talon, 1969), p.83.

3 Robin Mathews and Dennis Lee, 'Rejoinder,' *Saturday Night* 87 (September, 1972), p.32. This is an exchange over Lee's 'Running and Dwelling: Homage to Al Purdy', *Saturday Night* 87 (July, 1972), pp.14-16. This complicates Northrop Frye's famous observation about the 'stark terror' evoked by the land in Canadian poetry (in *The Bush Garden* [Toronto:Anansi, 1971], p.138).

4 The term cadence means different things in different contexts, literary and musical, and Lee agreeably confuses the issue when he says in 'Cadence, Country, Silence' that he is trying to heed in his poetry a cadence which comes from a source independent of him but which he recognizes in 'Hölderlin and Pindar. As in Henry Moore, The Brandenburg Concertos, Charlie Parker, John Coltrane, early Van Morrison'. (p.35) Given that cadence feels to be something like the language of Lee's muse, a certain latitude might be allowed in the application of the term. But another source, which should be reliable in this context, gives a more practical definition. In the glossary of the *Anthology of Verse* (Toronto: Oxford, 1964), Lee, working with Roberta Charlesworth, defined cadence as an aspect of rhythm: 'Cadence is the product of three elements: the natural grouping of words, the length and syntax of the sentence unit, and the speed of the line'. (p.506) For my purposes cadence is the local and cumulative patterning of units of sound and sense that make up what we usually think of as 'voice.'

⁵ Dennis Lee, 'Lee, poète du processus,' *Élégies civiles*, pp.110-111.

⁶ George Grant, 'Introduction to the Carleton Library Edition' of *Lament for a Nation* (Toronto: McClelland and Stewart, 1970), p.xi.

⁷ *Lament for a Nation*, p.3.

⁸ A.W. Purdy, ed., *The New Romans: Candid Opinions of The* u.s. (Edmonton: Hurtig, 1968), p.iv.

The Epistolary Mode

Towards Polyphony

Extracts From a Conversation between Dennis Lee and George Bowering

The following exchange is taken from letters written between June 1979 and March 1981, made available to us by George Bowering. Tracing the evolution of Lee's 'Polyphony' (which appears in revised form in this volume) from its origins as an interview with Jon Pearce in 1979, the letters refer to progressive versions of the essay. The whole of the correspondence illustrates why both men are known not only as important poets, essayists, and editors, but also as evocative and prolific epistlers. Lack of space has forced us to delete passages which show the personal dimensions of the correspondence, as well as the development of an articulated trust between a westerner whose voice is closely linked to Olson and the Tish movement and a poet who speaks from Toronto, Ontario, and Canada and whose voice has been trained by Pound and a choir of German poets and philosophers. What remains is of greater importance than two writers discussing the development of an essay: beneath that immediate concern one senses two minds reassessing their traditions and seeking new directions.

TO GEORGE BOWERING
15 June 1979

I've just finished another essay of sorts, which is a pendant to Cadence Country Silence. Called 'Enacting a Meditation' (another of my grabby neon titles). It poses as an interview, and in fact was written by me as a revision of an interview someone else did with me a year ago; I'd blathered on endlessly & only gotten to the starting point with anything interesting.

I miss the staircase reference with Poe, whom I haven't read for years. But the interview-cum-essay poked into the 'impossibility of writing a long poem' thing of Poe's, and essentially stood it on its head; I can see that a long poem was becoming impossible in many ways about his time, preparing the way for the burnished epiphany, few random moments of value in a de-valorized cosmos, all that stuff; and then the modernists finding a syntax for linking positive & negative epiphanies into myths of history, certainly not a 'long poem' as what a long poem had been understood to be for centuries. But it seems to me, if you cut into things from where I do at

191

least, that a 'short poem' is now a near-impossibility. (The fact that they're being written by the ten-thousand militates slightly against the case, you say? Humph!) I won't gab on about all that stuff now; I ended up leaving it out of the piece, because it was becoming self-indulgently long. There's just a little flick of a Poe reference left. But it struck me that you adduced him commenting on 'Cadence', when I'd just finished adducing him in this companion piece.   *Dennis Lee*

TO DENNIS LEE
24 August 1979

You sd I didnt have to feel as if I had to say pronouncements on yr essay/interview.

If I were doing it, as we all say, I would drop all the signs of orality, real or pretended, I think that you were trying to break up the length and embarrassment abt talking about yr own work (and you do the latter very well, in both senses of the latter). The irony in the pretended orality doesn't reach right thru, I think. One editor's suggestion.

I think I get what yr after with the discussion of the table, tho my purity hates the idea of SAYING 'tabling' etc, as much as yrs does, I am more willing to go along with the way the language works or doesnt, though I know that it is an arbitrary system that describes the speaker more than it does the world; but I am more at home in the arbitrary than you are, I think; that is, I distrust 'the real' . . .

I meant to say back there, that you can break up the text in ways other than the tipt water, etc.

Well, I also dont agree with the anti-'poetry' language, tho I see at the end a coming round to something more amenable. I am never unhappy to make art; I am likely to use the verb 'compose'. I trust in etymology a lot.

And it is odd, because then when you say that yr work is all a mapping of space, you're where DG Jones was in my kitchen a couple weeks ago, saying again and again that that is what Can poetry is setting about. I felt uneasy about it then and I feel uneasy abt it now, trying to apply it to my own intentions. I dont want the idea, I guess because of my old non-Ont prejudice, But that argues with my statement earlier that I can live with the arbitrary, because maps are meant to follow, and that puts space secondary, or space as a reifier of the map, for the second person coming that way. Well, that needs thrashing about.   *George Bowering*

31 August 1979

Now, your delight in making new worlds, your revelling (in *A Short Sad Book*, say) in the ways in which writing causes new things to exist on the page which never were before and could never be anywhere else — that is a quite distinct pleasure and vocation, and not one I participate in nearly as much (at least in the adult stuff). I suppose there's an overlap insofar as you are always consciously writ-*ing*; that the process of making it is to be included on the page, and to be known *as* a process. That's an active changing thing, like my trajectory of meditation. But apart from that morphological resonance in the two processes, your fundamental project is a different one from mine, and I wouldn't ask you to adopt my lingo (nor Doug's) — nor to feel excluded from being a 'Canadian writer' or whatever on that account, either . . . But as far as that essay of mine is concerned, I need to find some way of putting the thing that doesn't call up static fixed maps as the end-result, which the reader could presumably go to directly without having to use his musculature the way the poem has done. Your concession that your own principles should let you feel OK about that notion of 'poem-as-map' is always going to be somewhat duty-bound; and it does me no good at all, since I don't take any of my own poems to be maps, and don't much like poems that I do think of as maps.   *Dennis Lee*

TO DENNIS LEE
5 September 1979

Yes, and I am of course prejudiced, the long poem seems not only possible but called fr in the modernist and later period. That is to say, after the little rueful lyrics are all done with their job is over, goodbye to all that, and then you have to say: is there history? Is my one mind in any way determined by it or now lately a determinant? I take a lot of sustenance from Olson's *Special View of History*, of course, mainly because it puts to rest my feeling of obligation to the existential view; he attacks existentialism naturally from his view that it is a human universe, that history, as we live IN it rather than at its end or as effect of it, is created by our wills attacht to intelligence, i.e., the gathering man, now not of crops but of knowledge.
     George Bowering

2 November 1979

Further on the 'interview' method, prhaps. What I mean by drop-
ping the pretense of transcription — it seems to be to me, a kind of
fake dramatization that lets you see the mechanics, sort of like fol-
lowing the rules of he said she replied he uttered in the manufac-
ture of fiction dialogue, but maybe bad in another way. You can still
have a CONVERSATION without the printed one pretending it is a talkt
one. Check the Kroetsch-Bessai one in *Figures in a Land-Scape* I
mean in a *Ground* (sorry, Sheila); that is a little like the Lee-Helwig
one in Quarry, or the famous Mills-Hood one in Fiddlehead; those
were both interesting, very interesting, and even if the letters had
been doctored, they were still letters, somehow more interesting
than a bastard form. I see, though, that you were thinking of the so-
lution's being to go further in the dramatization. Well, maybe.
Maybe the further should be to do it as a dramatization, i.e. nerve it
up and do it on the CBC???? But I feel right now, so far, that the seri-
ousness of the argument is not served by the machinery of the
dramatized 'tape' — and I think that that is what yr feeling, too.
    You understand, I am sure, my remarks about the acceptance and
use of our language as constructed; but here is an article of my faith
— I do have a sense that there is a (is it Aristotelian?) universe of
language; that Whatever we find to do with the structure of our
writing, it has been got from the bank, from the holdings of that
universe. I agree with you that the way English works, we have been
instructed, can be viewed as Newtonian, one might even say Euclid-
ean; and I know that we live in a world that is Einsteinian and Heis-
enbergian, in a world where we act as and in a field. Mr. Olson and
before him Mr. Williams were working on that; how to get that said,
not said about — wcw in the 30's hated the poets who spoke about,
acted as if they were informed by, Mr. Einstein, but still made lines,
utterances that were characterized by a Euclidean mind — as if one
could add a line to another line and still expect the first line to be
the same; see Olson's enormous lecture, 'The Special View of Histo-
ry' — I have been reading it for years, and stupid me, it was not un-
til yesterday that I saw that word as connected to Einstein's Special
Theory of Rel. I say this: that once there was the stuff that we think
happened, and then James, e.g., wrote *The Bostonians*, and so that
became the stuff that was written before *The Bostonians*, and thus
changed; we, with every gesture we make, change the past, it then
becomes what happened in relation to that gesture; right?
    How I do go on. But Olson sd: (not in so many words — maybe I

am saying it) that is true about your poem. You cannot like Pope hope to add another fact and have added to the world's facts or couplets, . . . I agree with Blake literally — if you could make that grain of sand not-be, the entire universe wd have to rush inwards to occupy that space.

That is why you dont make a simile — it is Euclidean; when you extract a thing from its field to examine its likeness you posit with another extracted thing, you cant expect that you havent pulled with it the entire world it was glued to.

The trouble with a map, is the trouble that we experienced when we first read one as a child, isn't it? That it lies flat. It isn't a field. It is invisible. If you turn it on edge you can carry it thru the territory and it wont strike anything. It offers choices, that is its function, and we dont make choices. We do something that touches all the particulars of the field. When we are in a territory we are not in a coordinate of it, we are in all of it.

Is that too much shorthanded?

Instead of the map, maybe an electric eye, Dennis; when you walk thru it you ring a bell.   *George Bowering*

TO GEORGE BOWERING
3 December 1980

George, let me pick your brain. The final essay on this book, on which I've barely made a start, and into which I'm not going to launch till after Christmas, will be about long poems. Or perhaps The Long Poem. By which I mean, both things in the 500-1000-line league, and also things like the Cantos, Idylls of the King, Divine Comedy, etc. (Two different scales of 'long poem', obviously.) This will be the most speculative, investigative, question-asking but probably not question-answering essay in the book; the only one of that kind, really. I'd like to go back to about 1920, or maybe 1910, and say, 'Suppose the Imagist revolution had happened — Swinburne etc. had gotten scourged out of the language for another 75 years — but suppose Pound et al had found a different way ahead into the long poem from the one they did? (which seems to me to have been essentially a continuation and sophistication of the technique of juxtaposing discontinuous, cleanly-etched images). If you start from where they were just before the Great War, where else might you go?' . . . Now, I don't suppose that an essay is the place to answer that question as such; only way you could possibly do so would be to go write one yourself. Programmes very seldom precede the real writing. But that's the ground I want to plough. Want to understand better what they've done (Olson, Eliot, Williams, Olson, etc. — who else should I be cnsidering? Dorn? Ammons? Ashberry? David Jones? — that already blurs things a lot); and then, what got done by the types who tried a comparable but less far-reaching break with flatulent over-writing — like Owen, early Graves, Rosenberg — but either died in the war or didn't do anything interesting after. And of course trying finally to understand what I've been doing myself, the limitations on it I feel, where doors may open next; or are there more doors in the corridor I'm in at all? is it a matter of going back and finding another one? (I've rejected the vorticist way of doing a long poem so far, obviously, and found other, limited ways ahead which seem to me to have rung true, but also to have serious limitations built into them.)   *Dennis Lee*

TO DENNIS LEE
4 February 1981

I have again to hand (and teeth? bosom? not besom) your poly-phony (i got the joke on late page about 'this is phony') piece, and I am liking it, and you know why? because if there is one thing yr to be admired for Lee, it is your nerve. Here the nerve to try to speak to those things that are unnameable but experientially there. Experientially? Pah. I mean there. There. So much safer to do what I have been doing, a little observation on Newlove's poems, a little observation on Peggy's poems, etc; these for a collecton of literary not critical essays on poets in Canada. So what will I say about the essay? Well, as an editor yrself, I hope you dont mind my making remarks. I am glad to see the interview thing reduced. Because what you want, i.e. VOICE of essayist is still there, greatly there. In fact as I was rereading just now I remarkt that I wanted still a little more excision — pardon me, dont hit.

May I? I am a little disconcerted by the occasional maybe not gaucherie (I am not prjudiced; Thea is a lefty) but at least out of key slanginess, not respectable enough. This because the piece is LIVELY without them. May I mention? First 2 paragraphs of section 8. My personal taste/ear. I think you can do it elsewise. Later: 'Like in the *Symposium*.' Dont appreciate the 'like' rather than 'as' — smacks of condescension? But then the thing you say about Wallace Stevens (whom at the last minute I decided to teach for the first time this coming summer); that is just right. And tho he's obvious Eliot gets nearer to yr desire, at least as I read him on the page — tho he is on a performance stage, plotting it, eh? ... (Feb 5) ... now it is the next day, nearly noon, newspaper and fried eggs consumed, and I cant remember what I was talking about. Ho. No, I'll, as the guy in our favourite novel says, go on. I cant go on. I'll go on.

What I mean is, what I cd do without the '*Hmmm.*' for example. Perhaps you wanted to lighten up, take away from the reader's restless apprehension that this might be a hard to read piece. But I like to say again that it has enough elan in the rest of it to hold one as one is held by the earnest liveliness of the locution. The beginning of section 12 will perhaps touch on what I am failing to point at, the recognition — 'Shit! He's right! I have always noticed that but no one says it much.' You know? I keep priding myself on thinking yr writing abt such a poem as *Allophanes* but in that there is the pretense that there are a number of voices not mine. Actually yr talking about such a poem as *The Death of Harold Ladoo* . . .

These are passing remarks, Dennis, not organized, and I always feel so disorganized when I am talkin to you because I have the sense that yr so organized and able to see whether I am, etc etc. Once in a while I was aware that I wanted to hear the feet fall, I wanted to be reminded of the roots of the wd cadence, all the time aware of the particular way you use the word as fr yr earlier essay and this. Still I wanted the other too, the *cadere*, the sense of falling, dropping, the clunk we feel when the poem hits right, wch is the sister of the ping we feel when it takes off like a naval sea to air missile. Beckett again — All That Falls. It falls to one. See how the chips fall, etc. It is, to pick up yr image, the condition of the cosmos, wherein everything is in a movement called falling. We say it without gravity, eh? Sometimes it feels (I shd be using point-system here) as if yr kids' writing is intruding as in second para. of section 20, zoom to section 21, second para.: be careful, yr invoking the measurement of the cosmos, about the geometrical usage of the word 'describe'. Boy, the 4th paragraph of sec. 22 is sexy. I felt as if I shdnt have been reading, a flush rose from my breast and engulfed my throat and face. *George Bowering*

TO GEORGE BOWERING
23 March 1981

Your *ping* and *fall* anatomy is a honey. I never thought of it that way. (You're right — I'm *not* using 'cadence' with the latinate overtones — except with some distant sense of 'tumble', 'cascade', 'overspill'. But that's neither here nor there as far as your lovely distinction goes.) *That* is something I really wish you'd do a full-scale look at, listen at, sometime. I'd certainly learn from it.

Long poems. Yes, you did leave out a few that I presume you

don't mind reading — like *The Cantos* and *Maximus*, for two? . . . I've had an intriguing go-round with the whole thing. I won't try to re-capitulate, but I think the net result is likely to be that the whole (planned) 4th essay telescopes into one additional page or so in the 'Polyphony' essay. I conclude that I am finally far enough from the post-Poundian tradition, *in toto*, that it would be foolish to mount the gigantic wrestle with it that I had been planning. It's polyphonic, true; but the sense of organization or coherence in just about every-thing, from *Cantos* on, seems to me so radically wrong-handed (I conclude, to my dismay) that I can't muster the 4-6 months' energy to do such an essay. I'll try just to summarize instead . . . . I got to this, as the final catalyst, by the unlikely route of reading Stock's un-nerving biography of Pound. I remain knocked out by a great deal in Pound and his descendants — ear, diction, much more. But in the matter of overall coherence of a long poem, I simply have to dis-sent and take my own route. Not Milton's or Tennyson's or Brown-ing's. But not not theirs either.

Which leaves me with two piddling little queries. The first is, what the fuck route *do* I take? — since the convention of a single meditat-ing 'I', speaking from a (relatively) dramatic *in-situ* initial situation, no longer rings true for me . . . And secondly, have I scalped this es-say book back so far (to 3 essays) that I don't have a book any longer, but a kind of wordy epigram? . . . I'll worry about those two tomorrow.   *Dennis Lee*

Riffs

Riffs

Dennis Lee

A man and a woman become lovers; almost at once, the woman has to travel out of the country. She will return a month later, but then their lives will take them to different continents for good.

The man writes *Riffs* during the month in which they're first apart.

When I lurched like a blizzard of wants through the networks of plenty,
a me-shaped pang on the lam,
when I ghosted through lives like a headline, a scrap in the updraft,
and my fuckups and future were close & for keeps —

> when I watched the
> birches misting, pale spring
> voltage and
> not mine, nor mine, nor mine —

then
a lady laid her
touch a-
mong me, gentle thing, for which I stand still
startled, gentle thing and feel the
ache begin again,
the onus of joy.

2

But she is an
     ocean away, and

what is she
     dreaming?

3

When you're up to yr

homburg in
hopeless, & the

damsel is not here —

what merrie cheer?   zip zip no goddam cheer:

just
DIT-DAT-DOTS of biological/
ontological urgency —

pages of
empties,
late-night lady reprise.

4

Nudge of her snuggled head
      against my shoulder,
cool of her flank
      beneath my finger-trails;
all night, all
      prodigal night at the
tasks of
      passion —
sleep was the place we went
      as the sun came through.

5

Those perfect
conversations, as a lazy
clarity would gather . . .

Later:
skin that homed to
skin, confederate still across a
roomful of frantic chatter . . .

And fit of a life to a
lifetime: sedulous, incredulous, & OK downright

202

smug as we
basked around the block,
soaked up the glistening *is* of it all . . .

Doesn't anybody
know? we asked — not about us, about
acres of luminous storefronts, *camouflaged as storefronts,*
the sky in drag as sky, as blue as itself and,
free for the taking,
all breath & secrets of the newly-immediate earth . . .

Plus our non-stop, gut-bucket, cretinous bodily grins.

6

Capo and
fret, the
cumbersome flesh
arrangements — flexed by
what rare
air, what gifted melody trace?

7

. . . I'll tell you what's the matter.
When your body comes to in the
morning, it lacks one thing:

an excellent bedful of me, beatified klutz,
lazy & dozy & warm and noodling
out through the layers of sleep

into you, or not, no
matter — absurdly
smug to be hard by a snuggled-up bundle of you . . .

8

So I'll cook me some
thump & witness, raise a

bumper car in the dictionary:

stuff about low-
life us,
at play in the garden of words —

    remember?

Not that we were *good* enough.
But there was this new and, yes foreknown astonishment:
somehow we were being actively permitted to be reborn.

9

Hot po-
tato momma, got you in my

mouth all night.
Absenty

lady —
land o'

livin', I cd pay my
rent all year & still owe dues.

10

Acey deucey
    trey divide
I'm a guy
    with a fine wide-eyed

lady freckles too &
    squirms when she
feels good, I feel so
    good just

doin aw
    shucks
tricks and she's
    SOFISTIKATED!

11

Multifarious dodos:
notably extinct —

gangs of ex-
es copped their snuff & split —

nobody aspires to be nobody —

I just say I know you are fallible & gun-shy & still we cd

occupy one planet

and look in tomorrow's mirror and start to brush *one*
  two one two

12

  One thing
weird is,
    blowing

highwire struts of be-
    bop-a-
longing for

    lady in her moves, don't talk this
way — patrician
    dancer, *no-*

body's
    trick;
and has calm, and yes an olden chastity and whose

    pleasure is
classic, and breathes.

13

Take me again —

suite of longing, suite of

lies &
    take me again.

14

Pen-
ultimate lady, alive — sweet

skin and sesame:
why do we ever rub con-

tours, if not to conjure
shapes of what we aren't and

crave to be? . . .
Touching you I am

meat & pronto, I lounge in the chutzpah of
flesh; then woozy with

laughter & midnight &
caring, pure

carnal
panache — you, you, you in your frabjous parade —

how should I
reach for more?

Yet always beyond you — this is
courtly affirmation — barely be-

yond you
is

nothing at all . . .
Lady,

do not be offended when I
go there.

15

It is
        possible:

you could be flesh and tomorrow —
        colony

homage, *aere perennius* & you still yodelling back,
        'No, no, let them

eat *my* cake if they want it,' as your
        figurehead recedes into red-shift anthology legends.

16

Aw, nobody's
yen is an
ultimate:

just ache from the
boots, all

country 'n' blues, the

whole schmeer —

call me anything . . .

Just lie down one more time & grin yr famous tricky grin.

17

Not marble, nor the
        gilded
of (i.e.) these *canzone*

        cd sweeten this little

handy Arab
        hustler on the backstreets of lidderchur

18

Ho hum you
said — so soon attuned
to ecstasy. 'Ho
hum', it wasn't
cheap, it meant:
3 weeks ago we barely
knew the peaks existed, now they're
rear-view postcard vistas.
Ho bloody hum — it meant, already it's
too good to last   better
tempt fate fast   take it for granted & *past* zip
          past zip *past.*

19

For months before we lay down,
it kept going on, it kept going off like
gongs of force in my flesh . . . Sub-
versive inklings, yes &
mostly thanks to you: the waves of
homefree coming off you, how your
skin & your laugh & gravity were
seamless, at home with themselves . . . You
said things; did things; I got basement knowledge —
flash of belonging, weird immediates.
You had more surfaces than I knew about, and they fitted.

To me it meant (like a dare, and I got scared),
'The world doesn't
have to lose its tang?
That long-relinquished
hunch, in which a
life is indigenous radiance —
that's not just kitsch & wishing, while your
might-have-beens drag on . . . ?'

It meant, a man could stand again up
straight — straight, in the
difficult calling of joy . . . ?

(And then we laid-me-down. And got to know it.)

20

Will pass your place.
Will think of us in
two-tone pandemonium,
performing the belly the breast,
performing the stations,

referring all calls to the wizard of waist not
want. Your waist: your sultry waist.
My sullen want.

21

Heaven was plain &
painless;

god was a transplant.

You came along, liddle long-
legged dynamite nest & now sweet

nothing makes sense any more, thanks be to you.

22

We swam into
paradise easy . . .

That was in the flesh . . .

Now it's
drag the jubilee hunch through a
busted language, you not
here.

23

Why else do I squat like a rainbow
bruise in the night, arch-
ing in absence to you? . . .

It is for
lust.　　And
not just *you*; e-
lectric earth stood
singlified to our ken and I

will not let that clean impinging go,
itch of a glory norm and

why should I be here?
To hold to the molten temper of two whose
friction kindled it whole,
　　　　　　　　& hold in the language of molten.

24

Stir me again.
I cd be hoisted *how* high, I cd be
god in a pushcart: *bleep*.

Even the speechlessest rockface craves to utter its
　　　　　pendant climbers.

25

Smelting head foundries of ozone gravity breakage I
ached in a space & heard Keep keep keep

coming like something in flames
coming like nothing

coming like words are what a man cd burn and burn in, and
　　　　　for keeps

26

The angels'
cure for when they miss someone *very* bad is
    malt whiskey.

'Dja
    know that?
I never knew that.

    Found it out
my own way, special,
    just since you

went away and to-
    night at 2:48 a.m. I am
practising up being an angel twinkle twinkle mud . . .

27

How far can I
go?
Never been *this* far w/ no,
nobody, nothing . . .
Wanna go back; go broke; go
all the way?

28

    Aw, shd I
talk
    sociology?

    when where what how who

All I
    want, woman, is
crawl up your left nostril & snuff it for keeps in sexual as-
        thma heaven

29

Music of
        methodist forebears.

Flesh inheritance.

I say these dreadful things for
        what I got left, I got rites of
ache & legacy.

30

        Clear tracings in
empty space:

        from silence,

        nothing to
words to back to back to silence.

        I could go
drunk into

        jive-time, the
emptinesss, these halo lady

        tracings

31

Twirls on the face of
        silence.
What you are.

        After, there's time &
syntax.
        After there's prose.

32

    Am I in
love with you, or with an
    image of your

    layabout love-
play,
    by

    bed-lamps magni-
fied on the
    ceilings of Literature?

    Gawd I said, I don't want
Literature I just want
    you &

    changed the ribbon.

33

    To guzzle
grace

    I

lay myself,
    openly.

    But
you I crave like bedrock, you I could meet off the page and
        face into.

34

Look maw — no mind &
I cn

stick to the stony face of
nothing,

nothing-&-
you, & inch a-

head for one
more glimpse of the root of is.

35

Inch by
inch by inkling: niche by hunch.
Vertiginous thoughtface.

Rock at my temples; sheer drop, fingertip
grips & a piss-poor attendance record in the daily ad-
        hesive world.

36

Suppose a couple of
bodies, kindling rohrschach meshak abednego . . .

Was that sweet nothing-
doing going to

burn away the
heights, the pits, the cataclysmic heritage of the West?

37

Just
pitch the
crummy memos.
What I wrote I wrote for fame, & I wd

unwrite it all if you would
curl into me, be

woman around me
tonight.

38

Hey I scraped the
guywire limit — been so
high so long I don't know low from Lassie.
Flip me a fast past.

(& if you are leastwise interested, think to
salute as I shoot straight past you CLONK go push
        down brown-eyed daisies

39

Awright,
    jubilee:
le's pull off the
    mirror.

    You're looking like late-night
heaven.
    You're looking like rain.
You're looking like four on the floor & I thought I was
        hitching.

I thought we were quicksilver, now you're a
        ten-minute.
coffee stop.

40

You would not be-
lieve how ut-
terly strung
out I am for
you; I wd
rather be
dead.

41

Put it on Body controls, and fly the limit.

To live in a finch's wing; in any old stone.

To be, deep down. To drink air.

To come to intention by way of corpuscular grit & the
aeons of schist.

42

SKID skid, dopey li'l
juggernaut;
Molotov sidecar momma, wrench me a frog.

If you got happiness tablets throw some out the win-
dow way down opposite side.

43

Hey I'm too far headed.

You made a space I
went there: psycho-
whiteout, wired for sound.

Cash on my head, came barrelling thru off-
side splendours, fetched up quaint in a dollop of hell.

44

Goin' t'
psych-
o whiteout count-
ry, gonna

meet my baby there —

1. Whirling toward the centre: everything outside has
been translated into the music.
2. At the centre: there *is* no content — *not even itself*

3. Humans cannot live here

45

There is a pure
        over-
load, & it

        copes
w/
        modernity . . .

I want that. I also want
        chaucer and
water.

46

Crank it or
leave it, what
I got is a bad
case of you.
Can't handle it handle it Christ I can
barely talk back.

What I mean: it is *not* just
you, it's the privileged
access to
rich time.

What we lived from, in
grace.
What we hunger.

There is,
yeah there is unemployment & howl.
Want to be used . . .
                    And
you: you
triggered a norm.

47

All the left-out
corners,
faeces of living, the
lint:

dole lines,
bus queues,
old.

Show me a riff with straight-up
ejection & I want
those in too,
and count on your body to help.

48

    My
comrade of the
    ineffable:

let me take you
    down to
logos:

    pre-
logos,
    where

    stones stone,
light lights,
    hurt things & people hurt and go on hurting.

49

Downward of roses,
scumward of oceans of whales, darkward of stars:
deathward dimension of every substantial thing —

did you not have dominion enough? did men have to
    lend a hand?

50

Can't hold them together:
you and the

    (no you are not ad

    infinitum, you're part of the problem — you also

    kindled smthg: shut up)

you and the butchered, the
buried-by-shovelful
victims of Idi
Amin his reign on good green earth.

51

We two were given to emerge
to here & now, permitted to handle its radiance;
it was clear & quirky, as
rooted in daylight as grass,
bright with its own green sheen and very sane in its hide and
when we go, our going will not diminish it —

and here on the
planet, what news?
an 8-month child in Chile, electricity
up her vagina, the
sergeant is
pressing the button; he waits, flicking & flicking to
make the parents inform and they *cannot*, they've
never heard those names —

Queasy. Queasy. Quease.
If I
deny a slaughterhouse
world, if I
deny the numinous presence,
something goes numb at the core . . .

But open-to-both is

mayhem —
nothing beside that child's, yet
falling apart with static and
origin /incommensurable jangling /what is, and what is . . .

How can the one tormented world sustain such glints of
  beatitude?

52

From one half-wasted by
bourgeois heaven & hell, and some tonight
would crawl 5 miles to be gently discomfited so,
so great is their agony —

say it:
whom do I pray to?
what do I centrally serve?

the 41 years of a selfish, directionless life,
halfway to goners now,
with its jerkoff highs, no right to even blaspheme . . .

Scour me, deepness, somehow before I die.

53

How am I to live?

In the grey of day it
comes to this:
we are ringed and hemmed by commodities;
humans are being tortured as I write;
warheads shuttle above us, and
the race could be gone by Christmas.

What is the language of non-ecstatic time?

54

Barely, be

mouth . . .

Mouth to
terror:

*Now is
apocalypse* . . .

Mouth to
jags of

awkward, un-
prompted joy . . .

Be mouth, & after that & what about us I
do not know.

55

Just now I thought to your
doorway, you opened we
stood stock still in mind.
You were going to say, You *did* come but we
headed through the hall to your flat and
stood in the eerie surround — it was
locked recalcitrant wholeness,
so shattering I felt
relieved we could not speak; we were almost
unmade
to be together, we did not know,
Did things start here, or end, was it
good to have touched at all?

56

One month of
plonk & longing,

one more
rendezvous with you;

I came to coin new nerve-ends, fashion an
icon habitation, name of

be-when-your-reason-for-
being-is-snatched-away.

57

There's a
moon that shines on

lovers & I got no
part of *that* thank god thank god;

all I got
part of is

light of a
cellular day, sheer need like you & me give

blood for daily.
Bleed & rejoice, like hurting humans do.

58

If not for you
I would be homeless in my going through the world.
It does not
attach you, but I have no good
person to lie down in saving
yourself, and the
persuasion to.
If you hold to our jointure, I will be
strengthened in the holding which I do.

59

Blood on
    behemoth.

Tracts of pure
    unness.

Abyss and
    interludes.

I did that thing, I just can't walk home straight.

60

The dolphins of need be-
lie their shining traces.
Arcs in the air.

They do not mean to last. One
upward furrow, bright & the long disappearance,

as though by silver fiat of the sea.

61

Deciduate, on grounds.

Am *a capella* palp.

What oncely greens is a light in the always to-&-fro.

62

Am going soon, and I aspire to hear
what mortals cared for,
instep and desire.
Tell me what you cherished, I will not
break trust; give me lifetime,
not renege.
I have no other use. Living I flubbed.
But mouth to mouth I could sometimes ache into words.

223

63

Have walked some
planks since you been gone and now
wd love to walk straight up the plank to
you arriving.
'Take *that*,' I'd say, & hand you what has
happened since you left but I wd
take it back awhile, lie down &
breathing slow beside you hope to
ease your eyelid stress & coming home.

64

Radiance came and
kindled our bones in bed; OK,
that thing was real.
World is so daft it includes such dustings of paradise.

And OK, sorry, me, the world
includes all freaks & the lucid
torture of innocents:
lifesag, earthsag, end.

World is so various. I used to call it celebration;
now I say dementia.
But I will not shrink squint-eyed to just one world,
nor scoot off happy-skinned to loll in just one other.
Things don't resolve. Too bad.

        (And always the blitz by
        logos, skitters of rhythmic ellipse,
        and hunches that prowl the body:
        meanings *con carne* . . .)

Can't change the plenary cross-hatched hash of world, too
bad but
have to
live it piecemeal whole
in ache & joy & riffs of neighbourhood with
one or two like, many-radiant woman, you.

65

Nobody asked us
        to.

We were gratuitous, we
        mattered here on earth and we

also are gone.

66

Egg-
shell

a-
live-o.

Still, a
life &

living live-
o . . . Just

to be.

Piecemeal-

ly. Pang in bare
potency.

67

Lady, this is no-
where. I came you

went/you'll come I
got to

go again but
leave us leave with

loving fragments? one
hunk of what I

mattered? maybe some
you?

No large enlargements: elbows & angles &
caring, maybe a dog-eared good.

(Also, sing me to
someone, leave us be

people again . . .

Epilogue

Dennis Lee — Poetry and Philosophy

George Grant

IT IS SURPRISING for modern readers to find that a fifth of Aristotle's great book on ethics is devoted to friendship. I intend to write of Dennis Lee as friend because friendship is a form of love and love illuminates the intellect. In that illumination we come to know things about other people. The Platonic affirmation that our intelligences are illuminated by love has been darkened in our era both because our chief paradigm of knowledge concerns objects, that is things held away from us so that we can master them, and also because the preeminence we give to sexuality leads us to interpret all forms of love as too simply dependent on instinct. For example, Laurel and Hardy have been interpreted as completely understandable as homosexual lovers. Such a procrustean statement prevents us from understanding the many forms of love. I mean by friendship a relation between equals interested in certain common purposes which transcend either partner of the friendship. Such a relation allows one of the parties to see things about the other party. When one of the parties is a poet such things are of more than personal interest.

Yet I am very hesitant to write of Lee just because he is a poet. The accidents of my life have left me with a deeply neurotic fear of poetry. Apart from the uninteresting personal reasons for this, it is clear that the rejection of poetry in its completeness is widespread in modern society, and is closely related to the rejection of philosophy as more than analysis and ideology. The central reason for those rejections is that the control which is necessary to human beings who would be masters of the earth is the enemy of receptivity, without which there cannot be poetry or philosophy. By receptivity I do not chiefly mean that which is necessary in listening to poetry, but that which is necessary to writing it. Plato was indeed exalting poetry when he said that it was imitation; moderns denigrate poetry (indeed make it impossible) when they say that it is creation. To talk of 'the creative artist' is a contradiction in terms. For the poet is the being who must be immediately open to all that is, and who proclaims to others the immediate truth of what is. That openness, that receptivity, that imitation, is an ability difficult to sustain in a world where control for mastery is the paragon of human endeavor. Of course, poetry is so fundamental a stance, belonging to the deepest level of what it is to be human, that it cannot be destroyed amongst us; but it is liable to appear in our society as entertainment, as a turfing of the grave. As such its proclamations can neither be easily proclaimed nor heard.

Indeed at the heart of the tradition there has been a debate (of central importance in understanding politics) about the relation between the proclamations of poetry and those of philosophy. Is Heidegger right in saying that poetry and philosophy live at the top of two separate mountains? Or is Plato right that politics demands that poetry be ministerial to the truths of philosophy? But this debate can only be private and even secret in this era where only with the greatest difficulty can we participate in philosophy or poetry, as they are in themselves. When people have to hang on to what little they can make of these saving graces in the midst of the drive to change the world, it is hardly necessary to debate their relation. What is needed is to experience their healing balm.

My hesitation in writing about Lee's poems is then because the modern drive to control has vitiated my listening to what poetry proclaims. Therefore I must proceed to thinking about them through the memory of meeting him when he was a young man. Memories can, I trust, throw light on his poetry.

It was in the baleful glare which the Vietnam war threw on the United States and Canada that I first had the good fortune to become a friend of Lee's. In a fast-changing technological society, memory is put in question. It is difficult even to remember how many people were illumined by the sinister light of that war, whatever little public consequence that illumination has had. What struck me about Lee at that time was that of all the academics who were rightly moved by the searchlight of that war, he was the one who saw that at the heart of those events was an affirmation about 'being'. That affirmation (call it, if you will, a statement about the nature of the whole) shaped what came forth in the actions of our dominant classes. Along with many others he saw that Canada was part of an empire which was trying to impose its will by ferocious means right around the other side of the globe. He saw with many others that Canada was complicit in the acts of that empire and that that complicity was expressed in the politics of Lester Pearson. He saw with some others that the technological multiversity was not outside that complicity but central to it. This was true not only in the obviously technological parts of the university, but had taken hold in the very way that the liberal arts were practised.

It is more difficult to express what Lee so evidently saw beyond this. As words fail, let me try. He understood that at the heart of our civilization lay an affirmation about 'being' which was that civilization's necessity. The rampaging decadence of imperial war was not to be explained (within liberalism) as an aberration of our good system; it was not to be explained (within Marxism) as something understood in terms of the dynamics of capitalism. In the very roots of western civilization lay a particular apprehension of 'being'. From that apprehension arose not only imperial war, not only the greedy structure of our society, but also the nature of the multiversity and of poetry, the culture of the cosmopolis and the forms of our sexuality. When Lee left Victoria College he was not only saying with Chomsky that through research and consultation these institutions had become part of the war machine, but that their very understanding of knowledge, and in particular the understanding of poetry, came forth from an affirmation of 'being', the essence of which made poetry part of a museum culture. In that sense it determined what could be 'poiesis'.

Lee saw that the turn of the screw in that situation was that this affirmation of 'being', which was so necessary to articulate if we were to be free of it, was almost impossible to articulate because the very language which we could use for that articulation arose from the affirmation itself. It was therefore almost impossible to transcend it by knowing it. Lee expressed so clearly the baffling search to find language to speak what we are, when what is determining what we are has taken hold of language to fashion it into an instrument of its controlling power. The attempt to articulate our 'being' was therefore to enter the sad walks of impotence. What had happened to language was not only in the absurdities of advertising, the literature of entertainment and the pretensions of journalism, but in the very studies of language in which Lee had been trained so well. Language described as the house of being is likely to hide the extent to which we are squeezed in that vice. It is perhaps Heidegger's continuing pride in his Europeanness (despite all that has been) which makes this description slightly more cosy than Lee as a North American would allow.

Lee has not rested in this impotence, or he would not be a poet. Instead he has turned the experience itself into poetry. The last verse of *The Gods* achieves a magnificent stance, while acknowledging the price he must pay — a limitation on his speaking, a limitation of his knowing. Naturally, his own words describe it best.

for to secular men there is not given the glory of tongues, yet it is
    better to speak in silence than squeak in the gab of the age
        and if I cannot tell your terrifying
    praise, now Hallmark gabble and chintz nor least of all

231

what time and dimensions your naked incursions
announced, you scurrilous powers yet
still I stand against this bitch of a shrunken time
in semi-faithfulness
and whether you are godhead or zilch or daily ones like before
you strike our measure still and still you
endure as my murderous fate, though I
do not know you.

It is Lee's openness to the whole which enables him to face the po-
sition from which as poet he must struggle to be. The question of
the whole is present for him in all the parts including the parts
which are his own living. What is meant by openness to the whole
has been dimmed because the modern era has become a self-ful-
filled prophecy. Modern scientists like the modern thinkers in
Swift's *Battle of the Books* explain nature, human and non-human,
without the idea of soul, and not surprisingly they have produced a
world where it is difficult to think what it is to be open to the whole.
Ancient thinkers are compared to the bee which goes around col-
lecting honey from the flowers; modern thinkers are compared to
the spider which spins webs out of itself and then catches its food in
that web. If the search for honey is not the source of poetry, what is?

Indeed, Lee has described that openness beautifully when he de-
scribed his vocation as listening to cadence ('Cadence, Country, Si-
lence', *Open Letter*, Fall 1973, Toronto). The importance of the
idea of cadence for understanding what poetry and music are can
be seen in the fact that the most appropriate comment on it are the
words about his own art by a genius of the supreme order.

The question is how my art proceeds in writing and working
out great and important matters. I can say no more than this,
for I know no more and can come upon nothing further.
When I am well and have good surroundings, travelling in a
carriage, or after a good meal or a walk or at night when I can-
not sleep, then ideas come to me best and in torrents. Where
they come from and how they come I just do not know. I keep
in my head those that please me and hum them aloud as others
have told me. When I have all that carefully in my head, the
rest comes quickly, one thing after another; I see where such
fragments could be used to make a composition of them all, by
employing the rules of counterpoint and the sound of differ-
ent instruments etc. My soul is then on fire as long as I am not
disturbed; the idea expands, I develop it, all becoming clearer

and clearer. The piece becomes almost complete in my head, even if it is a long one, so that afterwards I see it in my spirit all in one look, as one sees a beautiful picture or beautiful human being. I am saying that in imagination I do not understand the parts one after another, in the order that they ought to follow in the music; I understand them all altogether at one moment. Delicious moments. When the ideas are discovered and put into a work, all occurs in me as in a beautiful dream which is quite lucid. But the most beautiful is to understand it all at one moment. What has happened I do not easily forget and this is the best gift which our God has given me. When it afterwards comes to writing, I take out of the bag of my mind what had previously gathered into it. Then it gets pretty quickly put down on paper, being strictly, as was said, already perfect, and generally in much the same way as it was in my head before. (*Mozart's Briefe*, ed. L. Nohl, 2nd edition, pp.443-44)

These words are perhaps not a perfect fit for what Lee is saying about cadence. Yet I always hold both statements together because in both of them the difficult question of the relation between hearing and seeing — the sense so related to time, the sense so related to space — is understood as this relation is illuminated in poetry and music. (I never reached Lee's poems so well as when I heard him read them). Both these accounts cut through the ghastly language about 'creative artists' found now on the pens of journalists and professors of English, of university officials and Canada Council executives. Obviously artists make things (not create them) but if anything great is to be made they do so by paying attention — by listening and seeing. (This is the trouble with Irving Layton's poetry.) To repeat creation is a dangerous word, because it denies the primacy for art of what is listened to or seen.

The expression of Lee's openness is evident not only in his writings, but practically in his work as an editor. That wonderful English word 'generosity' (for which there is no German equivalent) penetrated his work in setting up the Anansi Press and his editing a vast variety of writings. Whether for good or ill, a tiresome old manic-depressive such as myself would never have put the writings he cared about into a book if it were not for Lee's sane encouragement. And he dealt with equally queer types among the young and the middle-aged, always with that generosity which in human dealings is the mark of openness.

With hesitation I must now turn to Lee's long poems — the hesitation of my impotence before the proclamations of poetry. What I

233

will say is at a lower level than the essential. There is a great change between *Civil Elegies* to *The Gods* and *The Death of Harold Ladoo*. To compare the rhythm and form of *Civil Elegies* with that of *The Death of Harold Ladoo* is to know that much more immediately happens in the second poem than in the first. My comment upon this must be made in the accents of philosophy (*ich kann nicht anders*). To put the matter perhaps too simply: existentialism is the teaching that all thought about serious matters belongs to the suffering of a particular dynamic context; while traditional philosophy taught that thought was capable of lifting that suffering into the universal. Both teachings require openness, but traditional philosophy believed that the truth present in existentialism was only a preparation for its transcending. It would appear to me that *Civil Elegies* is written out of the struggle which makes human beings existentialists; while the two later poems have somehow raised up the sufferings of the particular dynamic context. *The Death of Harold Ladoo* moves back and forth with the fluidity of music, from 'the dynamic context' of a particular friend's particular death to the statements of self and otherness, love and hate, living and dying. Never does the particular dissolve into the merely general, nor does the universal flatten out into abstractions. Because the later poems are more universal, they are more immediate. Cadence is more upon the page. This is not meant paradoxically in any sense. Immediacy and universality require each other. Even at the end when Mozart writes that 'the ice is around my soul' he is still able to receive and imitate that which includes even that ice. It is dangerous and indeed pompous to try to state what is universal in the *Iliad, Las Menenas*, the clarinet concerto or *King Lear*, but to say that there is nothing such present in them is just the modern denial of the proclamation which is the work of art. Certainly the truth of existentialism is included in them all, but it is also transcended in them all. The beautiful is the image of the Good, and this includes the truth of existentialism because the perfectly beautiful has been crucified.

It is easier to write of *Savage Fields* for the simple reason that Lee has written about it so lucidly himself. ('Reading *Savage Fields*' *Canadian Journal of Political And Social Theory*, Spring 1979). Lee spells out there as in a finely honed legal document what he was doing in the book. It is therefore unnecessary to speak of its surface ambiguities when this has been done so lucidly by its author. Anyway, when at the height of his own enunciation of *Beautiful Losers* Lee comes to the point where Cohen drops away from what he might have reached, it becomes quite clear why Lee calls his book 'an essay in literature and cosmology'. Nevertheless let me end where I started with the relation of poetry and philosophy. At the end of *Savage Fields* Lee writes: 'Thinking proceeds by objectivity and mastering what is to be thought'. He asks: 'What form of thought can arise which does not reembody the crisis it is analysing?' The first statement is clearly true of our modern destiny. The second must drive anybody who asks it not only to what may be in the future but also to thinking of what was before the modern paradigm. The fact of this great change can be seen in Kant's statement that 'reason' is higher than 'understanding'; while Plato meant by 'the ideas' that 'understanding' is higher than 'reason'. I am not so foolish as to suggest that in the very midst of the modern fate we should try to avoid it by simply returning to ways of thought, the criticism of which was in the very substance of our fate. What I am saying is that as one looks at the height of modern philosophy in Heidegger or the height in the works of Céline, one must see the grandeur, the truth and suffering in both, but one must also see the ravages which are expressed in both. To overcome those ravages (which are oneself) one must look for sustenance to times when poetry and philosophy had not been ravaged in this way. In God's name I do not will Lee to become a scholar of poetry or philosophy: but rather to live in the midst of these ravages, and to try to re-collect what those proclamations were. To do so is not to become simply a useful scholar or an amusing entertainer, but to take upon oneself the mystery of things. Lee, of course, has done much of this. He is a highly educated human being. But *Savage Fields* says to me that he must do more, because the milk of the joy of eternity must be more substantially present, if the ravages of fate are to be looked on, and one is not to be turned to stone. Perhaps it is not possible for the modern poet to reclaim poetry's power from the honey of the past. The ambiguity that makes Céline the poet of European modernity (in his last books about war), is that the light of eternity is not absent, even for him. On the other hand, who can rest in Céline's proclamations of the word? Céline and Heidegger both must be known as inadequate if there is to be any real proclamation. In the apogee of technological science the attention necessary for re-collecting and detrivializing can only be a fearful and consummate act. As an older friend watches Lee at the height of his powers, one cannot help wondering what we will owe to him in this re-collecting and detrivializing. Luckily it is nobody's business but his.

Chronology and Bibliography

Chronology

1939, August 31st Born, Dennis Lee, in Toronto, Ontario.

1948 First published poem, 'If', in *Wee Wisdom*.

1956 First book publication. Poem, 'Free Verse', in *First Flowering: a selection of prose and poetry by the youth of Canada*.

1952-1957 Attended University of Toronto Schools, Toronto, Ontario.

1957-1959 Attended Victoria College, University of Toronto, Toronto, Ontario.

1959-1960 Worked in refugee camps near Linz, Austria, and Osnabrück, Germany, in work groups sponsored by the United Nations Association; travelled to Stockholm, Paris, Cambridge, and London.

1962 BA, English Literature, University of Toronto, Toronto, Ontario.

1962-1963 Work on *Kingdom Of Absence* at the British Museum, London, England.

1963 Returned to Toronto; began MA at the University of Toronto, Toronto, Ontario.

1963-1967 Lecturer, Victoria College, University of Toronto, Toronto, Ontario.

1965 MA, English Literature, University of Toronto, Toronto, Ontario; edited with Roberta A. Charlesworth, *An Anthology Of Verse* (Oxford University Press); started manuscript of children's poetry from which *Wiggle To The Laundromat* was excerpted.

1967	Founded House of Anansi publishing house with Dave Godfrey; first published book, *Kingdom Of Absence* (House of Anansi).
1967-1969	Resource person, Rochdale College, Toronto, Ontario; wrote first version of *Civil Elegies*.
1967-1971	Directed and edited for House of Anansi; wrote Spadina material.
1968	Published *Civil Elegies* (House of Anansi), *Sibelius Park* (Coach House Press); edited T.O. *Now: The Young Toronto Poets*. (House of Anansi); edited with Howard Adelman, *The University Game* (House of Anansi).
1969	Resigned from Rochdale College, Toronto, Ontario.
1970	Published *Wiggle To The Laundromat* (New Press).
1972	Left House of Anansi; revised *Civil Elegies*; published *Civil Elegies And Other Poems* (House of Anansi); won Governor General's Award For Poetry, for *Civil Elegies And Other Poems*.
1972-1973	Wrote first version of 'Cadence, Country, Silence: writing in colonial space'; taught Humanities, York University, Toronto, Ontario; started writing *Savage Fields*.
1974	Published *Alligator Pie* (Macmillan) and *Nicholas Knock And Other People* (Macmillan); published *Not Abstract Harmonies But* (Kanchenjunga Press); won the CACL Bronze Medal Award for the best Canadian children's book written in English, and the Toronto IODE Award for children's book, for *Alligator Pie*.
1974-1979	Consulting editor, Macmillan of Canada.
1975	Writer-in-residence, Trent University, Peterborough, Ontario, for the Fall of the academic year;

on the Hans Christian Andersen Honour List for *Alligator Pie*.

1975-1976   Wrote *The Death Of Harold Ladoo*.

1976   Published *The Death Of Harold Ladoo* (Kanchenjunga Press); edited *Moving To The Clear; poems from Trent University, Peterborough* (Private printing).

1976-1977   Wrote *Garbage Delight*.

1977   Published *Garbage Delight* (Macmillan); awarded the CACL Bronze Medal Award for the best Canadian children's book written in English, and the Ruth Schwartz Foundation Award for *Garbage Delight*; published *Savage Fields* (House of Anansi); published *Miscellany* (Private printing).

1978   Published *The Gods* (Kanchenjunga Press).

1978-1979   Writer-in-residence, University of Toronto, Toronto, Ontario.

1979   Published *The Gods* (McClelland & Stewart); published *The Ordinary Bath* (McClelland & Stewart).

1979-1980   Wrote *Jelly Belly*.

1980-1981   Holder of Scottish-Canadian exchange fellowship in Edinburgh, Scotland; revised the essays to be published in 'Cadence, Country, Silence'.

1981-   Literary advisor to McClelland & Stewart.

Selected Bibliography of Dennis Lee

Mary Macpherson

BOOKS AND OTHER SEPARATE WORKS

'Principles of Ekstatic Form'. M.A. thesis, U. of T. 1965. 126 l. A study of the formal strategies of modernist poetry, with extensive reference to the *Cantos* of Ezra Pound.

Kingdom of Absence. H[ouse] [of] A[nanse] P[oetry], No. 1, Toronto: House of Ananse, [May] 1967. 60 p. ('Ananse' was an early spelling of Anansi.)

'Wiggle To The Laundromat: Rhymes, Chants, Jingles, and Poems.' [Toronto: Rochdale College, 1967?]. 17 l. Mimeographed sheets 110 x 85 mm. Approx. 50 to 100 copies distributed free. 40 children's poems.

Civil Elegies. H[ouse] [of] A[nansi] P[oetry], No. 4, Toronto: Anansi, [Apr.] 1968. [48] p. Approx. 1,000 copies. 7 elegies. See also *Civil Elegies and other Poems*, below.

Sibelius Park. [Toronto]: Coach House Press, Fall 1968. Broadside 467 x 281 mm. Approx. 50 copies distributed free. A poem.

Wiggle To The Laundromat. Toronto-Chicago: New Press, 1970. 29 p. illus. Charles Pachter. Reproduced from original lithographs, drawings, and collages. 14 children's poems.

Civil Elegies And Other Poems. H[ouse] [of] A[nansi], No. 23, Toronto: Anansi, [Apr.] 1972. 59 p. 351 copies. Ed and expanded from the text of *Civil Elegies*, 1968. 16 poems and 9 elegies.

Civil Elegies, 1968, contains 7 elegies titled: First Elegy, Second Elegy, etc. *Civil Elegies And Other Poems*, 1972, contains 9 elegies titled somewhat differently: Civil Elegy 1, Civil Elegy 2, etc. The elegies in the 1972 publication are revised, expanded, and in some cases, reordered. The following chart identifies corresponding elegies:

Civil Elegies, 1968	*Civil Elegies And Other Poems*, 1972
First Elegy	Civil Elegy 1
Second Elegy	Civil Elegy 3
Third Elegy	Civil Elegy 5
Fourth Elegy	Civil Elegy 7
Fifth Elegy	Civil Elegy 6
Sixth Elegy	Civil Elegy 8

Seventh Elegy   Civil Elegy 9
                  Civil Elegy 2
                  Civil Elegy 4
Often, when the elegies are published in journals, periodicals, newspapers, and anthologies, the titles differ again. For example, they are named according to the first line of the poem; some are given the collective name, Civil Elegies.

Alligator Pie. The poems were written by DL; the pictures were drawn by Frank Newfeld. Toronto: Macmillan, [Sept.] 1974 col. illus. 65 p. 37 children's poems.

Nicholas Knock And Other People. Poems by DL; pictures by Frank Newfeld. Toronto: Macmillan, [Sept.] 1974. col. illus. 64 p. 30 children's poems.

Not Abstact Harmonies But. Kanchenjunga Chapbook, No. 1, San Francisco and Vancouver: The Kanchenjunga Press, 1974. 4 p. A poem.

The Death of Harold Ladoo. Kanchenjunga Chapbook, No.6, San Francisco and Vancouver: The Kanchenjunga Press, 1976. 25 p. A poem.

Miscellany. Toronto: N.P., [May] 1977. [24] p. 200 copies privately printed. 17 poems.

Garbage Delight. The poems were written by DL; the pictures were drawn by Frank Newfeld. Toronto: Macmillan, [Sept.] 1977. col. illus. 64 p. 42 children's poems.

Savage Fields: An Essay in Literature and Cosmology. Toronto: House of Anansi, [Nov.] 1977. 125 p. Literary criticism and cosmological theory.

The Gods. Kanchenjunga Chapbook, No. 9, San Francisco and Vancouver: The Kanchenjunga Press, [June] 1978. [10] p. Limited first edition of 400 numbered copies. A poem. (Not to be confused with *The Gods*, Oct. 1979).

The Gods. Toronto: McClelland & Stewart, [Oct.] 1979. 64 p. 3,500 copies. 15 poems, including a revised version of the poem 'The Gods' which originally appeared as the chapbook noted above.

The Ordinary Bath. Words by DL; pictures by Jon McKee; thanks for the original idea to Lou Fedorkow. Toronto: Magook Publishers Limited in association with McClelland & Stewart Limited, [Oct.] 1979. col. illus. [48] p. A children's tale.

ESSAYS

'Crisis in Liberal Education: U. of T. Full of Competent Mediocrity.'

243

Toronto Life, 1, No. 4 (Feb. 1967), pp.40-41, 52-53. DL examines contemporary university education and finds it to be 'post-secondary' as opposed to 'liberal', exemplified by his experience with the University of Toronto's undergraduate lecture system in the Humanities. He discusses the university's attempts at reform, including the Macpherson Committee.

'The Unreformed Universities: Part II.' *Toronto Life*, 1, No. 5 (Mar. 1967), pp.28-29, 41, 52, 57. The essay continues the discussion of a 'liberal' education, and includes an examination of the tutorial system.

'Getting to Rochdale.' *This Magazine Is About Schools* (Toronto), 2, No. 1 (Winter 1968), pp.72-96. DL examines the inability of traditional institutions to provide a 'liberal' education, discussing his personal experiences as a student and a lecturer at the University of Toronto. He outlines the goals and purposes of Rochdale College.

—————. *The University Game*. Ed. Howard Adelman and DL. Toronto: House of Anansi, 1968, pp.69-94.

—————. *This Book Is About Schools*. Ed. Satu Repo. New York: Pantheon Books, 1970, pp.354-380.

'Notes On A WASP Canadian Nationalist.' *Notes For A Native Land; A new encounter with Canada*. Ed. Andy Wainwright. Ottawa: Oberon Press, 1969, pp.19-25. An essay in the form of a dialogue which discusses DL's views of Canadian nationalism.

'Running and Dwelling: Homage to Al Purdy.' *Saturday Night* (Toronto), 87, No. 7 (July 1972), pp.14-16. illus. DL interprets Purdy's poetry as acts of running and dwelling — Canadians' ways of being tied to their land, neither at home in Canada, nor in the lands from which they originated. Lee compares Purdy to other poets writing in English, ranking him among Herbert, Dryden, Arnold, and Frost. In a letter (*Saturday Night*, 87, No. 9 [Sept. 1972], pp.32-33) DL replies to Robin Mathews' 'letter to the editor' in which Mathews criticizes DL's article: Lee refutes Mathews' letter, and discusses Mathews' approach to the Canadian tradition in poetry.

'Cadence, Country, Silence: Writing in Colonial Space.' *Liberté* (Montreal), 14, No. 6 (1972), 65088. An essay expanded from a talk given at the Rencontre québécoise internationale des Ecrivains held in Montreal, Spring, 1972, under the sponsorship of *Liberté*. DL discusses his writing as a Canadian artist, and the ethos of writing from that environment. He discusses the influence of George Grant's essays on his own work.

—————. *Open Letter* (Toronto), 2, No. 6 (Fall 1973), pp.34-53.

—————. *Boundary 2: A Journal of Postmodern Literature* (State University of New York, Binghamton), 3, No. 1 (Fall 1974), pp.151-168. Pages 82-88 of the *Liberté* essay were reconsidered by the author in the *Open Letter* and *Boundary 2* versions of the essay.

'Modern Poetry.' *Read Canadian: A Book about Canadian Books*. Ed. Robert Fulford, David Godfrey, and Abraham Rotstein. Toronto: James, Lewis and Samuel, 1972, pp.228-236. An essay on the appreciation of modern Canadian poetry.

'Roots and Play: Writing as a 35-year-old Children.' *Canadian Children's Literature* (Guelph), No. 4 (1976), pp.28-58. DL discusses his experience of writing children's poetry from the point of view of the children trapped within him, his sense of Canadian roots, and play — 'reanimation of repressed feelings'.

'Enacting A Meditation.' *Journal of Canadian Poetry* (Ottawa), 2, No. 1 (Winter 1979), pp.6-22. An essay by DL cast in the form of an interview between DL and Jon Pearce.

—————. *Twelve Voices: Interviews with Candian Poets*. Ed. Jon Pearce. Ottawa: Borealis, 1981.

'Reading *Savage Fields*.' *Canadian Journal of Political and Social Theory/Revue canadienne de théorie politique et sociale* (Winnipeg), 3, No. 2 (Spring-Summer 1979), pp.161-182. DL explains the difficulties of reading *Savage Fields* and recasts some of its arguments; he discusses, in detail, the critiques by Bradshaw and Godfrey.

—————. *Brick: a journal of reviews* (Ilderton, Ont.), 13 (Fall 1981), pp.32-39. illus. An altered version from CJP & ST.

TRANSLATIONS

Rilke, Rainer Maria. 'First Elegy.' Trans. DL from German. *Quarry* (Kingston), 19, No. 1 (Fall 1969), pp.6-9. 'Die Erste Elegie' from *Duineser Elegien*. Poem.

Rilke, Rainer Maria. 'Second Elegy.' Trans. DL from German. *Contemporary Literature In Translation* (Vancouver), 6 (Winter 1969), pp.9-11. 'Die Zweite Elegie' from *Duineser Elegien*. Poem.

Faludy, George. Poems. Trans. George Faludy and Eric Johnson from Hungarian. English version by DL. *Canadian Forum* (Toronto), 57, No. 678 (Feb. 1978), pp.21-23.

EDITED AND CO-EDITED WORKS

An Anthology of Verse. Ed. Roberta A. Charlesworth and DL. Toronto: Oxford University Press, 1964. 549 p. Poetry text for senior secondary schools.

T.O. *Now: The Young Toronto Poets.* Ed. DL. H[ouse] [of] A[nansi] P[oetry], No. 8, Toronto: House of Anansi, [July] 1968. 101 p.
The University Game. Ed. Howard Adelman and DL. Toronto: House of Anansi, 1968. 178 p. Essays.
Moving To The Clear; poems from Trent University, Peterborough. Ed. DL. [Peterborough]: N.P., 1976. 44 p. Poems.
————. [Toronto]: N.P., 1976. 35 p.

AUDIO AND VIDEO RECORDINGS

'Dennis Lee.' Read by DL. Toronto: High Barnet, 1970. Phonotape. (one cassette, 1 hr.). 23 poems.
'Civil Elegies And Other Poems.' Read by DL. Toronto: Toronto Public Libraries, 1972. Phonotape. (one cassette, 1 1/2 hr.). 16 poems and 9 elegies.
Dennis Lee. DL and Robert Fulford. Speaking of Books. Toronto: OECA, 1975. Videotape. (one reel, 30 min.). Robert Fulford interviews DL about the renaissance in Canadian writing and publishing. Lee reads poems from *Civil Elegies And Other Poems.* Interview and poetry reading.
'Alligator Pie And Other Poems.' Read by DL. Cond. and music comp. Don Heckman. New York: Caedmon, TC 1530, 1978. Front container illus. Frank Newfeld. Back container notes Sheila A. Egoff; includes poems 'Holidays' (4 l.), 'Goofus' (4 l.). Poems from *Alligator Pie, Nicholas Knock,* and *Garbage Delight.* Sound recording. (one 12 in. disc, 33 1/3 rpm). Children's poems.
'Keynote Speaker.' Read by DL. Prod. Audio Archives, Markham, Ont. Toronto: Ontario Library Association, Jan./Feb. 1980. Phonotape. (one cassette, 1 1/2 hr.). Adult and children's poetry reading with critical reflections, recorded live.

INTERVIEWS

Stedingh, R.W. 'An Interview With Dennis Lee.' *Canadian Fiction Magazine* (Vancouver), No. 7 (Summer 1972), pp.42-54.
'Enacting A Meditation.' *Journal Of Canadian Poetry* (Ottawa), 2, No. 1 (Winter 1979), pp.6-22. An essay by DL cast in the form of an interview between DL and Jon Pearce. See also entry under *Essays.*
Twigg, Alan. 'When To Write.' *For Openers: conversations with 24 Canadian writers.* Madiera Park, B.C.: Harbour Publishing, 1981, pp.241-252.

'The Dennis Lee Papers'. In January 1979 the Thomas Fisher Rare Book Library in Toronto acquired from the author his correspondence, editing files and notes, literary manuscripts, drafts, and related materials (reviews, clippings, publicity, etc.), lecture notes, and memorabilia, from the period 1948-1980. The collection fills 68 boxes, approximately 30 linear feet.